6 June

SCARPA

Bianca Albertini, Sandro Bagnoli

SCARPA
Architecture
in Details

Foreword by Stefan Buzas
Introduction by Maria Antonietta Crippa
English translation by Donald Mills

Architecture Design and Technology Press

First published in Great Britain in 1988
by Architecture Design and Technology Press Limited,
21A Gwendolen Avenue,
London SW15 6ET

All rights reserved. No part of this publication may be reproduced,
stored in a retrieval system, or transmitted,
in any form or by any means - graphic, electronic or mechanical,
including photocopying, recording, taping
or otherwise - without the prior permission
of the publishers. Such permission,
if granted, is subject to a fee
depending on the nature of the use

© 1988 Editoriale Jaca Book spa, Milano
all rights reserved

Original title
Scarpa, l'architettura nel dettaglio

Book and jacket design by Editoriale Jaca Book spa and Tre srl

Jacket illustrations: The gate on the Brion cemetery
at S. Vito di Altivole and a detail of the carriage (front);
sketches for the gate on the Brion cemetery (back)

English translation of *Introduction* by John Young

ISBN 1 85454 000 9

Manufactured in Italy

First printing 1988

Contents

Foreword by
Stefan Buzas
vii

Introduction by
Maria Antonietta Crippa
1

The Course of Invention
9

Thematic Elements
37

Dossiers
on the Thematic Elements
199

Index of Illustrations
223

Acknowledgments
227

Authorship of Texts and Dossiers
228

Photo Credits
229

Foreword

Everything is revealed to us through light. Blindness is indeed one of the gravest of afflictions.

The cosmic coincidence that created our small planet, and through an inconceivable chance surrounded it with an atmosphere that allowed life to be created, also has given us the miracle of forms, colors, and intangible transparencies. The familiarity with these miracles that make lesser mortals realize these without wonder becomes the constant stimulus for the true artist. To the painter through his individual harmonies or dissonances of colors, textures, and patterns; to the architect through his solids and voids and the majestic rule of perspective.

The intention of this exciting and beautiful book on the creative world of Carlo Scarpa is to present and—perhaps—try to explain the highly complex thinking of an architect. To express in words a visual process can only be peripheral and partial to the artist's innermost creative processes. Such processes are the drawings that suggest the way from innumerable ideas and a continuous flow of conceptions toward a singular and completed work.

Every individual is unique; his methods and his solutions are his very own and cannot be reproduced or recreated by anyone else. It is not often that one is able to trace the secrets of such a method as is the case with Scarpa. The mysterious connection between the "inner eye" and the hand guiding the pencil, creating images on paper, is sumptuously put before us in this book. "Maestro, infatti, è colui che esprime delle cose nuove che altri possono capire," said Scarpa during a discussion. A master indeed he was, as he was supremely capable of conveying his creations to others; after all, an architect's designs depend ultimately on the understanding of a multitude of those whose task it is to realize in physical ways the unreality of those lines on paper.

Josef Hoffmann said that "Architecture is decoration"; so did Ruskin. Although Hoffmann's period and culture did, at times, cause him to err on the "decorative" side, his statement is nonetheless true if one includes in that definition the hierarchy of detail. Order and articulation in architecture is a descending sequence of details. Each dominant element in the composition becomes alive through detail. The chosen materials with their characteristics of texture, color, surface, and pattern are decorations and, when integrated with logic and daring, result in richness, but are only successful when organized with sensitivity and care. Carlo Scarpa was a remarkable example of such ability.

His control of sequences of elements down to the smallest component parts was *achieved* with masterly skill and apparent ease. Such ease was arrived at by a relatively short *journey* to maturity. This *achievement* in a related field, that of painting—a field of which he had profound understanding—reveals the signposts of that *journey* with greater clarity. With one of the few exceptions, where the *journey* to maturity was a remarkably short one—I refer to Piero—most great painters show a distinct sequel from delicious, exciting youth to serene and clarified simplicity in late age. A dozen or so canvases by Titian, shown in chronological order, would reveal at a glance what is meant.

Scarpa's development, progressively more certain and refined, seems to have had characteristics similar to those few masters in painting. There were, of course, early ideas that were influenced by the thoughts and works of architects of his time he admired, not to mention the ever present and in his country so ubiquitous and majestic works of the past. He himself relates his joy in discovering Le Corbusier's *Vers une Architecture* which captivated his intellect, and there was Frank Lloyd Wright, above all, who captivated his imagination. But one detects remarkably early a very strong individual line of form, coupled with an already set system of integrating these forms.

His drawings are immediately explicit, relate directly to the essential forms and—oh, what inborn and rare capacity—are aesthetically most satisfying. It can be stated that no pleasing object or building was designed through ugly drawings. Even purely technical drawings will be aesthetically pleasing designs in the hands of a feeling author.

One of the puzzles of unending interest is the basic relationship between creation and drawing. In architecture, where functional and aesthetic values are essential and of equal importance, this relationship is fascinating. The plan of a building is the anatomy of its function, but it is far more than that. A small sketch, a seminal idea, of a circular church with a ring of semicircular chapels in the corner of a crowded sheet by the great Leonardo is, when viewed as pure *design*, a beautiful piece of jewelry. A plan by Mies van der Rohe, with its attenuated horizontal and shorter vertical lines, delineating the flow of spaces, is strongly reminiscent of the subtle, late compositions of Mondrian. What influences what is the intriguing and unresolved question.

The many drawings reproduced in this book are the best documents that can, post factum, prove the process of creativity at work. To "prove" is, of course, a debatable word to use when such an infinitely complex organ as the human brain and the mystery of perception is concerned. Much has been uncovered in laboratories and on the psychoanalytical couch, but both inherited and individually recorded experiences and reactions will, for a long time to come, remain the mystery they are.

All we can see here are the traces of this process of how, for example, a simple utility such as a metal hinge can be the source for an autonomous sculptural invention; or how an opening in a wall can result in a *composition* where light and opaqueness are used instinctively as *elements* for an abstract *design*. The generating force to the designer is that wonderful combination of two-dimensional pattern and volumetric vision.

In this sense and in many others the vast archive of Scarpa's drawings is the undoubted proof of his mastery of the solid form, of the control of light, of the exciting linear compositions and the use of color and materials generated by the magic of his pencil. The highly individual technique of his final drawings, with his use of colored pencils (they had to be a particular brand of English make) and on a smooth, cream-colored card, is a visual delight.

Carlo Scarpa was a happy man and his happiness stemmed from his inexhaustible enjoyment of the world as seen. By expressing his joy in such an obvious way, he warns us that there is a world of difference between looking and seeing. The world's infinite stimuli and the happiness he derived from them was the character of this man. The great gift of his visual memory and the recall of experience throughout his life were the fonts of his imagination as well as his logic.

"Architecture is the mother of the Arts," a classic phrase that may, on superficial judgment, appear elitist. In reality, however, the phrase is fundamentally true. From the humblest to the most exalted buildings, complexes, and cities we derive our sense of well-being or—if not from the minds and hands of true creators—our frustrations and sadness through inhuman chaos. Thus the responsibility as well as the joy of an architect is truly great. Joy and responsibility remain for a long time; no one needs to be more aware of this than an architect.

As the fruitful bearer of harmony, architecture is the instrument through whose power we are elevated, consciously or not, from existence to valuable life. Carlo Scarpa was one of these beautiful instruments.

Carlo Scarpa, Venice 1971.

Introduction

A fundamental inquiry into any aspect of reality is the relationship between the part and the whole, the fragment and the complete, the detail and the indivisible unity of a deed, of an object, of a thought. Disciplines with scrupulous foundations, exhaustively developed from the nineteenth century onward (for example, paleontology), are based on the deduction of organic forms from fragments preserved through the centuries. But this inquiry has not been answered conclusively. On the contrary, it dichotomizes current critical thought: oscillation without certitude between the acceptance of a reality characterized by the dissipation of energies and the hope of a balanced, plausible unity—albeit with the inevitable fragmentation of existence and experience.

It is an investigation particularly central to every kind of artistic production. Although only implicit in a vast majority of cases, the accuracy and validity of the interpretation of profound issues relating to individual figures, geographical areas, or specific periods in the history of art often are predicated upon a possible solution. Architectural production of indisputed value, such as Carlo Scarpa's, is endowed with potent imagery and evocative, incisive drawings. Work like Scarpa's is characterized by the project: each a compact and complete unit, richly filled with scholarly references.

The highly poetic[1] character of Scarpa's images, and the fact that as poetic images they "emerge from meaningful language," in the apt words of Bachelard, has been interpreted until now only superficially. Therefore, a kind of motivational vacuum has persisted, especially around the originating, inventive moment of his "imagining conscience."[2]

This book aims to discuss that vacuum, if not to fill it, choosing as its subject detail in Scarpa's architecture and entirely excluding any study of systems *in situ* or within a microurban context. The book focuses on minimal fragments: elements endowed with their own figurative unity. It searches for meaning at several levels; it relates the ideational phase, which may be traced in the drawings, to that of realization; it analytically describes both technical and construction characteristics.

Under the heading *Thematic Elements* come small-scale architectural themes, grouped in sequences formed without concern for systematic coherence. These elements are essentially structural aspects—support, connector-link, fixed joint-hinged joint—equated with perceptual phenomena—closure-aperture, solid-void, surface, and transparency. Even with the study of molding-profiling there is a strictly decorative theme. Justification for this approach relates directly to the quality of Scarpa's work. On the one hand, it permits the identification at detail level of novel thematic and figurative units, themselves immediately referencing a conscious elaboration of images conceived not gesturally but logically. On the other hand, it illuminates through unforeseen, rapid flashes of intuition that motivational vacuum surrounding the original moment of invention. One indisputable fact to emerge is that the detail—the tight control of flooding emotion—in Scarpa's architecture bears *poiesis* and urgency that go far beyond the canons and elements of style and composition defined by the architect himself or those who taught and influenced him. Detail itself becomes elevated to the status of *exemplum* in modern design, consciously transcending the limits implied by its scale.

Analytically dissecting an experience penetrates the vast subjective and cultural themes contained within it—a process sometimes indelicate but always fertile and fascinating. If such analysis is comparable to a dangerous voyage toward lands as yet unknown but hypothesized to exist, then venturing through architectural detail is like the strange and blundering progress of a man who must discover the size and form of a landscape without a high vantage point. As in close-up observation of a vast canvas, the explorer, immersed in a world with an unknown profile, must have great powers of induction. He must know how to discern paths leading to ways out of the uninterrupted sequence of architectonic forms that sometimes interlock and sometimes do not, by tracing their genetic morphology and formal coherence of the consciousness that imagines them.

Certainly a text of this kind presupposes and postulates studies of a different system relating to the same subject. There is also a serious risk of falling into formalism or emotionalism. The great advantage, however, is the highlighting of that *vie des formes* (described by Focillon in an influential study first published in France in 1943) as a permanently active form of life dynamically projected into a visible future and anticipated in forms that instantly establish a meaningful relationship between past and present. The text, then, has the value of restoring to Scarpa's architectonic figures their material consistency, technical resourcefulness, and plastic, spatial density, as well as the more debated and difficult value of metaphor. "The formal relationships in a work and between works [wrote Focillon] constitute an order, a metaphor of the universe."[3] He adds:

> "There is reason to believe that they [plastic forms] constitute an order and that such an order is animated by the movement of life. They are subject to the principle of metamorphosis, which perpetually renews them, and to the principle of styles, which, in unequal progression, tends successively to test, fix, and dissolve the relationships.
>
> "Hewn in stone, sculpted in marble...the work of art is only seemingly immobile. It expresses a desire for fixity; it is a suspension. In reality the work is born of one mutation and prepares another...but this mobility of form, and how apt it is to generate

different figures, is even more remarkable if one looks at it within more closely confining limits.... What could be further from life, its flux, its adaptability, than the geometric combinations of Islamic decoration...? And yet, within those rigid limitations rages a kind of fever, multiplying the figures.... Their very immobility flashes with metamorphosis...."[4]

The illustrations accompanying the text provide magnificent examples of the French critic's vivid formula. Indeed, one is tempted to dwell upon them at some length so as to place appropriate stress upon the tension among "desire of fixity," "suspension," and "flashing with metaphor" in the formal perfection of detail.

One example is offered by the thematic element of supports. The pillar on the Ottolenghi house at Bardolino is at once a static structure and a decorative form, as is clearly indicated in the orthogonal projections of the drawing, where the square section of the support is circumscribed by a circular form which, in line, dimension, and surface elaboration, enhances and enriches the supporting function.

Another example is the perspicacious architectonic design of the candelabrum in the Brion chapel. As a furnishing element, it is imagined and conceived with the accuracy usually reserved for complex, large-scale problems. The same painstaking care has been taken with the flyover for a square at Feltre, the bridge to the Querini Stampalia Foundation at Venice, the "Toledo" bed, the "Sarpi" table, and the door hinge of the Brion chapel, to mention only a few examples.

In all these instances, the book's drawings and photographs are a testament to the total, logical transparency of form; indeed, they highlight the process of its rational transformation into a communicative image. A similar approach can be formulated for the perceptual thematic elements. Lattices and decorative slabs are defined by a weave of solid and void, which creates rhythmical compositions of light and shade, transparent or translucent materials, architectonic elements placed to mark rather than to actuate, and spatial aperture and closure. This approach makes it possible to grasp in just how many ways consistency, grain, thickness, and texture of materials now can play an active role in the overall figuration by absorbing the energy of that impalpable but essential design element, light—sometimes modulating it, sometimes selecting it.

Finally, I must deal at least briefly with the importance of molding and profiling, offsetting and stepping, and edging of geometric combinations. This is an area where the fragment may absorb the significance of the whole. One recalls the formulae of Scarpa's inaugural lecture at the Architectural Institute of the University of Venice for the academic year 1963-1964. In this lecture Scarpa joined decoration, furnishing, and architecture under the common denominator of a categorical imperative of beauty for all time. He defended the need for decoration in order to achieve a life of expression and meaning in architecture and opposed the definition of spaces denoted by bare stereometry and simplistic formalism.[5]

The considerations outlined above exemplify, in addition to many other interesting points made in the text, the intelligence and careful, critical approach of Albertini and Bagnoli—one of conceptualization and serial organization of the illustrations. Independent of the relationships among the functional, structural, and spatial elements, or between the details and architectonic unit, such an approach not only permits minute analysis of detail but also institutes an interpretative horizon which brings to the fore the dynamic coexistence of perfection and instability, of fixity and metamorphosis, of formal richness (ancient and modern) and the morphemic force of an emerging language. It must be clear that within such a horizon the study of detail has no function to dissect, but can offer a fresh and revealing viewpoint.

The detail displayed, then, for syntactic study is valuable with reference to implied paradigmatic data. "Presence and absence"—the famous phrase of linguist Gérard Genette—is simultaneously in the artist's inventive genius; it opens an endlessly mutable space to his creative vision and resulting rational experiment. In other words, out of a meticulous investigation of architectural details emerges the metaphorical structure inherent in a design which carries, in strictly figurative terms, a particular horizon of culture and civilization. As has been candidly observed by Vincent Scully, modern architecture as a product of Western civilization, which has matured from the late eighteenth century to the present, has attempted to incarnate two human aspirations: to respond to the living and work space requirements of men in any given epoch and to represent the values to which men deliberately cling. That is to say, modern architecture has tried to give concrete expression to the collective aspiration of communities that bear positive, consolidated values, while at the same time struggling to preserve its own fundamentally unique originality.

> In so doing, architecture has certainly not confined itself to the simple role of a mirror: like all the arts it has revealed certain basic truths about the human condition; moreover—again like all the arts—architecture, too, has played a fundamental role in influencing the transformation and evolution of those same conditions which determined its genesis. From its very beginnings modern architecture has supplied us with a portrait of ourselves as contemporary men, recalling at one and the same time that which we are and that which we would have us be.[6]

If we concur with Scully, then we may well ask ourselves to what Scarpa's "system" of architectural details alludes, what it reveals, and what may be inferred from it. Perhaps Scarpa's system establishes a diagram of useful images for analyzing what we are or want to be; what we hide from ourselves but which nonetheless exists among us and in us; what we decide we want—which often remains suspended in figures born of our own intense desires. Or perhaps it puts forward a model of behavior—human rather than artistic—founded upon harmony, joy, and precise correspondence between fruition and the reality inherent in every object and in space.

I think it wise to stop here, at the threshold of the world of meanings and values of architecture in general, and of Scarpa's architecture in particular. Albertini and Bagnoli offer an informed study of Scarpa's planning methodology, and I will allow its rightful pride of place. I intend to outline a broader framework of considerations in which architectural detail, especially Scarpa's, may be adequately, even concisely, evaluated. The evaluation of Carlo Scarpa's work is still fraught with partiality, aversion, and a priori belittling. Recent architectural work and criticism, however, seem to feel an even more urgent need to symbolize, to respond to the pressure of widespread cultural desire for meaningful figuration, and to clearly understand and, to a certain extent, assimilate his lesson in design and personal language. They also have responded, or at least tried to respond, to his appeal—contained not so much in any formal denunciation as in the practice of his teaching—to leave off functional and ideological impoverishment and return to the full poetic richness of architecture. Scarpa is now seen clearly as a leading figure in the vast and varied movement in thought and design which emerged at the end of the last century and is still alive today, an era perhaps still wide open like a beginning, vacillating between ideological impetus and rigidity, and the early discovery (or rediscovery) of compositional formulae, formal links, and figures.

It is not a digression from our topic of architectural detail to shed some light on the theme of ornament—one of the most significant and illuminating in the history of the great debates of the nineteenth and twentieth centuries. The protagonists of these debates were of varied nationalities and cultural backgrounds. To mention only the most famous, there were the theorists Ruskin, Morris, Viollet-le-Duc, Semper, van de Velde, Boito and the architects Sullivan, Wright, Loos, Le Corbusier, van der Rohe. The question has become once again highly topical in recent years, both with the emergence and establishment of the postmodern movement, and with the attempts to draft a new line of defense of the decisions of the architectural masters of the first half of the twentieth century.

During the nineteenth century a seemingly irreparable rift opened between architectonic structure and ornament. Ornamental detail was contrasted with structural detail, and the overall dishonesty or honesty of a work was judged according to whether its decoration was or was not completely distinct from the purely functional, static organism. The debate itself is as notorious as the consequent moral judgments made on individual designs and buildings. Much archival source material, relating to both major and minor figures in the battle, recently has been brought to light and has further fueled the dispute. It is true that maxims such as those of Loos—"ornament is a crime"—and Mies van der Rohe—"least is best"—are no longer binding today. It is true, too, that the thoughtful consideration of decorative qualities—intrinsically linked to the nature of the material, and pioneered by the Modern movement—now is accorded the same status as entirely extrinsic decoration superimposed upon the construction materials. Allegations of dishonesty and illusionism in the use of materials have been replaced by admiring consideration of the effects achieved. And if all this is true, it is mostly and more frequently so because of the widespread formalistic and eclectic tendencies. These tendencies in the playful alteration of figurative disassociation and endless mirroring and quotation, often lie hidden beneath an architecture of mere performance, unable to define its own significance.

When looked at together, many of the more celebrated designs of recent years present a chaotic picture that is very hard to interpret, like an enormous puzzle. In this chaos, however, it is still possible to discern traces of an argument that usefully repostulates certain long-abandoned problems. Among these, the theme of the congruence of form and function, which includes the more restricted theme of the congruence of ornament and structure, is open to fresh consideration and is animated by various tendencies from postmodernism to neorationalism, and from organic to technological currents.

In particular there emerges—and only seemingly by coincidence—renewed interest for the long, illustrious tradition of architectural treatises, from the fifteenth to the eighteenth centuries, and for the manuals, dictionaries, and encyclopedias of the art of good building, from the end of the eighteenth century to the first half of the twentieth. Often these are organized catalogues on architecture, rich in detail and illustration. They are repertories in which, albeit by different means and in different cultures and epochs, a congruence is established between a complex architectonic unity and its details on various scales. Through this congruence, the architectonic element was allotted the fundamental and ineluctable role of a unit of composition, an essential and indivisible part of the design, linked to a stylistic definition that could identify large-scale architectonic works and sanctioned its representational value. The current interest in manuals and treatises is practical rather than theoretical in nature—hand in hand with the desires, recently grown quite intense, for at least some kind of formal regulation if not for actual rules and models of design. The complete absence of any such regulation often has caused a "liberating anarchy," as Scarpa himself put it,[7] heavily inclined to formal sterilization and the overrating in practice of quantitative rules and precautionary procedures, such as those prescribed by urban planning and building regulations.

Perhaps only via the capacity and opportunity to treat detail as architecture can a new "treatise" be conceived, a new regulatory diagram dealing with method, not form. In it the details, like windows upon a limitless space of formal experimentations, would be presented to the designer as coherent and prolific figures, as a vehicle for behavioral models. This fascinating hypothesis is fraught with danger, however. To accept, willingly or unwillingly, this hypothesis in the mind—if only as an antidote to the facile formalism, eclectic tendencies, and superficial mannerism increasingly rampant—makes it possible to evaluate the artistic stature of Carlo Scarpa in the context of the once-active influence of his teachings.

As I have attested in the past,[8] I believe Scarpa to have the proven ability to assimilate forms from artists both ancient and modern through a creative process of profound mimesis. Useful emphasis also is placed on this virtue by Albertini and Bagnoli in their study, which traces the most significant sources with an evocative description of the surrounding conditions, and the emotional environment in which such new elements in Scarpa's "language" of details were invented. This can be seen equally clear in many of the drawings reproduced in the book. Their lesson bears a message yet to be fully explored. Another reason why Scarpa may be counted among the great modern masters is his intelligent use of graphic representation as a means to invent and verify. His drawings were a kind of memory bank, a rationalizer of complex design processes developed simultaneously on several levels, and even as a partial substitute for vision. In drawing— usually geometrically—the designs of forms and spaces, Scarpa found the conditions to fertilize his intuition and to compose images that seem interwoven from strange *rêveries*, yet which can be decoded as logical prefigurations. Furthermore, the details of his architecture are always meticulously drawn and colored and may be related perfectly to the whole to which they belong. In line, color, and background they express at the highest level the creative energy and controlled mastery of the Architect.

Current criticism gradually is acknowledging a re-evaluation of the process of drawing in design, rediscovering its importance and content, which is expressive not only of fertile individual imagination, but also of the communicative force of collective codes. Thus critics are becoming aware of the potential and the transformations in drawings and of how they often contain phenomena of convergence and transgression. Moreover, although the rapid advance of technology would lead one to think of manual drawing as increasingly rare, architects such as Carlo Scarpa, perhaps eccentric compared to the mainstream, indicate prophetically how the capacity for experiment and invention is placed in man's hands; how concretely related they are to the materiality of things—their tactile, visual, even symbolic qualities; and how many patterns can be woven out of abstract geometrical constructions and the physical environment.

No one intends to propose a return to manual design processes as a panacea for the problems of architecture. But the intention is to stress once again that the central problem of contemporary design is its figuration, its context for significant forms, its being human—as Norberg-Schulz has recently written, with exceptional clarity: "The principal aim of postmodernism is to retrieve the figural dimension of architecture. This is the common denominator which today unites the most multifarious trends: everywhere the aim is to make architecture intelligible, that is, *human*, in the real sense of the word."[9] It seems to me that Scarpa has fully achieved this level of authenticity, in every detail.

---

[1] The term is to be understood according to its Greek etymology: *poiesis* signifies action.
[2] G. BACHELARD, *La poetica dello spazio*, Dedalo, Bari 1973, see *Introduzione*, pp 5-30.
[3] H. FOCILLON, *Vita delle forme*, Einaudi, Turin 1987, p. 5.
[4] *Ibid.*, pp 10-11.
[5] Tape recording preserved in the archives of Tobia Scarpa at Trevignano di Montebelluna, province of Treviso, Italy.
[6] V. SCULLY Jr., *Architettura moderna,* Jaca Book, Milan 1985, p 24.
[7] See note 5.
[8] M. A. CRIPPA, Carlo Scarpa: *Theory, Design, Projects*, The MIT Press, Cambridge, Massachusetts, 1986.
[9] C. NORBERG-SCHULZ, *Il mondo dell'architettura*, Electa, Milan 1986, p 238.

The Course of Invention

Premise

The chief aim of this book is to attempt to describe the working methods of Carlo Scarpa, covering not only the practical procedures of drawing up projects but also the mechanisms by which he slowly shaped an initial image to its definitive form.

Consequent to this premise, the text introduces the argument and clarifies the essential points. It is not the authors' intention to make out a list of Scarpian forms or to offer a source book, quite the contrary, their proposal is that the reader should view this particular type of architectural language purely as an incentive to furthering his or her own personal research.

The authors' prime concern is to draw attention to the methods that characterize Scarpa's approach as applied to studying both large-scale works and small objects for every day use, and to gain recognition for the latter as architectural works in their own right. Whatever the diversity of starting point from one case to another—due to the particular situations in which he was working—the process by which the idea takes shape is identical, almost always drawing on precise thematic nuclei—solid structural units on which the syntax of his architecture is based.

The more important of these *Thematic Elements* are identified as: "support," "connector-link," "fixed joint-hinged joint," "closure-aperture," "solid-void," "molding-profiling," "surfaces," "transparency," "play," "passage"... of which the first eight are dealt with in this book. Allowing one illustrated chapter to each, the authors attempt to exemplify these elements as they are employed in actual buildings or in unrealized projects. The essentially structural aspects are examined first, but attention gradually is shifted to take in the more two-dimensional factors and, lastly, their symbolic values.

Consequently, many works have been subjected to a sort of dismemberment in the course of these eight chapters so as to isolate these thematic elements severally, because, on careful examination, it may be seen that what makes many passages in Scarpa's work so enigmatic and hard to classify is the contradictory or dualistic meaning that attaches to the single element.

Of the various elements assigned to a particular thematic heading, with relevant visual documentation, certain instances are cited purely to stress the more significant exemplars and are excluded from the *Dossiers* in which technical and historical data essential to a complete understanding of the material handled are filed.

An *Index of Illustrations* reassembles all the works analyzed by parts in the course of the book in such a way as to facilitate consultation.

A profile

Anyone planning to take a closer look at the working methods of a great architect and to gain a better understanding of his style may find it interesting to learn something of the personality of the man and his private pleasures in a day-to-day context. But it complicates things when the man in question is Carlo Scarpa. His son Tobia holds the view that the figure of the artist represents his father better than that of the architect in the traditional sense and, in consequence, attempts to match the man to his work may be complicated by irrelevant factors. In effect, a curious aspect of Scarpa, not perhaps to be found in other figures of like fame, is the conviction of some people—still held by those who knew and have studied him—that they alone possess the key to Scarpa's true identity, that only they understand his world, by virtue of proximity, confidences, and repeated displays of affection which Scarpa was prodigal in showing toward almost everyone.

In fact, he was so liberal in sharing with others at any moment his thoughts, reflections, or real critical opinions relating to matters of art, architecture, or life itself that the confidant came to see himself in a privileged light. On the other hand, the inspirational sources of his work are so clearly identified that it seems that there are no mysteries about his preferences.

But then one realizes that these preferences were all-encompassing passions, that every expression of the human intellect has merit, as does every expression of nature, by reason of its being the object of observation, stimulus and interpretation by the intellect itself.

Like all artists, he probably appreciated grace. It is a quality he endeavored to assimilate in his projects, a quality he at once recognized in people, as well as its absence. It is something he knew how to turn to comic effect, for in his later years, by his own estimation too old and overweight to affect the elegance of youth, he adopted an odd, battered panama hat as a mocking tribute to his image.

In architectural practice good-natured mockery abounded, even at the expense of his admirers, when he amused himself in devising puzzling catches for windows or panels or unusual and totally unexpected solutions for opening doors. And in all his major works one observes that an integral part of his process of invention is always to transform his sources of inspiration: mere allusions that, as with a rebus, might lead anywhere.

The formal elegance of his art in no way inhibits its essential playfulness, even when the nature of the commission might seem almost to demand gravity. There are aspects of the Brion cemetery—described as a place where pure form becomes substance and space—in which the fusion of natural and man-made elements, by enhancing their intrinsic vitality, enriches playfulness with a lyricism and a heightened sense of the joy of life: the play of water, channeled into rivulets, then dissolving in pools, even the air and the light there respond to the changing angles of the encircling walls and the gradined surfaces of the concrete.

Insight into this predilection for levity and playfulness in handling forms, even though dissimulated at Brion, contributes to our understanding of the place.

Scarpa was a mixture of jest and earnestness. Just how seriously he took his abilities and subsequent fame is hard to tell.

There was always ambiguity between his recognition of self-worth and the fact that, unlike other celebrated architects, he never cultivated a "maestro" image or set his sights on prestigious appointments. It was museum directors and men of culture who respected him most: he was very proud of the few simple words of tribute that an admiring Roberto Longhi dedicated to his work on the occasion of the 1958 exhibition "Da Altichiero a Pisanello," when, commenting on Scarpa's first intervention in reorganizing the layout of the exhibition rooms at Castelvecchio he described it as "... handled with fitting restraint by the specialist in these things, Carlo Scarpa...."

Due to a kind of superstitious negligence, Scarpa gave no thought to cataloguing his work—a job for others, after one's death, he said. There was even a vagueness about where all his drawings might be. Indeed, they often had been discarded, considered simply as tools and certainly not as masterpieces to be exhibited periodically in magazines or architectural publications.

On predilections

In her Venetian home, Signora Nini Scarpa, wife and vigilant companion of a lifetime, presides over his personal possessions and works by his painter-friends, in the midst of hundreds of books. Most of these volumes deal with aspects of literature, poetry and art, far fewer with architecture. Observing this reminds one of Scarpa's belief that there are no closed doors where reading is concerned. In fact, he encouraged reading everything and, in his opinion, literature was supremely suited to the shaping of an architect: a difficult profession, to be undertaken late in life, when one has some understanding of things, when curiosity is sated and one has sufficient humility to make a start. More than any other, the architect's profession is for the mature.

Sifting through these volumes in search of preferences or key books would be arduous. To achieve an understanding of the type of culture based on these principles, formed over long years not only by reading and experience but also by encounters and companionship, one cannot overlook such factors as personal aptitude—certainly rather uncommon in this case—his great curiosity and roving sensibility. In the ocean of works that he as a cultivated man certainly dipped into, there were, however, titles or authors that came to prevail, and which, together with certain masterpieces of the visual arts, established the guidelines of his reasoning and choices.

La cognizione del dolore by Carlo Emilio Gadda and James Joyce's *Ulysses* were prime instances of the innovative style that a writer of this age might bring to revealing the human condition. Baudelaire was the genius who inaugurated modern poetry, and Pascoli and Carducci lingered in his mind with the greater serenity of their verses: "i pennacchi di color di rosa"—pink-colored plumes—aptly described the mimosa, and "la bruna capelliera"—a brown mane of hair—conjured up an image of energetic and radiant womankind.

Giacomo Noventa, moreover, was always remembered for the grace and poignancy of his words.

In fact, Scarpa readily borrowed a poet's verses to express a concept or even to indicate the necessity of certain spaces, whenever such verses were applicable to persons or situations that held literary connotations for him. Students or close acquaintances often were called by the names of heroes of novels or celebrated artists. Even more frequently he might liken the features of an occasional guest to those of some portrait by an old master. At a favorite restaurant, the complexion or lineaments of Titian's women might be discovered in the owner's daughter, while elsewhere, the modelling of Donatello might be espied in a young student's face, or in the great, deep eyes of another, the mythical stare of Carpaccio's basilisk.

The little flowers of the columbine or of the clematis were the most highly prized, and the skin of houris of the Moslem Paradise would be evoked to define the color of privet berries.

Differing from the customary view, which dismisses the forms of neoclassical art as mere cold imitation, he admired it, explaining what painting owed to the melting softness of Correggio's *Jove and Io* or his *Danae*, and how harmonious these forms in sculpture were—if one could only chop off the feet with their offending period sandals.

And among the supreme cornerstones of pictorial art there were, above all, the beauty of the light in Piero della Francesca and the transparency of Antonello's colors, as well as the peerless Leonardo.

Taking the example of a classical column, his habitual attention to surface quality was conducive to dwelling on the textural value of the rough pores of limestone in lending definition at its summit to the astragals and fusaroles, whose austere geometry was thrown into relief by piercing rays of light, or, along its shaft, the magical proportions of the deep-cut fluting.

He would have undertaken willingly a trip to Greece, the goal of all artists, sharing a comfortable touring coach with his students: it would be possible to check the measurements of the bases of the Erechthion columns and, together, probe the secrets of the harmony of the little temple of Athena Niké. The whole Acropolis should be the object of meticulous examination by all architectural students, the basic experience in educating the eye to see. There would be no end to the range of marvels: the vitality of the arrises of the walls, carved in gleaming white stone, its extraordinarily compact substance exposed by the ravages of time, the fine dentils or the minute friezes owing their superlative beauty to mere millimeters of relief.

At Vicenza, having only Palladio to hand, he often invited students who came to him for advice to visit the nearby Rotunda, because, naturally, one must understand Palladian space, and Villa Maser, in the Treviso area, always repaid a stop-over if one were passing that way by car.

To his great surprise and pleasure, when measuring the interstices between the ledges of two small, adjoining balconies on Palazzo Thiene at Vicenza, it turned out to be 5.5 cm, his own module. Earlier he had been emphasizing the perfect finish of the plaster covering the columns of another nearby Palladian building: the ancient lime-wash was standing the test of time well, it had become like stone, which was indeed the intention of that supreme master. The stylobate of Palazzo Chiericati was almost as noble as that of a Greek temple. As a child he had played bowls between the columns surmounting it. He attributed the secret of good architecture to "proportion," and its preeminent expression was perhaps to be found in Florence. After noting the perfection of the arrises of Palazzo Strozzi, sharply defined against the ingenious furrows cutting across the full height of each rusticated front, one must visit that hidden treasure, the unsurpassed jewel of proportion by Leon Battista Alberti, the sacellum of S. Pancrazio. Scarpa was obliged to admit, however, though much to his regret, that the marvels of Florence, owing to the frequent use of a softer stone, would not last as well as those of Venice. And here, he would add: "se non fosse per le gambe"—were it not for the legs—recollecting the foundations of Venetian palaces, immersed in insalubrious waters. Then there was Brunelleschi, the unrivalled master of perfection: the Pazzi chapel was both a personal myth and a consolation for what he saw as his own unsuccessful attempts to offer something worthwhile in his projects.

Be that as it may, any occasion for talk was a pretext for lifting veils, pointing out links, exemplary works or authors.

Returning from a visit to the Monreale mosaics, he commented that the Christ Pantocrator at Cefalù surpassed them in beauty.

Enthralled by the beauties of Palermo, he recalled an earlier visit, when, engaged in remodelling Palazzo Abatellis, he would linger each morning before the regal tomb of Frederick II of Swabia (King of Sicily and Holy Roman Emperor) in the cathedral, bearing the tribute of a flower and attempting to steal a little of its "energy" by touching the oriental porphyry.

It goes without saying that it would have been impossible for him not to find some trace of the perfection of antiquity in the rigorous, formal investigation of the early twentieth-century Viennese School of architecture, and of the arts in general. Much has been said about the bearing these had as sources of inspiration for many areas of his work, but his real affinities were, above all, with the elegance and refinement of taste of Josef Hoffmann. However, as this book will attempt to explain, everything that had been achieved up to the thirties lodged in his mind, and it was this that sustained him during planning research.

Late in life he advised a student consulting him about a thesis to take a house by Mallet Stevens as a model for his work, explaining the high quality of its spatial organization and the modernism of its conception. He always proposed the early twentieth-century as a source of reliable sustenance for current architecture.

He claimed, though, that true modern taste stemmed from Japan, the superlatively refined Japan, even though he sadly admitted to the coarse fiber of certain modern Japanese works. He admired the elegance of its prints for the sinuosity of the figures, and the landscapes captured with a few simple strokes, with an unsurpassed naturalism, yet so different from Western graphic devices, as in Klee, and the colors so remote from the nuances of Rothko, or those of Joseph Albers, who were also his models.

But above all he admired the imperial palace of Katsura, at Kyoto, with the calibrated geometries of its interiors—assuredly a source for Mondrian—and the metaphysical spaces of the gardens, in which the various materials almost sing out their harmonious presence. The cobbled walks, the hedges and fences, the shape of the stone lanterns, and the bamboo with its periodic clack against the stones as it channels water into the fountain. Nostalgic evocation and dry narrative often combined as he explained the contribution of fog and dusk in creating an authentic structure from those rounded landscapes.

He had tried to conjure up the hidden essence of the art of Katsura in the garden of the Brion cemetery, and one may well understand the pleasure that visiting this garden by moonlight must have given him, and his longing for a photograph to capture its most eloquent moment, the night of the February full moon.

Why this particular choice of moment, it is impossible to know, but some mysterious assonance brings to mind the exuberant ceremony inherited from his friend Arturo Martini, who customarily performed it wherever he was: interrupting anything he was doing when he suddenly caught sight of the crescent forming, he would bow before the slim, luminous figure, and intone three times "Bonsoir, Madame la Lune!"

Scarpa at work

What struck one immediately was his lively, searching curiosity, his eyes noting everything and his memory that, almost like a camera lens, recorded everything. He made no display of his competence and had no need of obscure foreign words to emphasize his meaning, indeed he played it down with his informal turn of phrase and dialect.

He had total recall of the works of other architects. He studied the solutions and layouts of their drawings and plans in books, and wherever possible then confirmed his impressions by a visit to the actual building. He could bring it all back when he glimpsed analogous planning situations or some aspect of similarity of intent or solution. And while he was planning, explaining and discussing with others, it might seem to be they who were being persuaded, but in reality he was convincing himself that he had had a good inspiration, a good idea.

This idea then underwent prolonged elaboration, following a pattern that can be traced back through his drawings. It might happen that this first idea would give way to a new one.

His mental vivacity and ready wit showed in the most surprising and provocative ideas, such as, for example, certain proposals made to students in the course of a scholastic assembly in those years of student unrest; but they, with their minds on other matters, could only reject them, taking the view that any proposal must be reactionary when made by a teacher to "studenti che non studiano": a common enough form of address—non-studying students—that denotes his firmness in the face of juvenile arrogance and presumption but also his approachableness and the conviction he brought to his attempts to fire them with enthusiasm for study. An entire lifetime dedicated to teaching speaks no less for this.

During the final years of his professional activity, Scarpa lived in Vicenza, not too far away from the university faculty in Venice, nor from the building site of the Banca Popolare at Verona. His workspace was nothing like the typical architect's office, with assistants and secretaries; he always had worked from a home base among his books, accustomed to convenience and comfort, with "la Nini" in charge of organization and running the house.

For the jobs that were beginning to trickle in, he relied on student collaborators, who took over the preparation of drawings on which he later made corrections and introduced such changes as the pace of planning called for. He had an entourage of enthusiastic admirers, university students filled with veneration for their teacher and eager to lend a hand in carrying out his projects. Collaboration lingered on after graduation, on a more occasional basis by this time, whenever there was an opportunity for work in the area. There have been ex-students associated with him on official commissions, who were by then respected professional figures with greying hair, or else youngsters, few in number, who, in his last years in the house in Vicenza, were engaged in laying out plans, drawing to scale a sketch or a quick rough, in accordance with his instructions or suggestions, work that was later regularly corrected and recorrected in his own hand.

A constant rhythm was maintained in the elaboration of drawings, primarily to keep pace with work on the site. But this also allowed him to give personal attention to the definition of the more delicate objects, such as those unique and particular pieces that complete the furnishing of the Brion cemetery. The little "pavilion"—long at the stage of a concrete platform set over a void—the candelabrum, the crucifix, the headstones for members of the family, the holy water stoup.

Onorina Brion had become a kind of obsession with him. It was absolutely necessary to throw her off his trail and answer over the phone that "il professore" was not in—he was in Venice, in Genoa, in Palermo, on the building site—and, if anyone could come up with a better idea, to go ahead and use it. He himself, with his nose deep in a handkerchief, had once answered that "il professore" was at school. He had promised her that everything would be finished shortly, but he just wasn't ready. He had to think, come up with a good idea, draw it up, check it, correct it, and then, if everything measured up, carry it out. And all this was, of necessity, long-term work.

Objective difficulties sometimes obliged him to make changes on an already approved project. Paradoxically, he welcomed such difficulties, at times real setbacks, because although they took more out of him, they resulted in more significant solutions, which were satisfying. A good architect, he would say, is one who knows how to turn obstacles to good advantage in the course of a job.

A case in point might be that of the round windows for the Banca Popolare di Verona, which were originally identical in size. Obliged for structural reasons to make one of them smaller, he consequently had a chance to reexamine the balance of the façade. Instead of reducing all the windows to the same scale, which was, perhaps, too obvious a course to take, his brilliant solution was to strike a rhythmic balance between the two different dimensions, and to repeat it on the other side.

The models and the module

The objects Scarpa kept about him were rarely of intrinsic value but always exemplars of fine workmanship. Heterogeneous in function, made of the most unexpected materials, each of these, whether in wood, metal or stone, was perfectly suited to its specific purpose and the fruit of manual dexterity.

The seductions of a semi-precious stone drew him more than the glitter of a jewel because the slow process of sedimentation of the material together with the nuances brought by time, the accumulations and transformations were all there to be seen. These stones differed one from another; when he came across one with unusual colors or markings he purchased it at once for the pleasure of having it about him. Small wooden boxes, of enchanting proportions and delicate structure; drawing instruments made of ivory or boxwood, discovered in old-fashioned stationers' shops in England and Austria, and an ebony set-square with the correct angle for drawing an octagon, that might prove useful only in exceptional circumstances. Small round silver cups, for champagne toasts, were held to be authentic treasures, on a par with the fragile origami animal forms that a Japanese friend devised from colored paper to delight him. Things made by hand alone, with patience and discernment, were what attracted him most, and he always would admire manual skill, but sigh regretfully that he himself "could only use his hands to draw with."

They were never quirky things, but rather forms conveying tradition or invention, thought-provoking forms and models. The point of all this is the contribution it makes to defining Scarpa's role as an educator of taste, teaching discernment, the avoidance of gimmickry, and an understanding of the fact that the real difficulty lies not in coming up with ideas, but in singling out the right one.

His preferences, sympathies, even his obsessions are well-known, but what perhaps has been overlooked is that he schooled taste by his choice of objects, by surrounding himself with certain things, which carried over into his professional activity in his very individual way of using his materials.

There are grounds for the argument that there can be no such thing as a school of

Scarpa: he was a master without followers but he taught a method, that of seeking, and of learning how to recognize something done well. He suggested that the best already had been achieved by the ancients or by one's predecessors, and that the fundamental thing was to find the key, if only to attempt to approach them. Therefore the method consists not of copying or interpreting but of grasping the mechanisms of choice.

When the project for Feltre prompted steps as a solution to the change in level between piazza and road, his mind turned to certain Indian structures for bridges, a kind of gradined barrier alternating with platform areas—an image clearly evoked by association with the same functional requirements of a connector modulated in tiers. Instead, when the time came to complete the arched roofing over the sarcophagi in the Brion cemetery, what came to mind was the exquisite ceramic revetment of the vault in a chapel in S. Job, the only work the Della Robbia carried out in Venice: a sacred place with an analogous intrados, the same need to underline its importance—he even used the same hues for the yellow, blue and green tesserae, made to order at Murano. The result is very personal, everything about it—the materials, his way of plotting out his colors to obey alternating or irregular alignments difficult to trace to their source, the model, the place that prompted the solution—everything about it spells out Scarpa.

Another useful illustration of this ready habit of drawing on his store of knowledge, a constant recourse fostered by "knowing how to see, and not merely look"—a favored dictum with him—is the inspiration for the spaces of the Ottolenghi house at Bardolino. Whoever observes the building, attempting to take in the complexity of its articulation, has to come to terms with the pillars, powerful structural entities formed of alternating stone and concrete courses, contrasting in color, materials and handling. It will be grasped at once that these dictate spatial organization, determine the volumes, harmonize the asymmetries and tie in the angularities. The subtle appeal of this organism will register, the inventiveness will be admired, but it is doubtful that the observer will be able to see, beyond the trimming divide and successive layers of memory and imagination, one of the seeds from which that concept sprang. It is doubtful whether those superimposed spools will provide a clue to the sturdy contours of Palladio's columns on the Villa Sarego at S. Sofia di Pedemonte. There too they are the determinant structural elements of the building, the true spatial protagonists, notwithstanding that their classical alignment and the visual continuity of the balusters make such an emphatic scenographic contribution. This solution certainly was suggested to Palladio by the particular setting in which the Villa stands, a luxuriantly verdant zone of serene, fertile countryside, sheltered by hills.

The pillars at Bardolino follow apparently casual rhythms. They stand singly or in groups. Other memories overlap, Wrightian reminiscences bind interior to exterior and modern architecture cancels the "façade." In place of Palladio's honey-tinted limestone there is concrete and the surface of the pink and white stone is rough hewn. It is the subtle scenographic factor that provides the analogies, suggested here by the green hills, greyed by olive groves, sloping down to the lake shore.

His constant attention to history and models, the manner in which he draws on a variety of sources before contributing a very personal statement, can also be seen from smaller things, from detailing, from the minor works: we are no longer startled when the idea for the stone connective element crowning the parapet of the main staircase in the Banca Popolare di Verona is seen to trace back to the escalation of the marbles delineating the parapet of the bridge of Tiberius at Rimini, those acute and sharp-cut profiles supplying an elegant solution to the camber. There is no mindless repetition in this. Once the concepts of others have been assimilated, a personal language must assert itself. Everything must be new to make a clean break with the past, but seeking to be original at any price, or bizarre, is to be avoided as much as banality or any uncritical and perhaps involuntary dependence on conventional praxis.

His conscious detachment and urge to deviate, even if only minimally, from the accepted norm are undoubtedly at the root of his adopting a yardstick of his own, the module that has been applied throughout the planning of the Brion cemetery.

Let it be said that there is nothing odd or maniacal in the use of the 5.5 cm unit. It is an attempt to experiment with unusual proportions derived from a minimal deviation from the accepted convention of 5 cm, it corresponds to a slight shift in the central viewpoint, from which, perhaps, the novelty of things will be enhanced. It is no longer 5, but five and a bit, then 11, 16.5, 22, 27.5, and so on, in a sequence of rounded-off, imperfect figures. This numerical approximation perhaps will introduce margins of imperfection in the materials used and reflect individuality even in the dimensions of an object.

Nonetheless, the use by others of this ubiquitous 5.5 module amused him, and with a habitual vein of sarcasm led him to deny the efficacy of belief in the relativity of things and the choices that have been made.

Yet this particular yardstick was a constant point of reference, and when one of his projects was ready to be drawn up on Bristol board, its multiples and submultiples would be scrupulously observed to establish relations between parts in the desired proportions. One is taken aback to find recourse to the module in a quick rough in soft pencil on tracing paper: even as early as this, the scale of 5.5, 11, 44, etc. had been envisaged.

From tracing paper to Bristol board

On more than one occasion Scarpa explained what he meant by working method: perseverance and constant commitment, long periods of concentration over the drawing board. This was the only system that brought him results. Any easing up of tension, or even occasional detachment, broke the thread of concentration by which he dominated the whole. Each job, from start to finish, was a dogged pursuance of this method; and everything had to sort itself out in the same setting, his home, with its familiar decor and the tools he was used to readily available.

Naturally, it fell to him, his mind intent on what to do, to sketch in the first lines on tracing paper laid over a drawing showing the location plan with the surrounding buildings, or the bare bones of a structure, as the case might be. There is always a peremptoriness and conviction in these first marks on paper—an intricate network of lines, some fine, some heavy. For Scarpa, more than for others, this was a real language—no concessions were made, display was absent.

The idea was woven into shape from these lines, just as threads form a piece of cloth. In this initial phase Scarpa helped himself along with just a hint of color, which would be used more extensively later on in the process. Lines and color, to supply a semblance of reality—the first to delineate, the second to identify and flesh out. At this stage he was intent on correlating the vital spaces. These must be convincingly harmonic and evolve in equilibrium throughout the entire process, from the first outlines, the first masses in black and white or in color—almost always planimetrical—from which Scarpa customarily derived a portent of the success of a job.

If there is an easy flow of ideas the marks are expressive, a complete statement supplying the general picture, but the detail soon follows, either as a check or a backing. The large scale prompts elaboration so as to grasp the potential of the small part, which may be decisive for the rest.

When an idea is lacking, forcing is useless. Things have to be slept on. One waits while they settle and take shape within. Only then, whenever that may be, will the required solution come.

Taking stock of functions is the prime consideration. Their set proportions and concrete presence shape the forms, and these dilate or set up harmonious rhythms and relationships.

A wide-ranging visual education sustaining formal composition and certainly stemming from a deep feeling for art, above all for painting, is the first support in focusing on these harmonies, but Scarpa's thinking certainly was shaped by a hidden store of detailed memories of everything that he had seen or understood of the best in architecture. Sometimes, as in the case of work in an historical context, the link is more direct, more fortuitous, occasioned by whatever pretexts the residual structures offer for immediate connection. It is as well to emphasize that in such cases insertion of the new structure is by no means mimetic. In such an event, the intervention is dialectic: the assonance is filtered, transformed almost beyond recognition; its charge of novelty must submit itself respectfully.

Asked to name the master of modern architecture he most admired, Scarpa would answer that they had all contributed something, he had no particular preference. In fact, one finds odd correspondences to each of their voices in the plans for his buildings, roughs for unrealized projects, as well as in those subsequently carried out—rather suggesting that what had been most taxing had been the job of selecting the best from each of them.

Testimony to this was the continuous explaining, digressions on the perfection achieved by the "great ones" in this or that place, which accompanied the drawing up of the roughs, or else his smiling comment that, after all, what he was drawing "wasn't the Pazzi chapel," so he might just as well content himself. It was all one long inventory of places, epochs and styles. Painting was his prime inspiration, inclining him to fine detail, such as the tonal subtleties, the imperceptible glazes Raphael had devised for his *La Gravida*, or Giovanni Bellini for his Madonnas. He explained that these were precise indications of the scrupulous striving for harmony in what one is doing, of the humility in taking everything into consideration, even trifles, just like these great artists, who overlooked no aspect of reality, each with a style of his own, but all capturing life for us by the use of their medium.

And Donatello, "the Son of God by direct descent, on a par with Mozart," knew all about it—"had understood everything"—it was enough to look at the clothes his David wears: the fringes, laces and folds, displaying all the infinite variety of style and form that reality offers.

For this same reason, the jobs of focusing, proportioning and detailing call for the ability to visualize all the measurements of a building contemporaneously, or all the plans of connecting space if one is handling an elevation. Even the surrounding fabric must be seen, the whole must be checked because every detail has to be respected. In the end, all this pays off.

Bristol board is effectively the most ductile surface to work up a drawing on. One can erase without entirely losing one's preliminary work, the first idea or drawing that will serve as a reference. A nucleus of notes or conceptions can be stratified, an important detail, specifications for a material or the measurements of a fixed point, some essential intuition, all these can be jotted in a margin, ready to hand. When the scale drawing was submitted to him, Scarpa applied colors to enhance its legibility, and to isolate sequences or levels. This color never was applied in a painterly way, to lend the object reality, but always in an abstract manner, appropriately enough to accompany the abstract nature of the line. He almost always used the same shades of yellow, pink and green, to indicate thickness of walls, the heights above and below, a cutaway in a partition, or a strategic point because some detail had been planned for it. Consequently, for a better grasp of the creative process, this phase too, illustrated in the book, has to be taken into account: work resulting from combined efforts, the preparatory stages laid in by others, his coloring, light or heavy retouching, alterations and clarifications superimposed, almost to the point of obliterating what lies beneath.

Days would go by, the previous phases were continually checked over, second thoughts occurred, changes were made, certain parts slightly shifted: trimming started. "La lima hassi a fare"—trimming is called for—a statement frequently heard at this stage of the project, evoking his beloved Leopardi, who teaches careful finish, pruning, keying and polishing.

This was perhaps the most delicate moment, decisive for perfect coordination of axes, multiple alignments, balanced rhythms for forms whose corporate definition was established in the previous phase, the one characterized by an almost obsessive concern for fitness to purpose. A kind of scrupulous deference to reality stayed Scarpa in his dealings with precise function and concreteness, the material that prompts, invites, obliges or convinces; only later could his imagination give wing to his ideas or draw on his models. Then trimming brought clarity, the decisive choice between two and three or even three and a half centimeters, if the ratio should prove more appropriate.

Such ratios were established by his own empirical methods, still stemming from his grounding in the balancing of parts. They never were calculated mathematically, even though he always had great curiosity about the exactitude of mathematics and for those who used them with confidence. One of his student collaborators, who fascinated him with his slide-rule, was to be dubbed "the scientific Tommasi."

Trimming and tallying—axes, alignments and Gestalt

The study for the fronts of the Banca Popolare di Verona provides a good illustration of the previous phase of the planning process—from tracing paper to Bristol board. The front on the square is the more complex of the two, not only because it addresses public space, but also because of the number of elements involved. Nevertheless, the design for this front was completed first; only later did Scarpa produce a definitive solution for the front on the court, incorporating certain features of the façade.

The studies on Bristol board bear all the traces of the stratifications that accumulated over quite a long period, during the progessive definition of the various parts. In order of importance, they show the structural axes of the building, those of the façade, followed by the axes of the loggia supports coinciding with the center line, and those of the spans between the bases of the colonettes; then the floors, the longitudinal joists of the façade, and the demarcation lines of the partitionings.

This network of vertical and horizontal lines determines the clearance of each element of the front. The interior spaces must in fact have windows and, while a shift of a few centimeters may be irrelevant for lighting, it can be decisive for external composition. Once all the necessary spatial definitions have been dealt with, the study can then move on into a strictly two-dimensional field to effect a balance between solids and voids and establish their interdependency. What results is a gestaltic order, reached by trial and error in placing the elements.

Each of the vertical axes functions autonomously as an axis of symmetry, but the overall effect, tempered by mixing and overlapping, prevents any single axis from predominating.

However, there are also numerous anomalies that often elude the non-specialist eye.

For example, facing the façade and reading from the left, it is possible to identify the dominant axes in defining the whole: the first axis of symmetry is picked up in the center line of the first span of the loggia, coinciding with the center line of the inverted molding on the cornice, an alignment that, as the eye travels down, takes in the center lines of the two stiffeners of the wing of the big girder, the round window and its dripstone, tying into the left-hand molding of the rectangular window beneath. The second axis starts in the next span, runs down through the center line of the small balcony to coincide with those of the projecting window and the window beneath. The third, instead, is that of the third base of the colonettes, which falls between two stones of the cornice, coincides with the axis of the girder riveting plate, that of the gilded-spheres motif, and ties in once more with that of the round window, its dripstone, and the rectangular window.

Moving to the right, the fifth span mirrors the situation of the first. In direct succession, the axis of the next pair of colonettes states itself forcefully between the two bay windows, determining the trend and the molding of the red stone fascia and the aperture below for the basement.

Proceeding to the next span: here, because of its greater breadth, the axis determines a duplication of the cornice stone molded on its lower extremity, and of the girder stiffeners. It subsequently runs between the two narrow balconies and the quadrangular windows beneath, of which the left-hand one is aligned exactly with the right-hand one below. Moreover, the interstices of the two bay windows are identical on both levels. There are also less discernible axes, whose action is confined to minor elements. Clearly, there is nothing rigid about these axes of symmetry, each has a bearing on a given point but may then give way to another axis, occasionally to reappear elsewhere.

The alignments also are studied horizontally: the first of these is indicated by the stone revetment, then by the height of all the mezzanine apertures. Finally, the base of the glazed wall on the main staircase establishes the sill course of all the windows, larger, smaller and quadrangular; these in their turn determine the position of the transversal girder of the glazed wall itself. It may be noticed that the height of the mezzanine bay windows is less than in those of the upper level, where the height equals that of the larger round windows. This same rhythmic pattern carries over into the glazing bars of the windows.

It is nonetheless apparent that the façade is quite asymmetrical. The large window on the right has no counterpart on the left, but is compensated by the compact surface beneath it. The position of the main entrance is completely autonomous in respect to the rest. The zigzag course of the glazing in the upper zone is echoed lower down in the stone fascia. Both motifs are dynamic by virtue of their asymmetry in relation to the motif of the round windows. The cornice is the stabilizing element of the whole. Even in the first roughs, when its configuration still had to be determined, it brought the front to a close and harmonized the various elements.

Finally, the stone curtain wall, which Scarpa intended to resemble thin cartilage, is, in reality, a solid load-bearing structure that even incorporates a Vierendel beam which allows the large aperture at the side of the main entrance.

A pair of colonettes is perched above this void and another pair, also apparently mock load-bearing, stand above the windows.

"Nobody notices," Scarpa commented, implying by this that the façade by no means transmits a sense of instability; indeed, it derives its harmonic character from so much diversity in its elements and from the balance achieved by the painstaking study of the axes and ratios between the parts described here.

Analogous asymmetries and anomalies are not hard to find on the front overlooking the court. Additionally, two round windows appear, larger in size and set close together, that, in conjunction with the positioning of their dripstones, determine a larger-scale rectangular window beneath: a feature subsequently repeated twice on the right-hand side, so that an anomaly would not be mistaken for an error of judgment or a failure to dominate the elements.

In the first roughs, the front addressing the court was conceived as sequences of glazed bands at different levels.

Only later, after the definition of the front on the square, did it follow suit with the two types of windows, round and rectangular, but without projection, and the red fascia, but with a rectilinear trend.

The overall asymmetry of the court front also is legible at first sight. It is slightly reentrant on the left, to allow for the insertion of the suspended walkway on the first floor, while, on the right, in the upper part, the curtain walling is interrupted by the presence of a terrace connecting with the spiral staircase. The white surface of the front, however, partially shields this sudden void, indeed, it even sets a pair of colonettes against it, before producing itself as a "flag" that links up with the two tall columns at approximately mid-height. These elements of the structure support the girders that cross the void, but not the cornice, which, logically, turns back in the direction of the elevator core.

Genesis of the working drawing

The Bristol board now offers a perfect representation of what the actual building will be, because nothing has escaped attention in the trimming process. It is now possible to change scale and go into smaller detail. The study process is identical: from the rough to proportioning, from refining to trimming, etc., a process that is repeated for subsequent enlargements, progressively focusing on parts, almost all of which already have been foreshadowed in the previous phases.

From the stratifications on a single board, the separate items are extracted and drawn up in India ink on tracing paper, thereby producing a number of different drawings. These are the working drawings, copies of which were to be handed out to the various skilled workers involved on the job: masons, smiths, bricklayers, etc. Scarpa also colored these copies, certainly to enhance their legibility, but also, perhaps subconsciously, in an attempt to modulate the technical drawing and soften its rigidity. These had to be scrupulously elaborated drawings, immediately legible, with measurements and proportions explained, symmetries marked in, accompanied by notes and specifications for materials. Certain parts might overlap, as much to exploit the space of a sheet to the maximum as to enhance its visual appeal.

At the last moment there might be further retouching, second thoughts penciled in on the copy, accompanied by more precise instructions or recommendations to the worker involved.

In his final years, second thoughts at the executive phase were infrequent because of the meticulous preparatory work that had preceded it, and it is extraordinary to see that, when realized, certain details are exactly identical to their projected image on the board. True, Scarpa would sometimes change his mind, even improvise, but only when the drawing had not been adequately perfected or patiently checked over. There are, too, items laid aside over a long period, and only a sudden rush of inspiration could resolve these.

Emblematic of this situation are the studies for the Brion cemetery, truly exemplary for its yield of deposits and inventions, especially where details that eluded definitive drafting are concerned.

The idea for the holy water stoup, of Carrara statuary marble, came to him unexpectedly, derived from the rounded contours of a small nineteenth-century tobacco jar, made of thin briarwood, which captured his attention in an antique shop during one of his trips to London. He discovered on the screw top his favourite motif of two intersecting circles: an authentic portent of pertinent inspiration for the holy water stoup that had been awaiting a form for months.

Cross references within the canon

In this last instance we have an illustration of how a planning idea may appear suddenly after any amount of research and effort has proved fruitless, or else been judged unacceptable. When the object of planning lies outside the usual run, one has to wait for the right inspiration to come along. If, however, there were aspects of similarity between projects, Scarpa resorted to a little device, which consisted of lifting some relevant part from another of his projects and temporarily transplanting it into the new context, until some definitive idea should turn up.

Observing his various projects, it can be seen that he has, at times, made use of this expedient to enable him to get on with areas that could be more rapidly elaborated, postponing confronting the more difficult parts, which would require greater attention.

This is what happened in planning for the Monselice branch office of the Banca Antoniana di Padova, when, reluctant to deprive the township of public space, he thought of raising the building above a portico, and his spontaneous reaction was to design pillars similar to those being built in the Ottolenghi house at Bardolino.

Only at a later date did he note with satisfaction the inspirational source for those pillars, having found it in the covered walkway designed by Frank Lloyd Wright for the Florida Southern College at Lakeland. From the designs it is possible to observe this change, as well as the fact that Wright's pillars are certainly not those of Scarpa's project. All they have in common is a vague resemblance in the pronounced flaring at the head of the shaft, but the general conformation is entirely original.

It was planned that the structures beneath the Monselice bank should feature twin pillars of reinforced concrete, twin rectangular pillars, set close together but independent of one another, each with a powerful lateral projection at the head of the shaft. To introduce greater variety, each file of pillars on the regular but incomplete grid turns through 90° in respect to its neighbor.

An analogous situation arises at the Faculty of Humanities and Philosophy in Venice, in the former convent of S. Sebastian. The aula magna fanning out into the vast courtyard has supplanted the hall on a square plan, which temporarily occupied the area to be developed and originally was designed by Scarpa for the Bailo Museum in the convent of

S. Catherine in Treviso. Both are supported by pairs of round pillars turning through 90° to define the perimeter of the square plan.

There is also the case of the pillar typology for the covered walk, sealed off by glazing, on this same project at S. Sebastian, which was later envisaged as an evolution of the Ottolenghi house pillar: a revetment composed exclusively of two types of prefabricated elements, alternating both in the make up of the single ring and in the sequence of rings forming the shaft.

One may sum up, therefore, by saying that when Scarpa, for whatever reason, was hard pressed to get drawings ready, and the time for thought was less than he required, he borrowed certain concepts from his other buildings until such time as he could replace them with new and more appropriate ideas.

Memory and invention I

Among the numerous projects left incomplete in the preliminary planning phase is his intervention on the conventual nucleus of S. Catherine in Treviso, to inscribe the Bailo Museum. It offers an exemplary illustration of the course of research.

Obviously, the first set of relations that Scarpa felt compelled to evaluate centred on the context, sited in the ancient district of the town, where, flanking the convent church, lay an area in which residual volumes were to be restructured and others built ex-novo. The location plan best reflects the reality of the situation, suggesting where new organisms were to be delineated and old ones revitalized.

In the layout of a museum, as in this case, in a preexistent nucleus, the self-same principles that animate all planning interventions in ancient contexts apply even to the connective tissue of display areas, staircases, ramps, entry points, etc. Research must lead to a natural, near-organic articulation of the various walkways and communicating spaces, to convey an idea of the uniqueness and the inevitability of the whole, as if the building itself had dictated its function. This, however, as Scarpa was well aware, is pure illusion, as a thousand different approaches are possible. Nonetheless, the important thing is that there should be no straining, no violation of what exists. Everything must look natural. The aim is to build up the vital relationships within this place, primarily by means of full exploitation of factors of assonance and dissonance, as the case may be, modulated in near-musical terms: broadening-narrowing, sheen-opacity, light-dark, color-monotone, wood-iron, etc., in a word, contrasts; but also like themes: light-white, gold-color, rough plaster-stone, etc.

And here, in the case of the Bailo Museum, massive volumes, created ex-novo to supplement the residual structures, fall into place with extreme clarity, evincing characteristics of lightness at variance with their bulk. On the other hand, thanks to those subtle, near-musical associations, minimum apertures or some sudden isolated void have sufficed to animate the vast, sweeping surfaces of the complex.

It is wise to stress Scarpa's attention to the innate vocation of a space and his progressive focusing on parts of organisms so as to ensure clarity and detail, almost as if some uniquely right solution to that function would ensue.

This is so marked as to imply that successful issue is inescapable, the solution is as if preordained, and the various elements, notwithstanding their autonomous vitality, seem to come together of their own accord.

Development of the elevation of the project, or of some part of it, submits to this same law, as the drawing calls for attention to this or that detail, or enhanced definition of the volumes.

In the project for S. Catherine's there is a point on the front addressing the street that clarifies this process, revealing meticulous research. What has been interpreted elsewhere—in consideration of Scarpa's prevalent attention to context—as an act of homage to the missing apse of the church, is a slight convexity in a portion of the wall flanking it. Yet this feature itself is quite clearly a pointer to an overriding concern for the aspect of modernity required of the new insertion, perhaps the most interesting and personal aspect of the project. Granted that the convexity of this structure is generated by osmosis, or as a reflection of the presence—absence of the church apse, the mainspring is to be seen in Scarpa's plans for it. This convexity must, in fact, allow space for the full loop of a stairway, and the evident intention here, beyond that of isolating this connective element from the static enfilade of container spaces, is to express its full, steep ascent on the exterior. In this way, the sharply defined form, apparently deriving an almost organic flexion from the accelerated pace of ascent, is virtually transformed into an engine part, a laminated gear box enclosing its vital mechanisms.

At the same time, this example offered by the front of the Bailo Museum draws attention to another important aspect of Scarpian invention: the sudden tautening and expansion of the wall as if in response to some force within. The phenomenon never develops beyond the bounds of the initial phase of distortion, a flexion, an almost imperceptible curve not unlike that produced by finger pressure behind a sheet of paper, and its expressive virtues can be sensed. It is an insight prompted by simple juxtaposition, the fitting together of two surfaces separately subjected to a subterranean charge of dissimilar potential. This is not, however, merely an encounter between flat planes and curved planes but rather the sudden, slight incurvature of a taut membrane, and its disengagement from the background plane. The almost perceptible sound of this is what communicates to an attentive viewer the joy of formal achievement, the profound motivation of an architectural volume and its total absence of gratuitousness.

The continuous plane surface on this same front, broken only by ribbon fenestration high up—a feature not remote from Le Corbusier—makes another important point in the slim cylinder attached to it, housing another tiny staircase. This container is suggestive of a sheet of paper rolled up to form a scroll, the inner corners adroitly left exposed above and below in an impulse of ingenuous, almost ironic naturalism, and notwithstanding its almost accidental nature, the element succeeds in animating the front. Scarpa's approach in respect to this front at S. Catherine's shows how he proceeded by fragments, by almost imperceptible observations, by sudden, lively intuitions of forms germinated in the most dishomogeneous soils, but each secreting its own vital lymph, each born of a previously untried process but accompanied by familiar hereditary traits. Apparently incoherent and disconnected forms in a single organism, graceful, detached entities that all together achieve coalescence by virtue of the prior claim of perfect synchronization of the vital spaces; even though Scarpa himself cautioned that the processes of coalescence might prove versatile, and that what results may not be the final word.

The elevation, therefore, brings us back to the same formal principles that were expressed in the location plan. In synthesis, one of the aspects of invention is the sense of organic unity, innate to those earlier described volumes that break free on the front, the sense of a perfect exterior suggested by that which is to be contained. The second aspect lies in the attribution of a precise expression to each part, a specific identity to the single element, which calls into play his inflexible rules of balance, contrasts, and agreement of proportions.

The great masters and the lessons to be learned from them surface once more. But in this subtle handling of sources of inspiration not even the minor figures are overlooked: Hugo Häring, for instance, whose presence may be felt strongly in Scarpa's other buildings, or in sections of them, as in certain areas of the Zentner house in Zurich.

Any attempt to discern influences and tributes would be long and difficult, but this brief mention, stemming from the analysis of his method, may suffice to convey the complexity of this aspect of Scarpian poetics, hitherto dismissed, albeit with expressions of esteem, as sophisticated handling of regional idiom, or the product of aristocratic isolation.

Another of these tributes to the rich and multiple aspects of modern architecture in the twenties and thirties may be seen in the cylindrical form and mushroom cap of the third staircase, the same design which is manifest in the Bailo Museum.

It relates to a phase in which Scarpa, with evident pleasure, was thumbing through illustrations of buildings by Robert Mallet Stevens, pointing to them as supremely elegant examples of a reserved, disciplined, and informed art.

Memory and invention II

Similarities to the Bailo Museum in the former convent of S. Catherine also are to be seen in the plans for a new house for Giovanni Chiesa at Vicenza, alongside a nineteenth-century mock-Palladian villa by the architect Ottone Calderari; but here there are other aspects to be considered.

The project was to provide a new nucleus to replace a structure—a kind of "barn", wholly insignificant and adjacent to the villa—which was in such a bad state of repair as to be uninhabitable. At the start of the nineteenth century, moreover, "an unworthy period turret" had been added, and this, in Scarpa's opinion, disfigured the whole. Besides conservation work on the villa, the quite unassuming project envisaged the new nucleus as a day zone on the ground floor, a night zone on the first, and also offered interesting detailing, especially on the fronts. Analysis of the drawings shows that the new nucleus was articulated in unobtrusive projections and allowed for the presence of small areas outside the house, beyond the garden facing the villa. The front was modulated by tonalities of chiaroscuro, a gestaltic balance of solids and voids in respect to the windows, and the positioning of shutters, aligned either to right or left as the case might be. The pitch of the roof was so low as to be hidden from view and the main block brought forward in respect to its original position, because it was set too far back and hidden by the staircase at the front of the villa.

The most interesting innovation occurs in the ground-floor perimeter wall to a court at the entry point to the house, to which access is gained through a round aperture, as in Chinese gardens. The scene is completed by a pool, situated between the villa and the new wall, thereby excluding traffic near the heavy pronaos, a rather ill-proportioned structure casting over-long shadows. The wall itself, which is the connecting link between the residual nucleus and the new house, from the entry point runs the full length of the house and beyond, delimiting the garden, a "hortus conclusus." The garden is on the same level as the day zone, slightly sunken in respect to the surrounding countryside.

Bureaucratic difficulties and failure to obtain the necessary permits forced Scarpa to review the project. Planning regulations at Vicenza called for pantile roofing and a request also came through that the project should not differ too much from the existing edifice. Pantile roofing therefore appeared above a façade of extreme simplicity that contrived minimum displacement of windows. The roof follows an irregular course, and is pitched rather low, as in the Palazzetto house at Monselice, built in the same period, or later, on the Ottolenghi house at Bardolino. The final blow to the project came when the authorities concerned rejected the plans and ordered conservative restoration, even of the turret.

In his dealings with tutelary bodies for ancient monuments and civic offices of works, the definition of the important remnants to be respected was disputed at times, and his ability to make new insertions in ancient contexts sometimes underestimated. A negative judgment was passed not only on this last project but also respecting the Bailo Museum in Treviso, and for the restoration and extension of the convent of S. Sebastian for the Faculty of Humanities and Philosophy at the University of Venice. Here, too, only the parts relevant to conservative restoration were approved.

Instead, when there was perfect agreement of intent with the tutelary authorities, the result is exemplary regarding the regulations governing restoration. The interventions at Possagno, Verona, and Palermo are proof of this.

5.5 x 5.5 as a signature

In his work on the Brion cemetery at S. Vito di Altivole, near Treviso, Scarpa made systematic use of the 5.5 x 5.5 cm module and its multiples and submultiples.

Applied to reinforced concrete, this module generates form and decoration, structure and surface. It becomes one with the medium, instrumental in determining and bonding solids or in cutting into them to create voids and shadows, modulating the light in variable depths of chiaroscuro. Scarpa turned to this flexible yardstick to create innumerable variants and combinations in all the diverse solutions his imagination provided, before choosing among them.

In conversation and interviews Scarpa declared that he had been influenced while planning the cemetery by images that had lodged in his mind in the course of readings many years before. It is a fascinating hypothesis that he may have adopted this module to compete with the innumerable images evoked by Paul Valéry in his *Cimetière Marin*. The hour, the light and the reflections from the sea brought continuous change to the appearance of the little cemetery. At S. Vito it is form that challenges immobility by creating a variety of situations and inflections, but here, too, light, the hour of day and the seasons are instruments of change. Scarpa tempered this propensity for change by coupling it to the sense of stability implicit in the calm and serenity of a garden, a refuge for rest and contemplation, a respite from oppressive feelings and anguish, a place to linger.

In a short space of time Brion became widely known and was as commonly associated with the name of Scarpa as the module that generated it. So much so that the author justifiably concluded that he might assume proprietorial rights to this theme and its variations, using it as his "signature."

Consequently, in subsequent projects this module, varying in proportions and in the material it is applied to, no longer appears exclusively as a structural yardstick, but also as a decorative feature of the revetments or in the modelling of a surface. It may be seen on the cornice stones and the fascias on the Banca Popolare di Verona, where it also decorates the interiors. It inscribes his "signature" on such projects as the stonework on the entrance to the Faculty of Humanities and Philosophy in the former convent of S. Sebastian, the guest rooms of the Querini Stampalia Foundation and, also in Venice, on the entrance to the Architectural Institute at the University. Here the module is once more applied to concrete, but exclusively as surface modulation: the dimensions varying in proportion, one of them much larger than the other, and the depth scaled down to the minimum the planks of the mold would accept. The module appears in marble on the commemorative monument in Piazza della Loggia in Brescia, with meticulous relief in the order of 11 x 5.5 x 3 mm.

The cornice stones of the Banca Popolare di Verona illustrate another peculiarity of Scarpa's method: at the center of each span on the second-floor loggia, one stone of the cornice has been up-ended and its molding, in contrast with neighboring stones, faces downward. Initially he had studied a version of both fronts in which all stones, regardless of size, were plain above and carved below. The working drawings were ready to leave for Verona when everything was called in question again by a jocular remark that the weight of the stones would prevent the crane from positioning them. Fearing that he had exaggerated their bulk, he therefore resolved to up-end them so as to enable him to carve deeper and lessen their weight.

This is the genesis of the pinnacles so reminiscent of the Venetian tradition in crowning palaces, and especially of the Fondaco dei Turchi. However, he decided to retain one centrally placed stone with the molding pointing down as a reminder of the first version, and to demonstrate, both to himself and others, that the problem had been redimensioned.

In the end, he came to the conclusion that these echoes of the past and the variety they introduced made the new solution more significant than its predecessor.

Building traditions

Constant fidelity to tradition, to Venetian tradition in particular, was expressly proclaimed. His first thought when faced with a problem was how it would have been dealt with in the past. It was the discipline and method he sought to emulate, not the idiom, for which he attempted to work out an equivalent more attuned to modern sensibility, while pursuing traditional procedures and materials. This can be seen clearly if one looks closely at his works.

The floor of the Ottolenghi house at Bardolino, for example, is like a continuous carpet for which the ancient Venetian "terrazzo" was the immediate inspiration: the stones, selected by size and in a color range from beige to brown, are bonded with a pale cement paste mixed with minute black and white pebbles. The colored stones form casual and irregular sequences subordinate to an overall pattern reminiscent of the large stone paving blocks of Roman roads, but also serving the practical purpose of lessening the risk of surface chipping and cracking.

Another sign of this is his frequent recourse to stucco, *marmorino* and *calce rasata*, the use of which has fallen into neglect almost everywhere because craftsmen today have lost the techniques. Tinted stucco is a constant and precious complement to Scarpa's work. Its handling was entrusted to the firm of Eugenio De Luigi, the only firm still employing the classic and traditional procedure that lends stucco those peculiar characteristics of sheen, transparency, softness and tone-color. Scarpa himself was reluctant to talk about the application or the components of this magical substance, for fear of saying anything detrimental to his friend's interests by divulging the secrets of his work.

The elementary rule for having a job well done, he said, was to place oneself in the hands of the right man, and he confirmed this belief throughout his activity by working, almost without exception, with the same craftsmen. He knew their specific professional capacities, his relationships with them were marked by esteem, and even friendship. He employed them wherever he was working, whether in the Venetian region or in Sicily, in Switzerland, or even in Montreal when he was invited to collaborate on the Italian pavilion at the 1967 World Exposition.

He knew by now that he could rely on their abilities. They in turn showed an intuitive understanding of his requirements without need of long explanations.

He was demanding, but not bizarre, if he was punctilious it was over important matters, and he made a point of never demolishing anything that had been made to his order. When anything dissatisfied him, he set about correcting it.

A single form and its potential

Since he liked to see "a job well done," as he put it, Scarpa's ideal was to study everything down to the last detail.

Analyzing his projects and examining his drawings soon reveals studies for secondary parts of some complex that, in a manner of speaking, no one has ever considered. In the case of the Gavina store in Bologna, which he worked on without assistants, preparing all the plans personally, even the working drawings for the craftsmen, he gave undivided attention to every item, including the door to the meter cupboard, the back entrance, the garbage-closet door—all subjects designed with his customary attention, precision and coherency: his declared aim was to overlook nothing, to give even greater attention to what was out of sight than to what was there for everyone to see.

On occasion, his solutions may be grasped immediately—they are the fruit of straightforward graphic procedures, empirically proportioned and selected without recourse to such mathematical ratios as $\sqrt{2}$, the golden section, or other formulas. In fact, he showed a certain reluctance to make use of the pure forms, geometrical loci, or perfect figures by which the great civilizations of the past achieved their supreme harmony of expression.

Modern form language is a barrier to using a simple square figure appropriately today: one can play with the relationship between the two dimensions, conjure up an equilibrium from whatever slight margin of difference exists between their measurements, but it would be meaningless to take a pair of compasses to a piece of paper, inscribe a circle on it, and then transfer it to a building of our own times. On the other hand, with contemporary aids, admittedly technologically advanced, but remote from a spirit of perfection in any classical sense, realizing these absolute forms also would be difficult—whereas a sudden intuitive grasp of the imperfection, the desired margin, is tantamount to rediscovering a lost "rule." A characteristic instance of this is the circular form with two centers Scarpa utilized from the fifties onwards, and which came fully into its own in the motif of two intersecting rings at the entrance to the Brion cemetery.

He stumbled on this in the course of planning the spiral staircase for the Veritti house when, needing to augment its total volume, he took a slightly off-center point for his compass, inscribed another circle and, to his surprise, "the staircase seemed to pulsate." This was a confirmation of his theory that a form containing an imperfection in respect to a pure geometrical figure is more "natural" and consequently more expressive. The impression of movement establishes the character of the staircase and the precise positioning on paper of the two centers. This was later to be expressed in the actual staircase by means of two vertical elements running its full height. In fact, a flash of insight touched off by a line on paper often would take its place alongside reasoning in the course of planning—the linearity and abstract nature of the drawing itself proposed alternatives, suggested new solutions, and Scarpa would allow himself to follow them up.

Almost coinciding with work on the Veritti house, this twin-centered motif acquired a third dimension, applied to a small depression in a tombstone in the Quero cemetery in Belluno and, very shortly afterwards, pluri-centered arcs combined to shape the Gavina store windows in Bologna. Subsequently, at Brion, the special pieces cast in bronze repropose variations on the same motif, three-dimensional once more, as indeed are the two large intersecting metal rings at the entrance to the cemetery. Scarpa certainly must have made up his mind from the start that a fitting motif for the cemetery would be an abstract design suggestive of the union between a man and a woman, with its echoes of ancient symbologies. But this also gave him the opportunity to satisfy his criterion for "a job well done," using mosaic to introduce a note of color and framing the sward beyond so as to make it clear that out there was a different place from the usual oppressive country cemetery, with its clutter of headstones and wretched corpses crammed into "shoeboxes": in essence, there was a garden, with water and flowers, where death had been put to rout.

The graphic construction of this motif is of extreme simplicity, as he himself admitted: a circle is drawn, its radius is halved, from this center-point the radius is produced horizontally and a second circle is centered on its terminal point. The gap between the two centers corresponds therefore to a radius and a half: that this distance should equal 3/2 of the radius did not trouble him at all. Once the two centers had been found, he described another two circumferences, concentric to the earlier ones and allowing sufficient difference in radius to accommodate the glass tesserae.

Last on the list, this motif of intersecting circumferences reappears at strategic points on the Banca Popolare di Verona, as if to provide an endorsing "signature" wherever the sharp note of gilding might be called for. Moreover, here the bank windows constructed with two arcs of circles spaced out along the horizontal axis are in some aspects similar to the Gavina store windows, which also have quite close-set centers, but where spacing is determined by the vertical axis. In both cases, however, any tendency there might be for these dynamically constructed elements to drift is checked by the surface grids of their respective fronts. At Bologna, the windows are stayed by the gilded fascias furrowing the concrete front—cross-references between the three voids tie them in; at Verona, their dipstones, anchored by the stability of the rectangular apertures beneath, act as stays and commit them to a role in determining the balance of the total frontage.

Large scale, small scale

Another unusual aspect of Scarpa's style and method is his marked consistency of invention, whatever the scale. Detailing, in fact, obeys the same principles observed in spatial organization. The great lessons of the past are there, the high tradition of craftsmanship, perfect adherence to purpose and context, strict observance of functionality, and the unmistakable penchant for an organism that must evolve naturally. The individual parts take shape slowly, each pursuing its specific role, initially schematic in concept, gaining in complexity as it contrives to evolve into a new form. At this stage, the processes of articulating, connecting and interlocking must combine harmonically to produce a precisely machined, perfectly efficient and near-organic whole.

An example will clarify this best: the candelabrum studied for the Brion chapel was an inspiration. The first sketch Scarpa jotted down shows a gossamer tangle descending from the height of the ceiling to the side of the altar: the words "candelabrum like this," scrawled hastily beside it point to his conviction regarding this inspiration. Deriving a form for the individual pieces from the idea underlying this simple scheme—simple after the fashion of all successful things—was a very long job. The first element—almost as if to mark the start—is simply a bar, albeit enriched in composition by a miscellany of woods, let into the masonry of the cupola in the manner of a crossbar: a common enough structural element to hang things from. The second element, which must branch off perpendicularly from the first, could not be resolved in a single piece: "one must keep it simple, but not over-simple," and, to avert this danger, it is contrived by combining three slender rods, jointed together at alternating points so that unity is preserved, while resorting to a sheaf, a "simple" assemblage, to state the vertical supporting the lights. An articulating joint is needed to secure it to the crossbar; it must rotate on a plane to be unobtrusive, but it cannot be either a pin or a screw. Instead, it will be a tiny hinge, equipped with a round bulb and a tassel of gilded rods, which simulate a knot tying the two bars together. These are "complex" rather than complicated forms, quite unevocative, simply themselves. In situ, seen against the vault, they are sculptural. The sculpture-mechanism will be completed by the transparent plexiglass candleholders; these too are exposed, fitted to silver-plated brass rods, rotating in sockets clamped to the perpendicular wooden bar. Each element as can be seen, is complete in itself, clearly stated without confusion or sloppiness, its function undisguised; an almost elementary counterplay of forms. Yet the whole appears complex, a study in neatly-balanced proportions and weights.

The crucifix planned for the same chapel is the result of analogous extended experiment and reflection. It too is an elegant organism of interlocking elements and functions. It must hold its place in a precise point on the altar, almost the center of gravity for the whole, an elaborately turned, multi-faceted assemblage of parts and materials. All the objects for the Brion tomb were to make time to evolve, a demonstration of the sacred respect in which he held not only the place for which they were planned, but also the freedom from deadlines his imagination required to produce them.

Thus it was for the low gated apertures on the water: simple and straightforward in comparison with other pieces, but, just the same, held up almost until the very last, until he was convinced he had found the most fitting materials for the symbolic form to inlay the hinged slabs of white Clauzetto stone by means of which closure is effected. These were a chance find by his marble-worker, two pieces of ancient stone, oriental red porphyry and Stella green serpentine. The circumstance stands as a reminder that often only certain materials fit certain uses, that these and these alone are right, and without them it is better not to make a start. Yet despite everything, one very small part of the inlay on the back of these same slabs was never to be placed. This offers an indication of analogies in handling procedure between the tiniest objects and his architecture, whereby everything must be allowed to come of its own accord, only when it is ready, when the time is ripe. More than in his architecture—where he also had to contend with external factors, often quite determinant for the building process—the occasional difficulty in coming to the right idea, and the consequent, sometimes permanent delay, is seen more explicitly in the objects, or at least, in the small scale elements. It was the case with the angel which should have taken its place on the corner projection of the chapel, a gesture of warning and an emblem. Over the years, dozens of sketches were made for it, but the idea would not come. Even an angel of near-Romanesque inspiration was considered: awe-inspiring and evil-averting, both monster and insect, the bare bones of human attributes, but conviction was absent.

Neither craftwork nor design

Scarpa may have passed from the smooth, transparent forms of his vases to the necessarily more solid and complex structures of his furniture quite naturally, without any transition form, but this is something we cannot know for sure.

However, working with glass, whether exploiting its plasticity, its opalescence or transparency, whether dripping colors on, fusing segments of glass together or swathing the form in a uniform glaze, he never lost sight of purity of line. If he remarked how much a bowl gained by the absence of a foot, his comment revealed the response of instinctive taste and reflected his sensibility towards changeable things, and also towards freedom of invention. With glass the marvels of light can be captured, the depth of a color that would look flat in other materials.

From the thirties onwards Scarpa designed for the Venini glass factory in Murano and also produced furniture for his own home, as well as for shops and private houses. Whereas defining form for objects in glass provides a pretext for creating attractive ornament and allows one a more or less free hand, the factor of function where furniture is concerned obviously imposes decisive constraints. Sturdiness for a table, for example, is essential, and Scarpa, deploring the slightest wobble, often would discourage undiscriminating admiration for novelty of form or elegance. With furniture, a thorough grounding in the specific tensile properties of one's materials is fundamental for their correct usage. The resulting aesthetic pleasure is then far removed from what the purely formal essay obtains.

The entirely individual quality of his objects and, above all, their remoteness from craftwork products, needs no comment. There was never any indulgence in manual skill, which was transcended, or at least disciplined, by his noble tradition of respect for materials. Technologically, his solutions were always beyond criticism, there was no wasteful indulgence in ornamentation or fanciful aestheticizing. But the term "design," with its connotations of perfect mechanical reproducibility, of formal results geared to providing a precise and reiterated solution to functional problems, is also inapplicable.

He himself had a particular aversion to the word, observing that a good designer was his son Tobia, who had a perfect understanding of industrial processes, spent long hours in the factory, and came up with ingenious solutions in response to new procedures. Anything of this kind was quite extraneous to his own nature. A sound knowledge of the limits or merits of a type of wood, for example, gave him an immediate grasp of the correct thickness for a board to be used or the right treatment to obtain maximum aesthetic and practical advantages. It is impossible to get to the bottom of his negative reaction towards production in series, when, instead, an eye for innovation was perhaps the most significant facet of his way of grappling with a conception. So much so that his products and, by extension, his most successful buildings, are not just formal achievements; they bear within them the seeds of their development, the evidence of transformation, and herald future taste.

What perhaps lies at the root of this reluctance to give himself wholeheartedly to production in series is a desire to stay with an object and keep a sharp eye on measuring his materials. He felt that any reliance on machines would deprive him of this. By contrast, he was reconciled to the intervention of the latest technologies in architectural production, where scale and the intrinsically composite nature of architecture provides its own justifications.

An encounter with Dino Gavina, in the late fifties, allowed him a more direct hand in attempting to adapt certain of his ideas for furniture to production in series. This rather uncommon manufacturer was the first to sense Scarpa's possibilities as an inventor of new forms, indeed as an arbiter of taste, and eventually persuaded him to adapt a table originally designed for the Zentner house in Zurich to production in his workshops. There is little that is not already known about how the splendid "Doge" table, its pared-down structures shorn of the embellishments fitting it to shine in an already elaborate and striking private setting, turned into a perfect example of the application of his earlier-described capacities and convictions to steel and glass and the interpretation of form.

Of all furnishing elements, in his opinion, the structures of the table were closest to those of architecture. It was this factor that won him round and convinced him that, here, he could express himself with greater precision and turn out his best results.

When designing a wooden table he drew on the fifteenth-century forms of a convent table, and seeing it photographed in Pier Paolo Pasolini's house, he came out with an ironical and, for one so little motivated by financial return, unexpected comment on the eventuality that this fortuitous piece of advertising should prove a boost to sales. The same amused attitude can be seen in a marginal note to a handsome colored drawing of the "Toledo" bed, inviting "high production at high prices."

In reality, he was convinced to design furniture for industry solely by virtue of the polite but firm stand taken up by Gavina, who on several occasions, proving a match for Scarpa's natural averseness, obtained drawings and even stirred enthusiasm.

The request that always was made to him was to try to make designs simpler, to hone down the structures of pieces that, in the past, he had entrusted to skilled craftsmen, pieces that he himself owned. But, certainly, this was no easy task and the best way of almost forcing commitment on him was to appeal to his innate drive to improve, perfect, or even make something new of an earlier idea.

Thus it was that submitting to him the required piece, drawn up on a board by others, provoked the automatic and immediate response of "touching up" in pencil, thereby suggesting new possibilities and even new objects. And this took place even without the client's specific request, when some collaborator took a sheet of paper to try to draw up and proportion some idea of his own, or one of the hundreds of roughs Scarpa habitually kept by him on sheets of extra strong paper to amuse himself in pauses between more arduous commitments, inventing all manner of chairs, armchairs, and tables. Should any of these sketches work, drawing it up was a lengthy process, subject to ups and downs of morale such as no other planning activity caused him; his reserves of constancy, punctiliousness and patience were put to the test. Every job lay dormant on Bristol board for a long time. Indeed, certain studies still remain there, even though worked up to quite a fair degree of finish, because toward the end of his life they met with a categorical refusal to put his hand to them.

Instead, in propitious moments these projects were submitted to the same meticulous procedure of individuation he employed on his architectural work, as the images in the book attempt to convey: passing through refined focusing of parts, the definition of detail, slowly but surely to reach an image of an organism perfectly articulated in every part, such is the image his furniture projects. A case in point is an unpublished drawing, the last study he worked on, carried through to the prototype stage and approved by him. Here he clearly defined a cylindrical support in heavy iron tube, into which, parallel to the ground, other slimmer cylindrical elements were fitted to afford a base. But notwithstanding that this was an established feature from the outset, delineation of the point of insertion proved such a delicate operation of proportioning—passing through quite complex formal evolutions and transformation, richly charged with even organic associations—as to suggest that he was driven to condense into this point all the expressive implications of the object, which otherwise was of exemplary structural simplicity.

An illustration of his need to thrash out any problems arising from at least one detail of an object destined for partially mechanized production is offered by the study for the device by which the head of the "Toledo" bed is attached to its supporting structure.

Having seen it drawn up and eloquently colored, he anticipated the difficulties in carrying out the fine detail its rounded forms called for by having a model made in plasticine. He then labored over this to produce a more convincing definition that made subsequent changes and adaptations in the foundry negligible.

Drawn to the Viennese tradition, he was prompted to design a piece of furniture in homage to Joseph Hoffman, over three meters long and fitted with a special hinge in cast muntzmetal. This arose out of his passion for experimenting with flexible joints: finding solutions to opening these kept him enthralled. At the same time he dreamed of making special wooden structures in series, nothing particularly elaborate, just simple assemblages. These would substantiate a favorite tenet of his and provide an answer to critics who viewed him as an aristocratic producer of costly custom-made items.

Basically, it was that if but given the opportunity, his desire was to plan very simple objects in humble materials. It would have given him immense satisfaction to demonstrate that the least expensive buildings might be elegant and that good taste and harmony are not synonymous with luxury and costly materials.

Thematic Elements

Note

*The captions printed in smaller capitals
refer to instances extra-dossier.*

SUPPORT

A pillar, an entirely solid component, but also an iron or wooden display stand, a suspended or supported frame, an object of complete definition: all of which, whether large or small, architecture or object of use, are constituent units, spacemakers even when isolated, almost always strongly expressed but subordinate to context or function. Forms rarely bizarre, odd, or predictable, more often innovatory and eloquent of a taste and a style: a fusion of impressions and memories charged with future potential.

1. Pillar on the Ottolenghi house
2. Support on the Brion pavilion
3. Trabeation on the Vicenza condominium
4. Display stand for the bust of Eleanor of Aragon
5. "Sarpi" table
6. Lamp, Querini Stampalia Foundation
7. Fruit stand

INSTANCES EXTRA-DOSSIER

1. Pillar on the Ottolenghi house

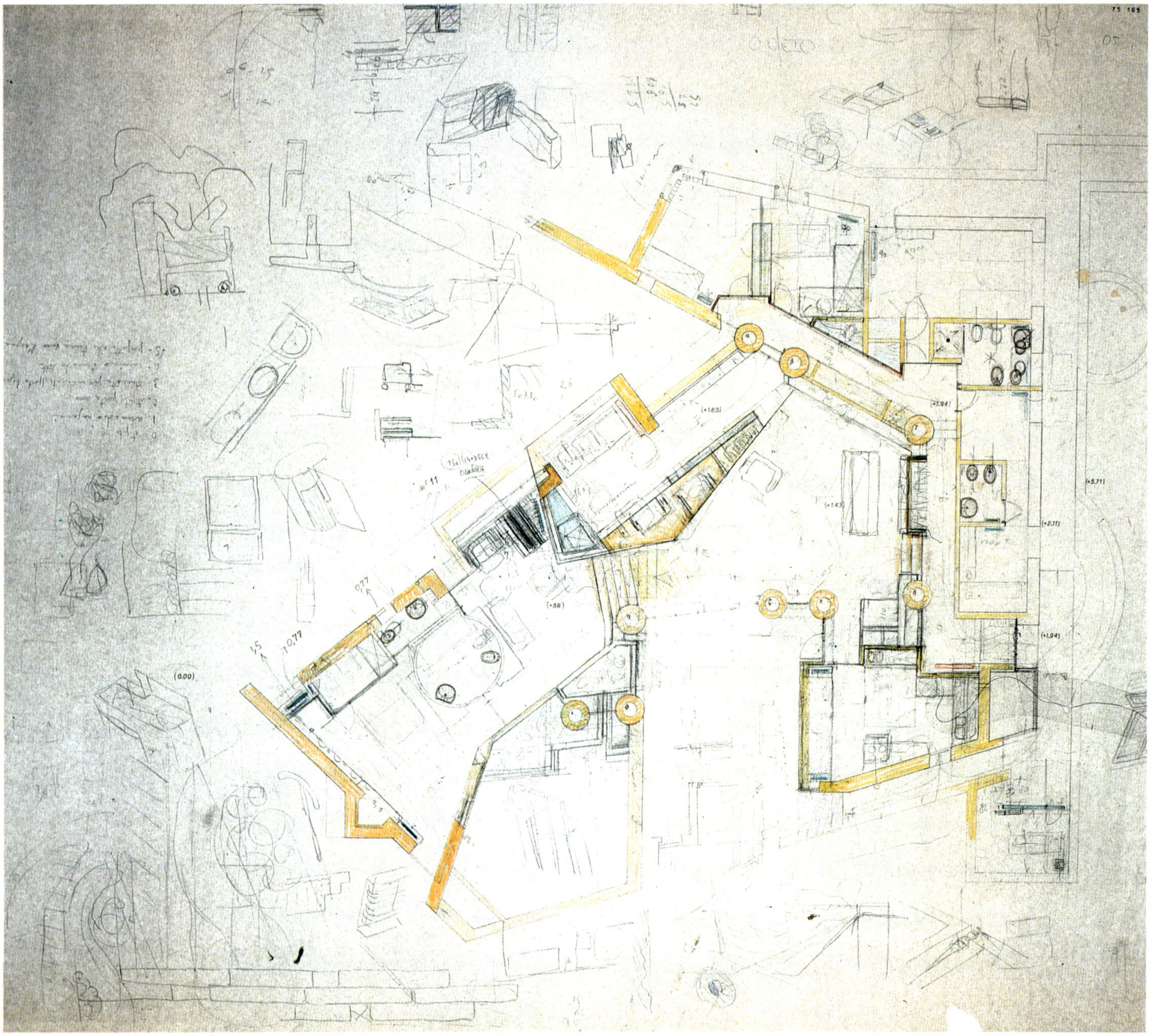

1

2

3

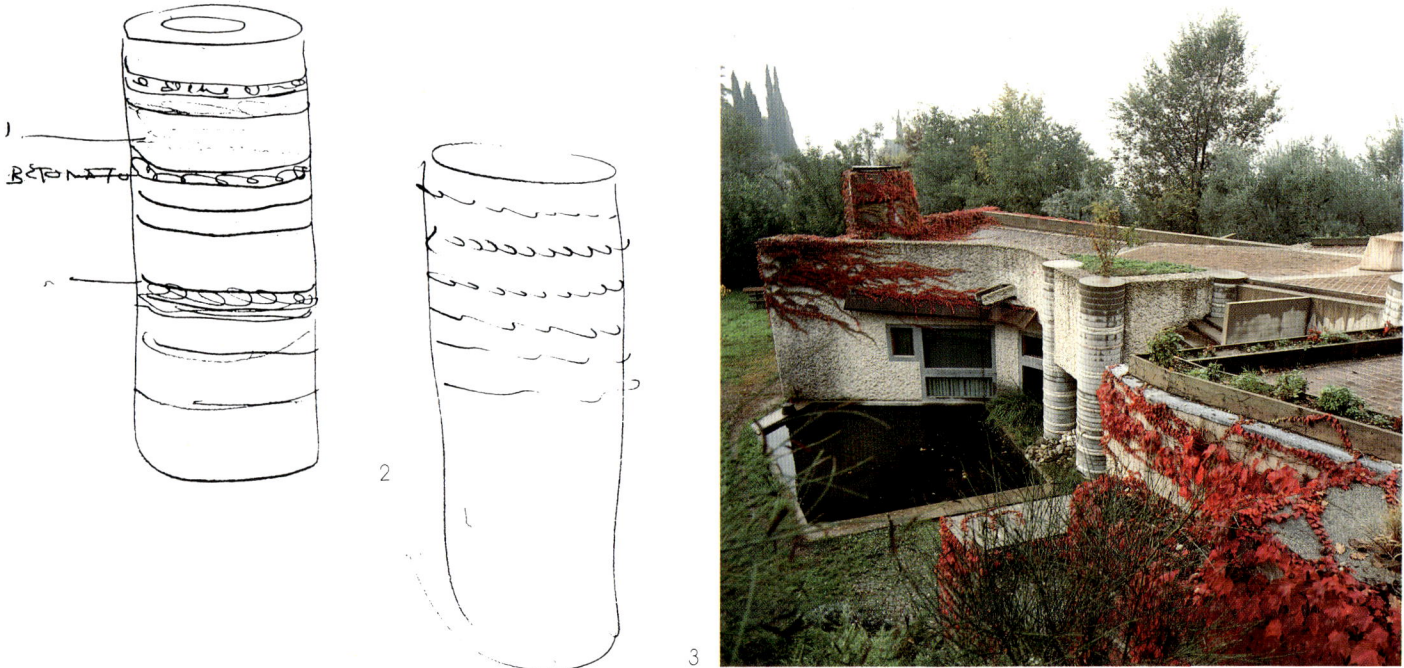

1. Plan of the Ottolenghi house, Bardolino (Verona). Pencil and crayons on heliographic print

2. Sketch for a pillar. Pencil on paper

3. Exterior of the house

4. A pillar on the interior

5. Plan of a pillar. Pencil and crayons on paper

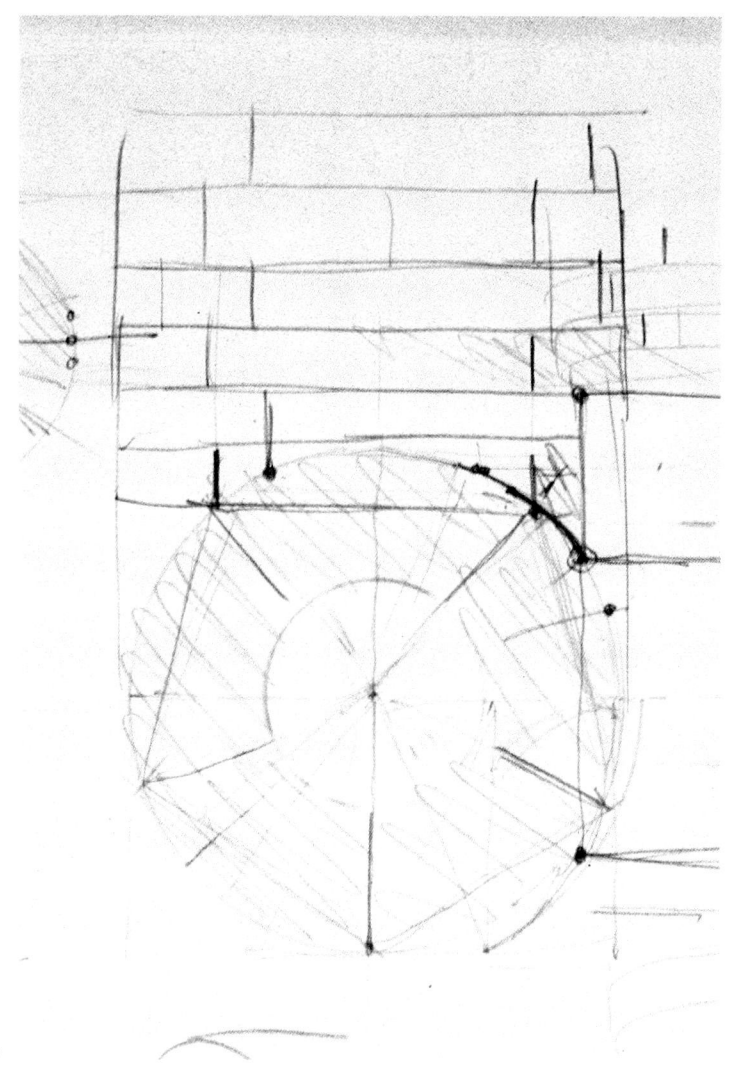

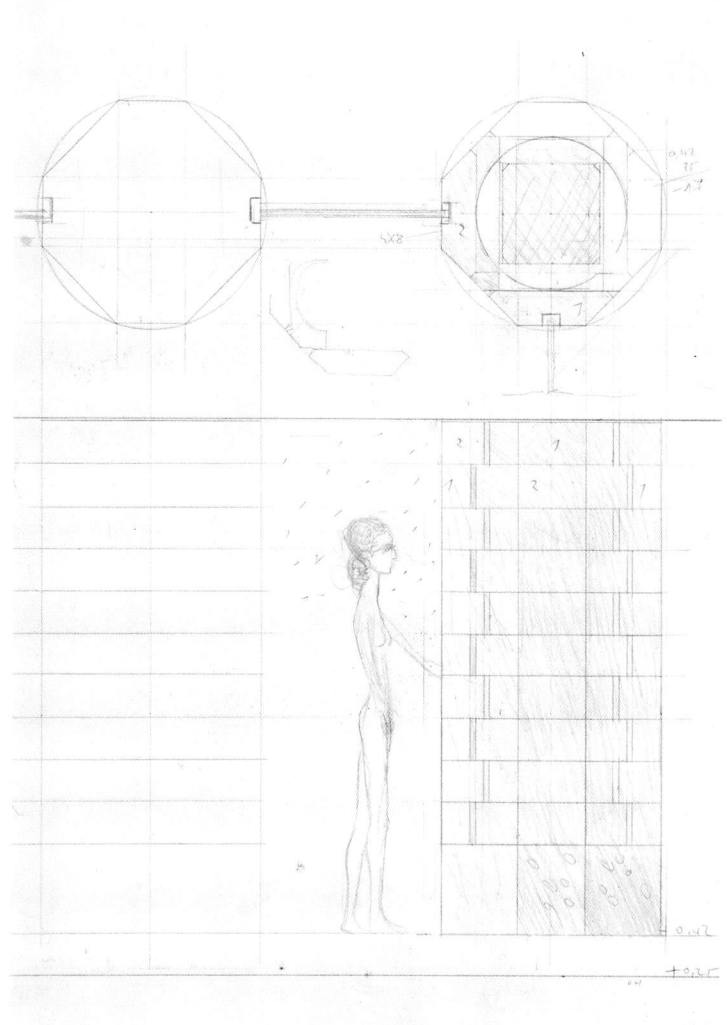

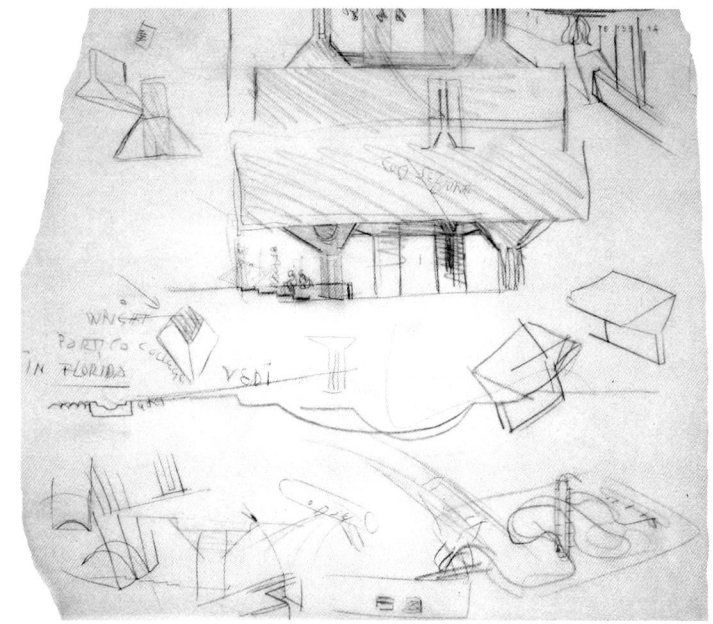

6. Plan of a pillar. Pencil on paper

7. PLAN AND ELEVATION OF A PILLAR, PROJECT FOR THE FACULTY OF HUMANITIES AND PHILOSOPHY IN THE FORMER CONVENT OF S. SEBASTIAN, VENICE. PENCIL ON BRISTOL BOARD

8. SKETCH FOR PILLARS ON THE OPEN GALLERY, PROJECT FOR THE BANCA ANTONIANA, MONSELICE (PADUA). PENCIL ON TRACING PAPER

9. SKETCH FOR PILLARS ON THE GAVINA STORE, BOLOGNA. PENCIL AND RED BALL-POINT PEN ON PAPER

2. Support on the Brion pavilion

10. Detail of pavilion support in the Brion cemetery, S. Vito di Altivole (Treviso)

▷

11. Sketches for the support. Pencil and crayons on onionskin

12. Working drawing for the support. Pencil and crayon on onionskin

13. The support

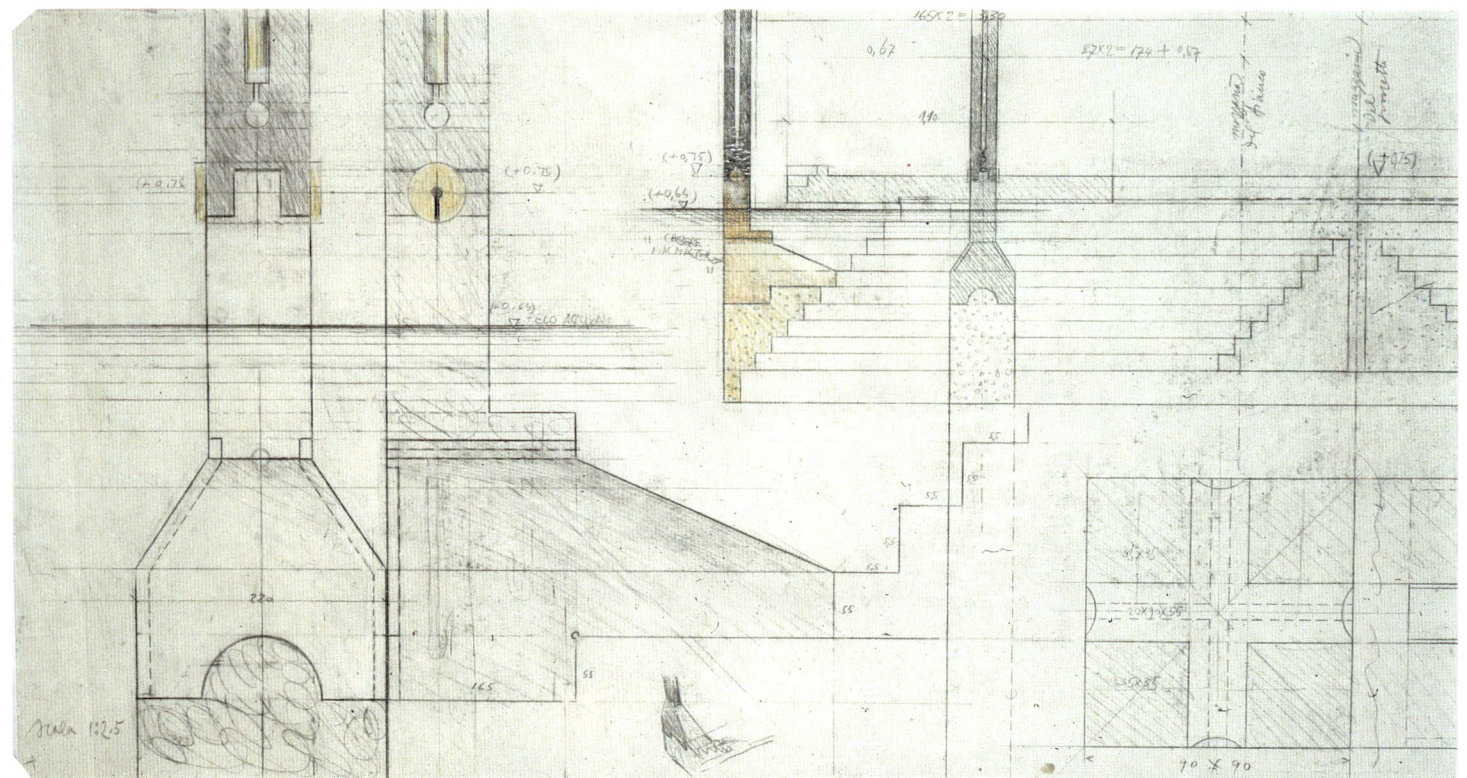

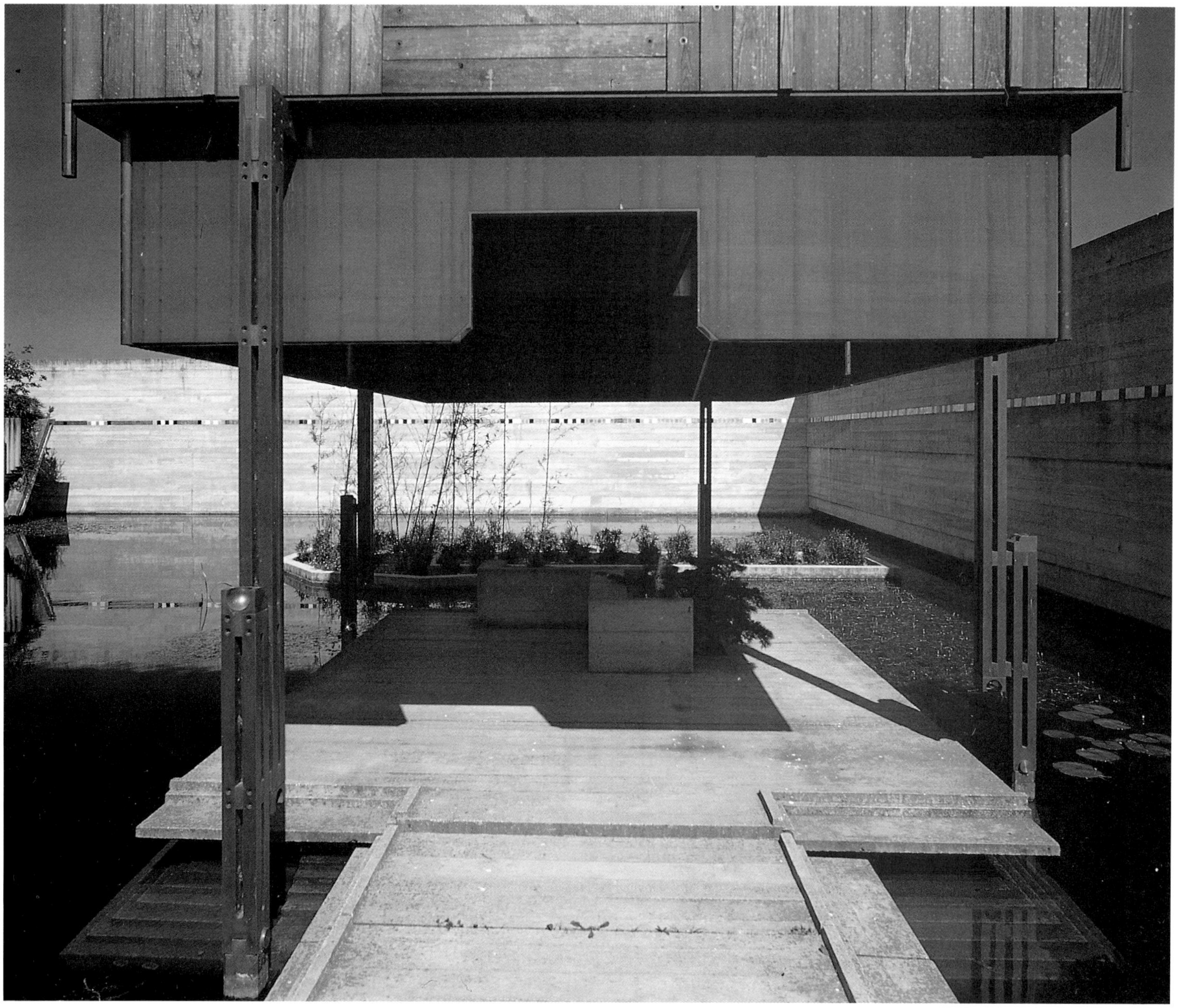

14

14. Detail of the pavilion

15. Study for the pavilion. Pencil and crayons on Bristol board

15

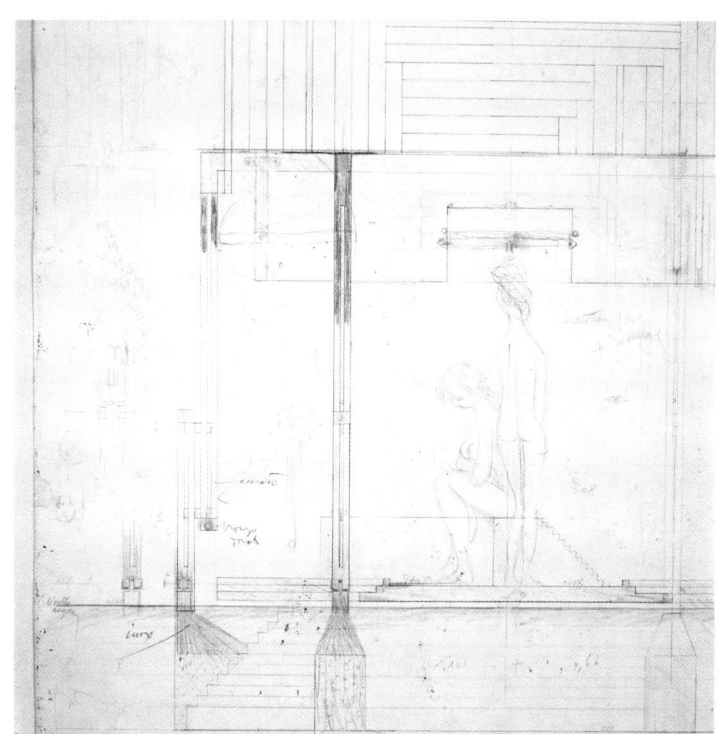

3. Trabeation on the Vicenza condominium

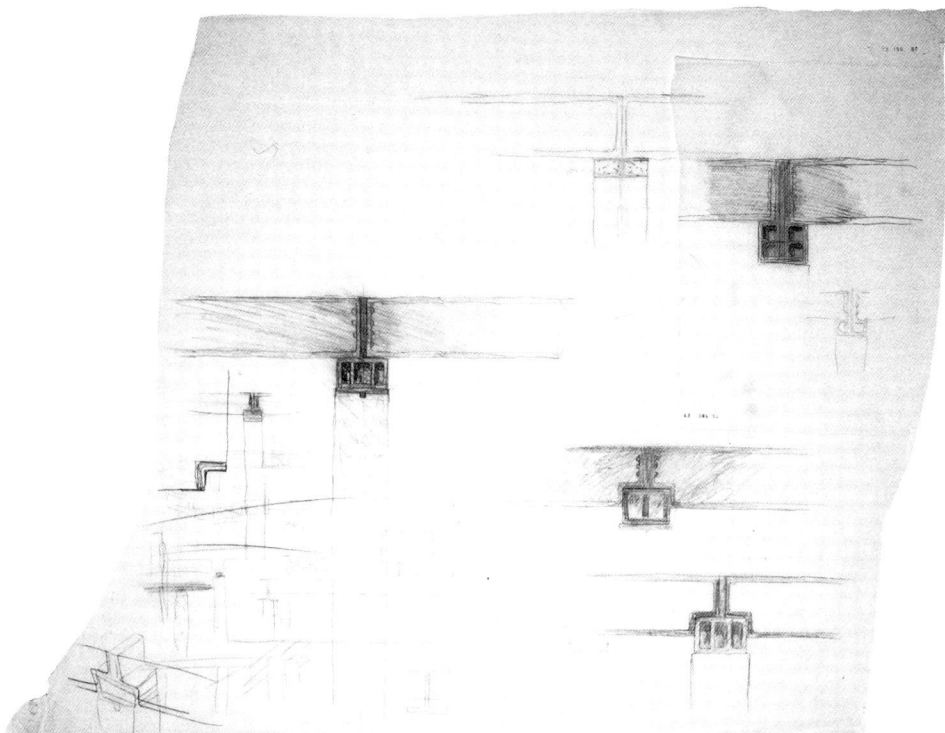

16
17

16. Trabeation and twin capitals on the condominium in Vicenza

17. Studies for the capital. Pencil on tracing paper

▷
18. DETAIL OF A BEAM ON THE CASTELVECCHIO MUSEUM, VERONA

5. "Sarpi" table

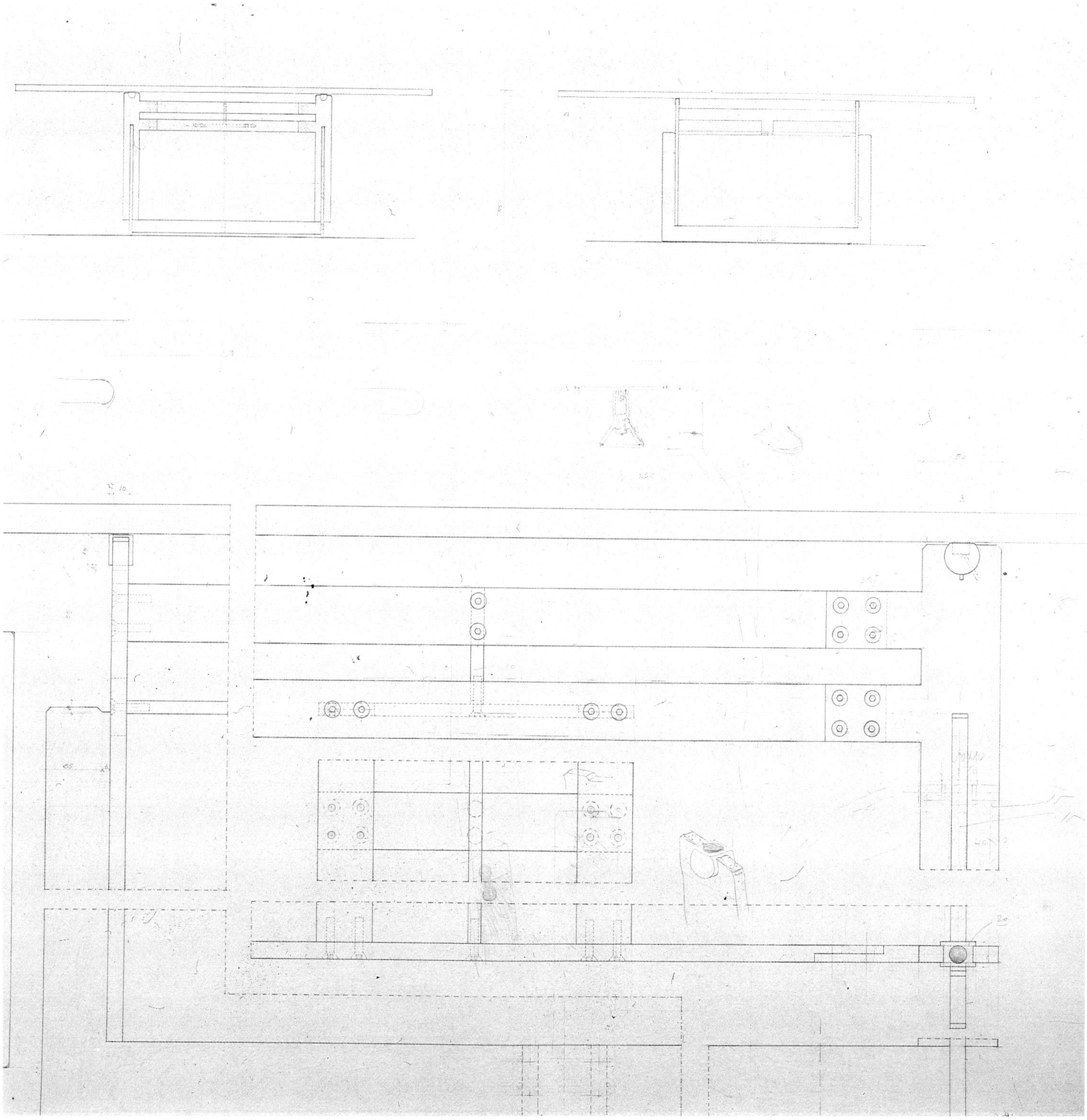

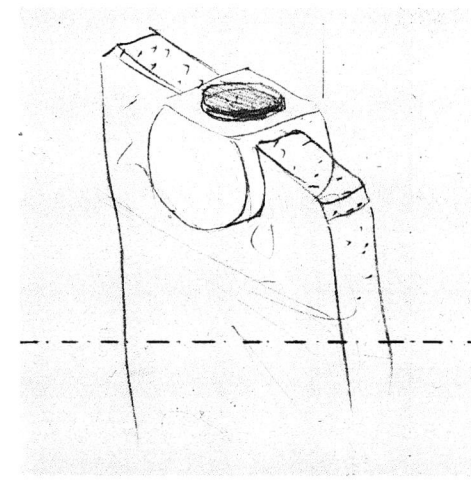

4. Display stand for the bust of Eleanor of Aragon

19. Display stand for the bust of Eleanor of Aragon in the National Gallery of Sicily, Palazzo Abatellis, Palermo

20. Study for the "Sarpi" table. Pencil and crayons on Bristol board

21. Support with buffer for glass, detail from previous board

22. BASE FOR A CRUCIFIX, PALAZZO ABATELLIS, PALERMO

23. THE CRUCIFIX WITH BASE

24. DETAIL OF BASE

7. Fruit stand

26

◁
6. Lamp,
Querini Stampalia
Foundation

25. Lamp (seen
from below) in the
Querini Stampalia
Foundation, Venice

27

26, 27. Silver stand for fruit

28

28. Working drawing for the lamp. Pencil, crayons and ball-point pen on heliographic print

29. Sketch for the fruit stand and study for a tray. Pencil on Bristol board

29

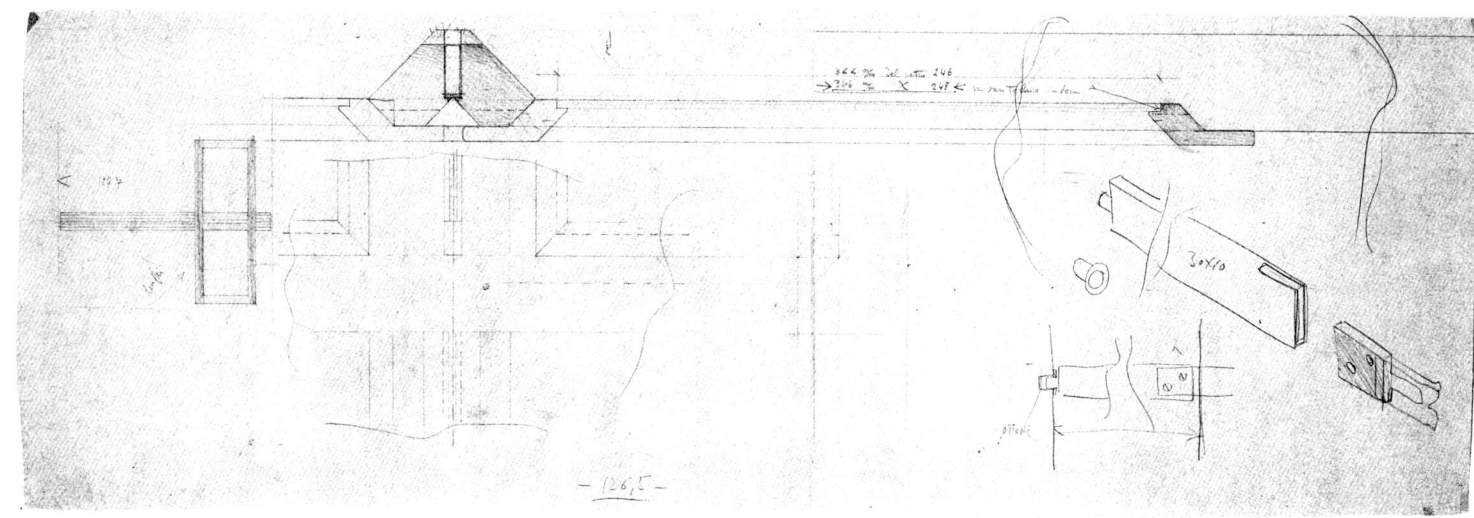

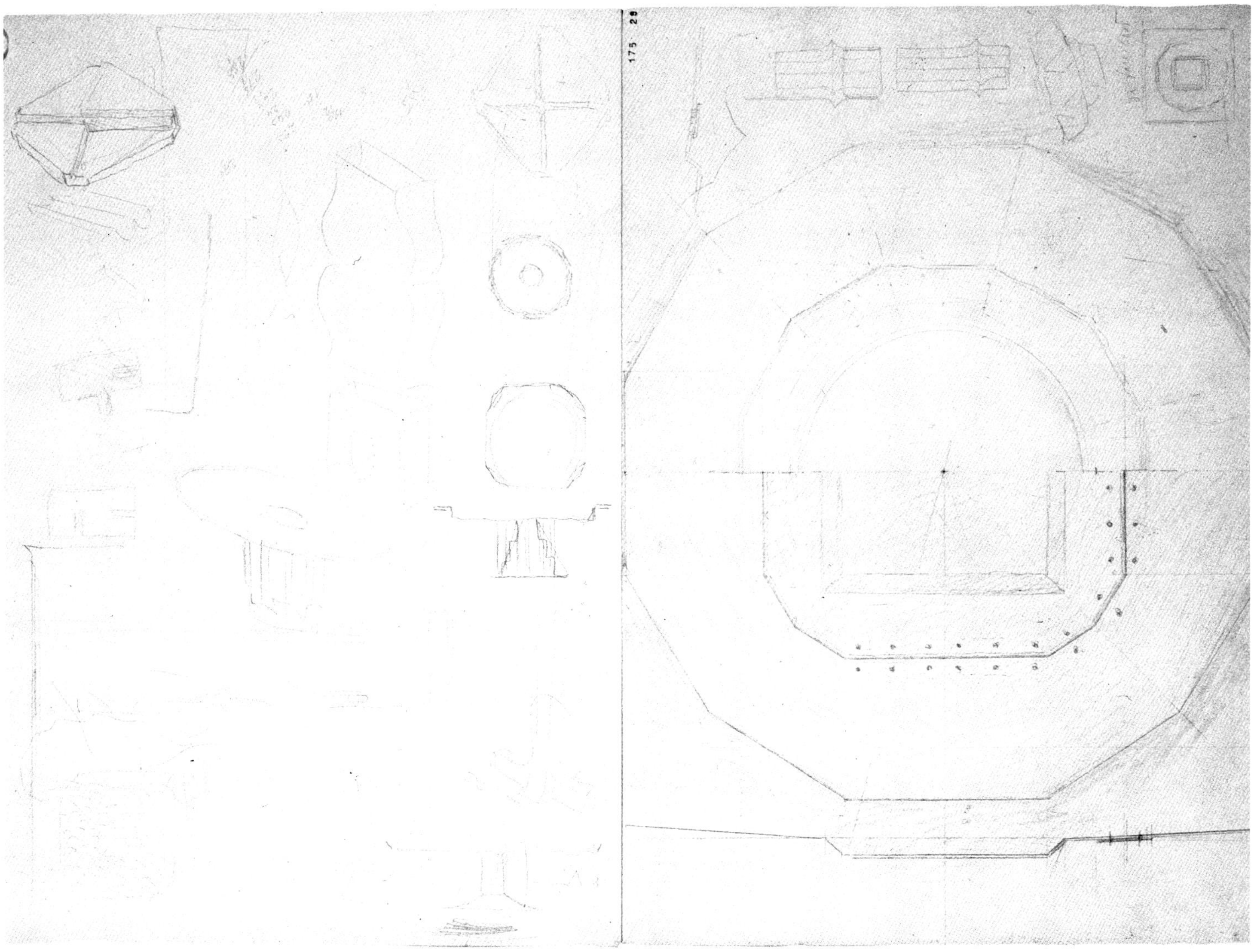

CONNECTOR—LINK

A transitional structural element, the connector shapes the sum of assembled parts. On occasion the initial nucleus of the project, determining the various spaces, even when its detailing may be the last factor to be dealt with, the connector is often the essential complement, providing an outlet for differing formal tensions or, vice versa, a means of harmonizing contrasts.

The link is a smaller-scale element connecting less important parts, but, in itself, it is pre-eminent in identifying, characterizing and lending refinement. In this phase of invention, seen as proceeding by enlargement, it is the "connector of connectors."

8. Flyover on a square at Feltre
9. Bridge, Querini Stampalia Foundation
10. "Tunnel" on the Banca Popolare di Verona
11. Staircase in Palazzo Abatellis
12. Trabeation on the Banca Popolare di Verona
13. Staircase in the Muraro house
14. Unpublished table
INSTANCES EXTRA-DOSSIER

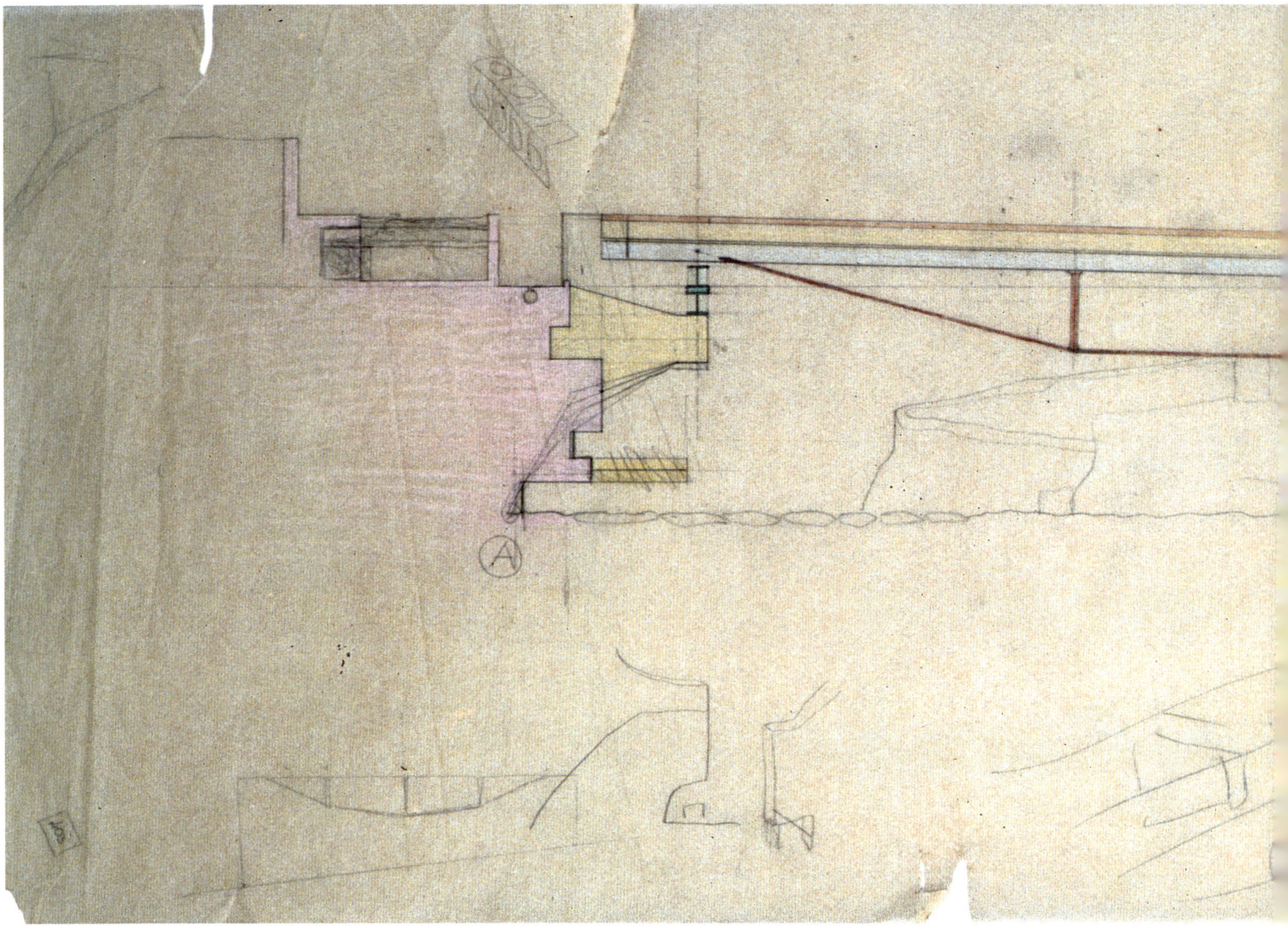

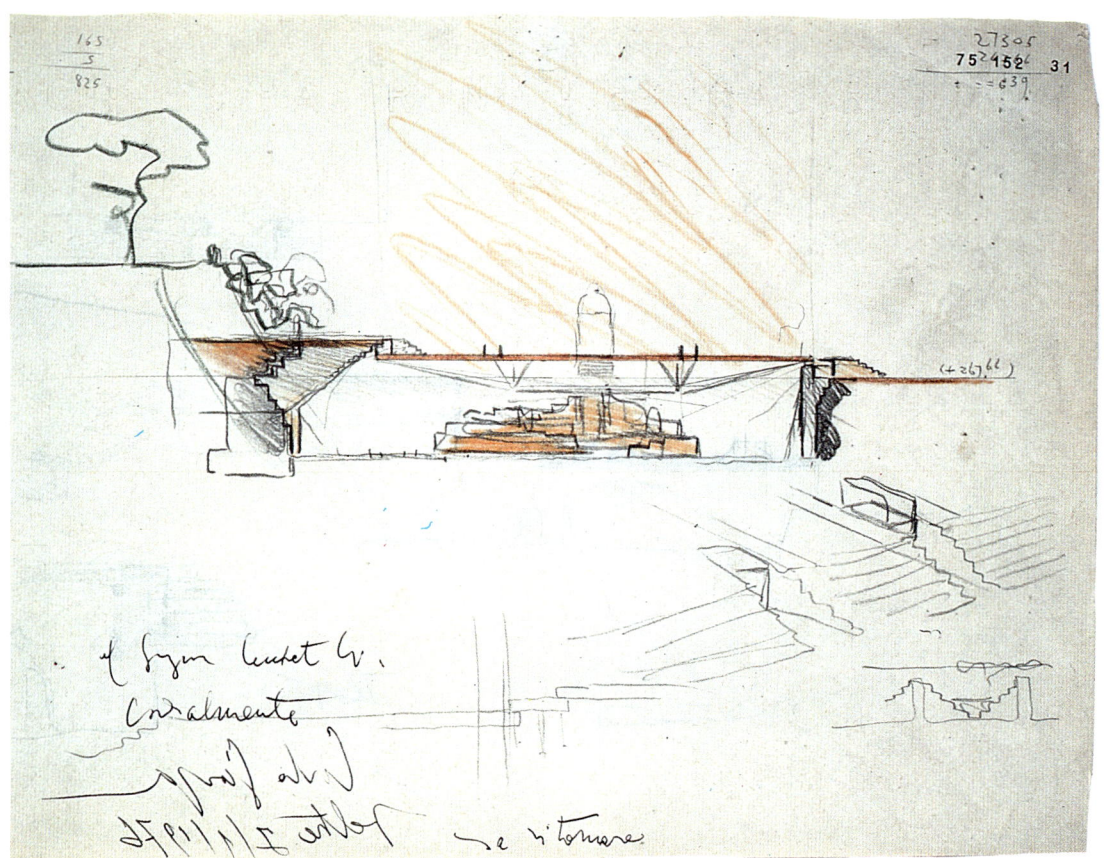

30. Study for the flyover planned for the cathedral square at Feltre (Belluno). Second version, longitudinal section. Pencil and crayons on heliographic print

31. Sketch of the longitudinal section. Pencil, crayons and ink on paper

32. Plan of the project. Pencil, crayons, red ball-point pen and India ink on Bristol board

33. Preparatory sketches for the girder. Pencil, crayons and ink on paper

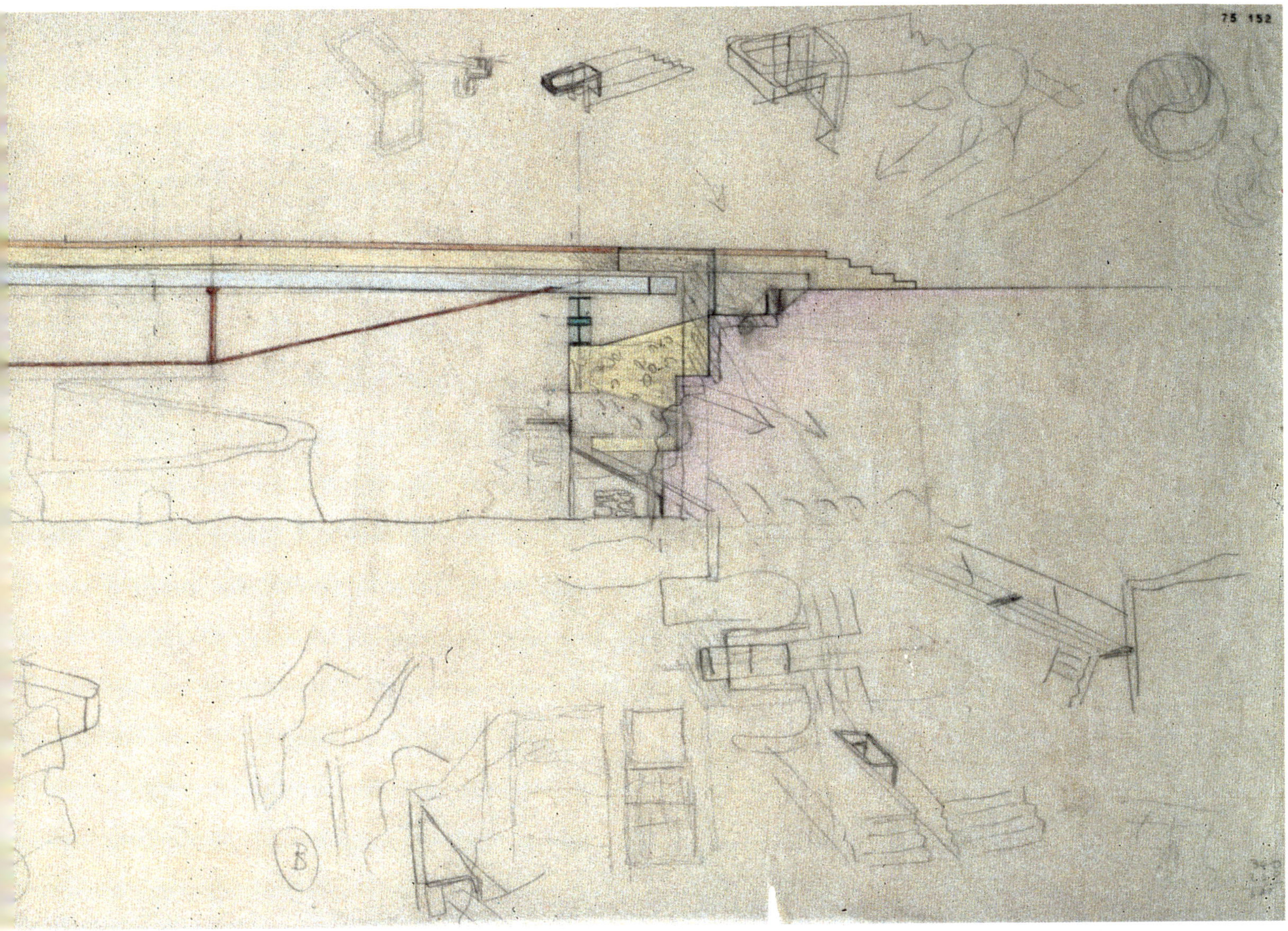

8. Flyover on a square at Feltre

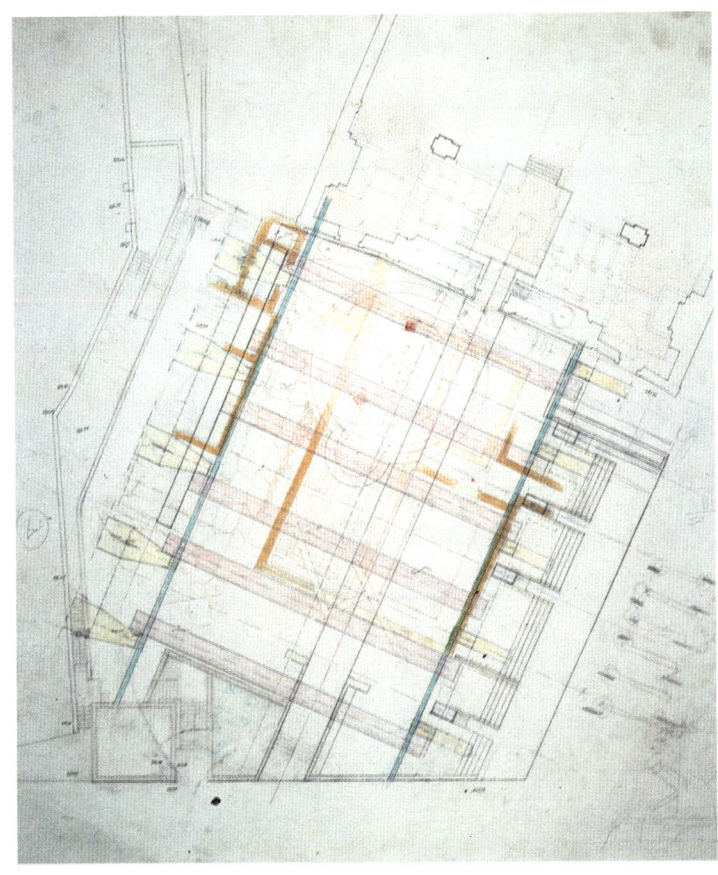
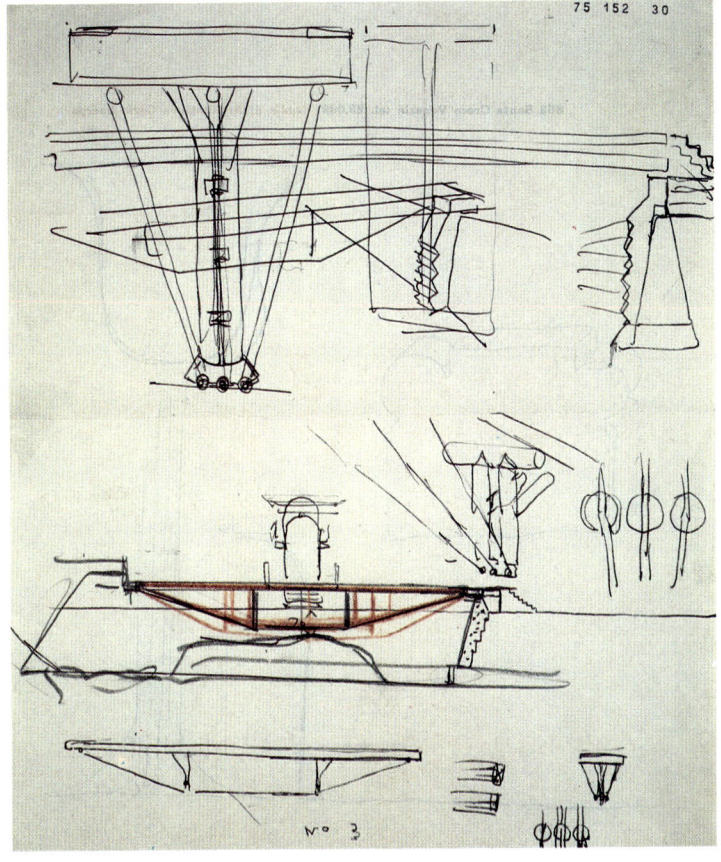

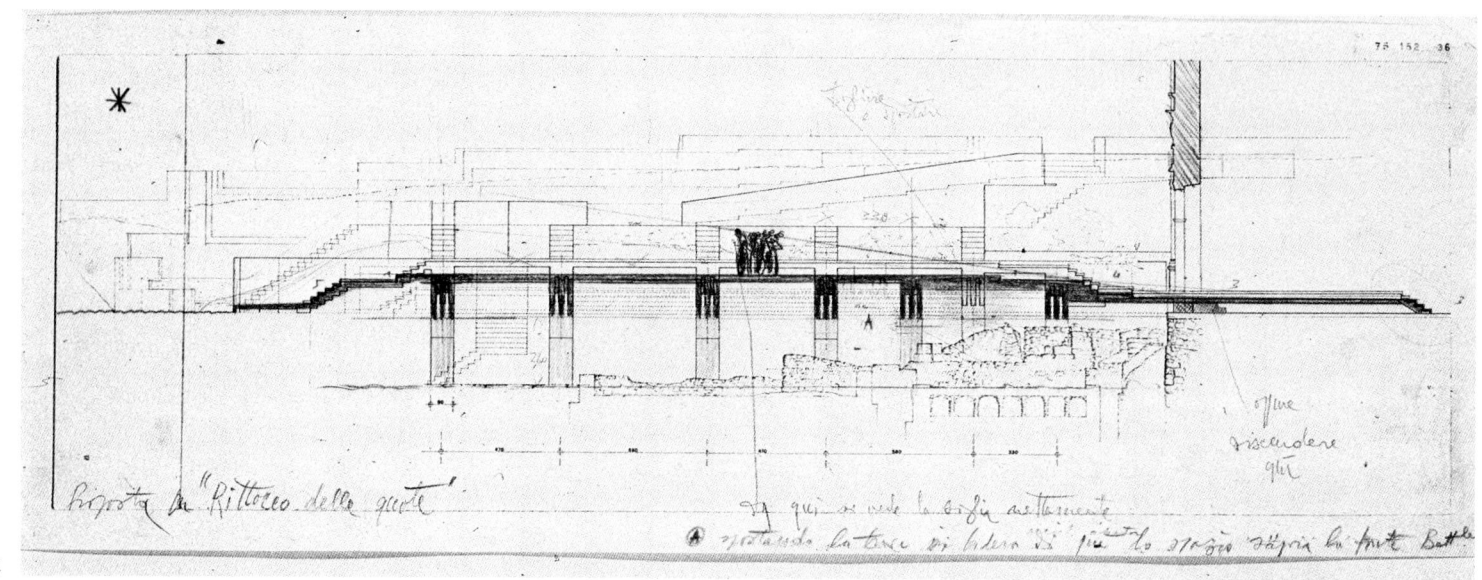

34

35

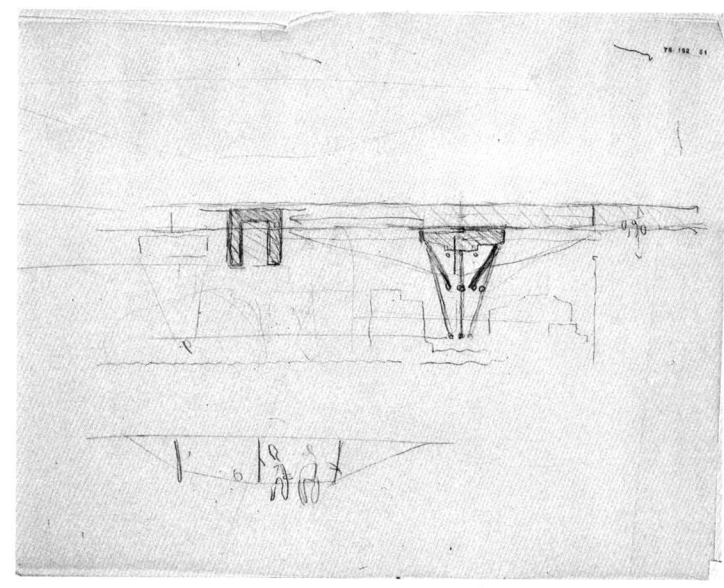

36

37

34. Study for the flyover, first solution, transversal section. Pencil and red ball-point pen on heliographic print

35. Sketches for the girder. Pencil on tracing paper

36. Sketch for the transversal section of the girder. Pencil on tracing paper

37. Study for the anchorage of the girder. Pencil and crayons on tracing paper

9. Bridge, Querini Stampalia Foundation

38. Detail of the handrail on the entrance bridge to the Querini Stampalia Foundation, Venice

▷

39. The bridge
40. The handrail
41. Handrail support
42. Front view of the bridge
43. The bridge seen from above

39

40

41

42

43

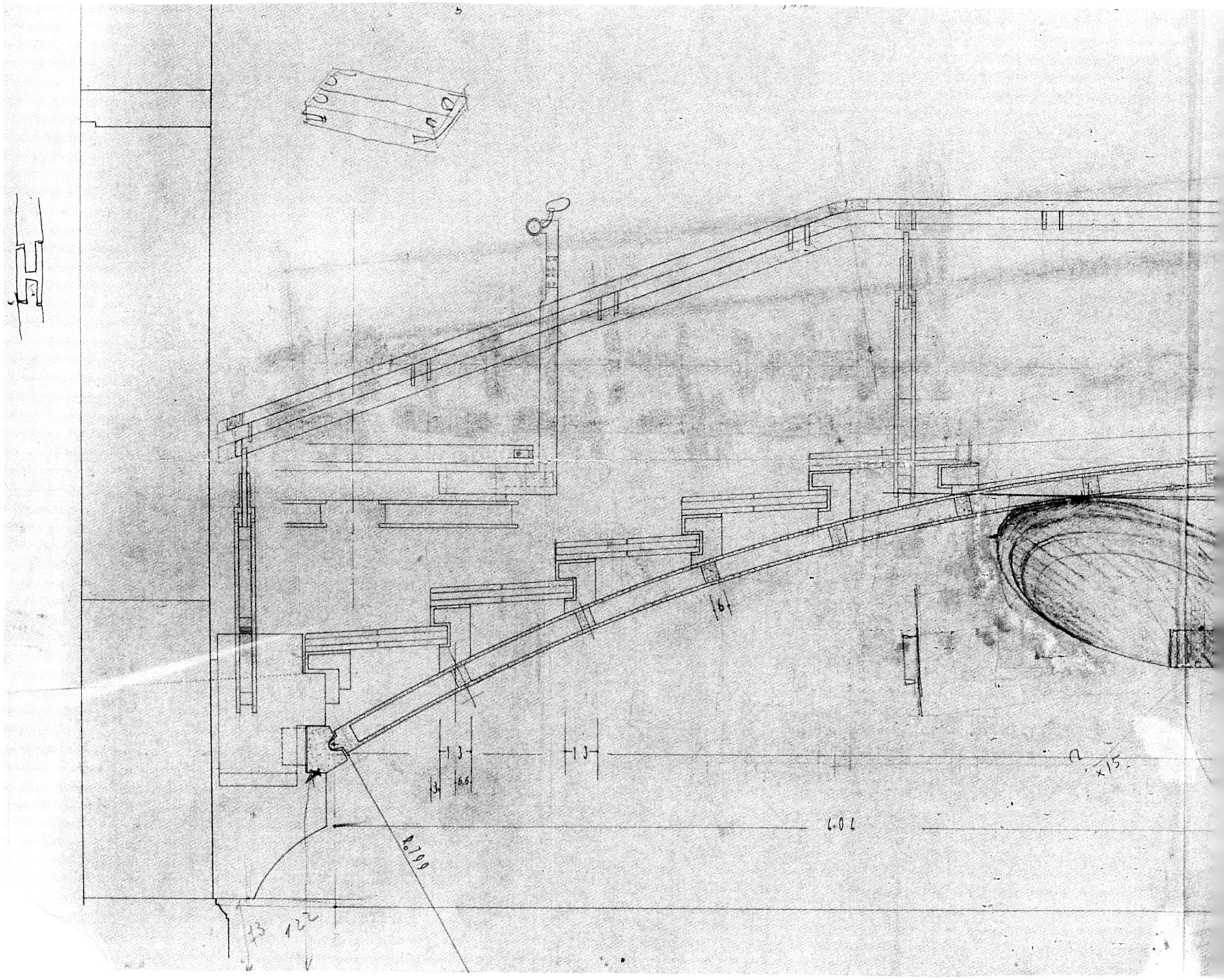

44. Side view of the bridge and detail of the handrail. Heliographic print of the final version

45. Sketches of the first idea. Pencil on paper

46. Preparatory studies nearing the final version. Pencil on tracing paper

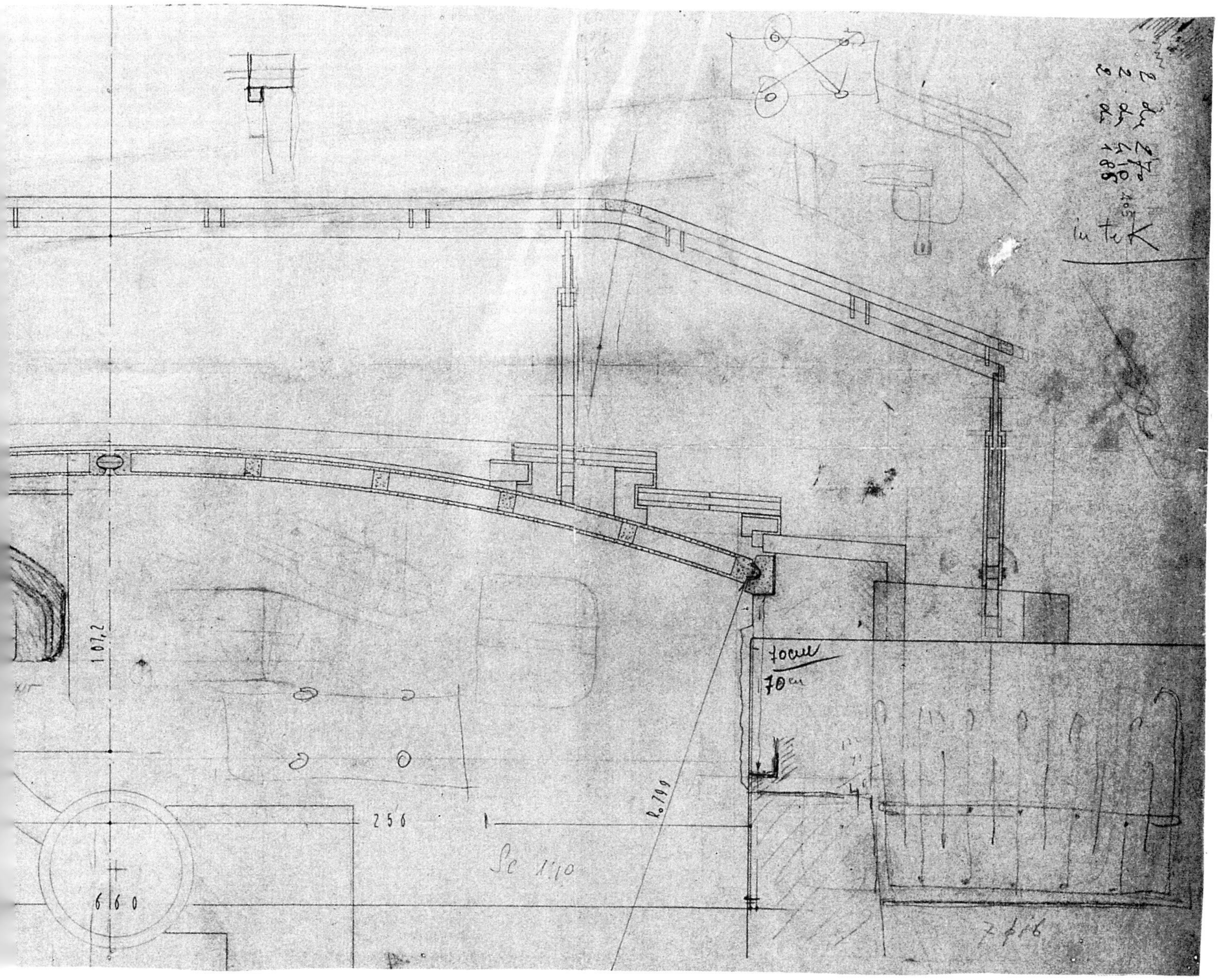

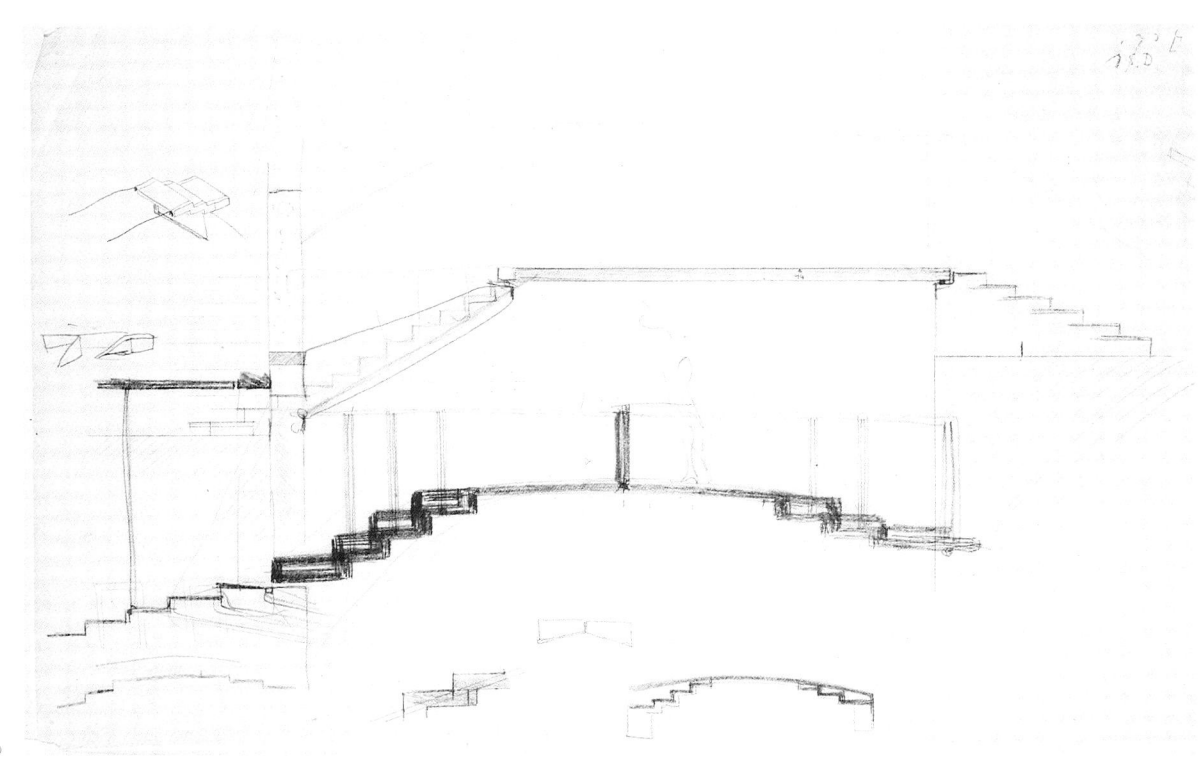

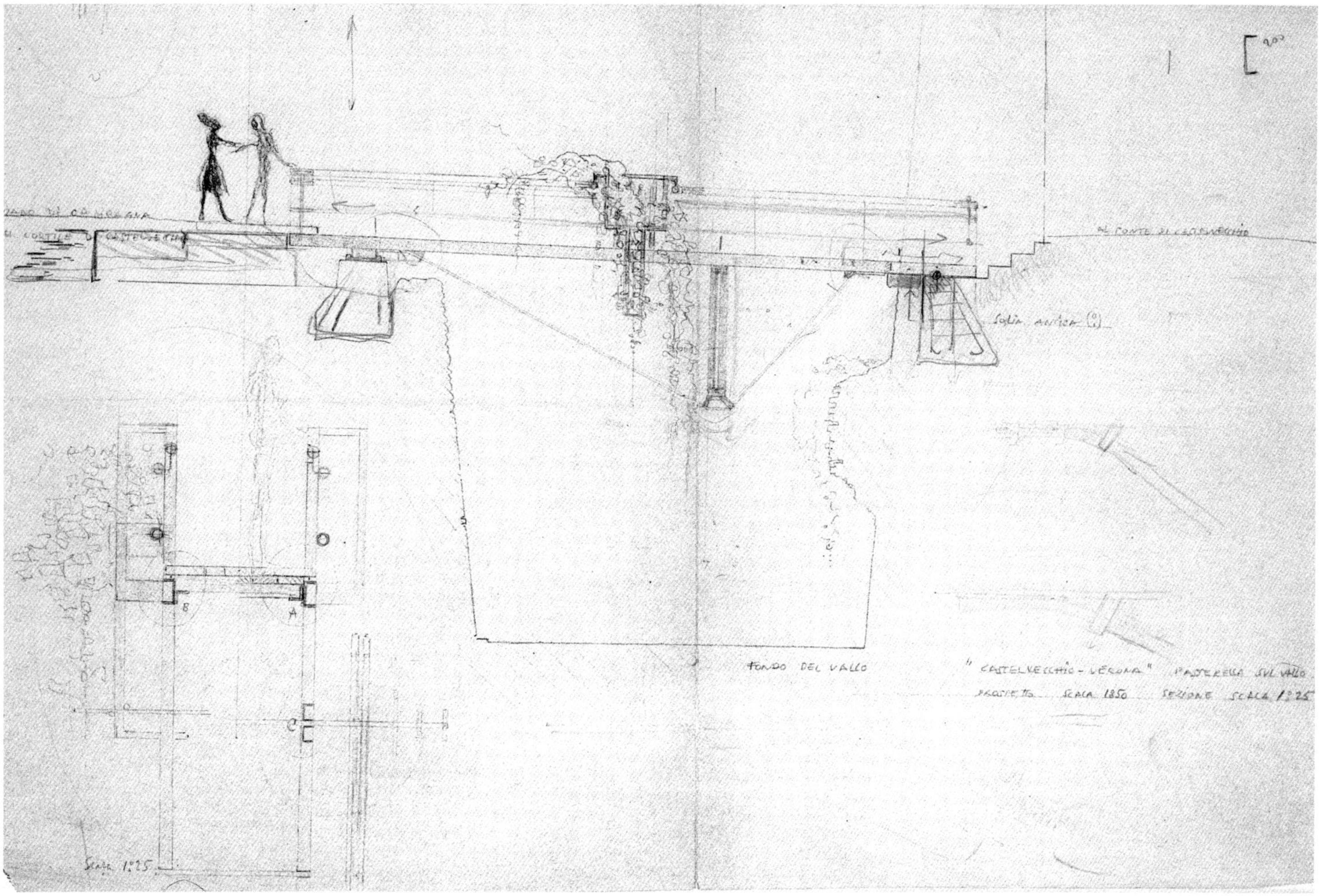

47

48

47. STUDY FOR THE SMALL BRIDGE OVER THE DITCH IN THE COURTYARD AT THE CASTELVECCHIO MUSEUM, VERONA. HELIOGRAPHIC PRINT

48. VIEW OF THE SMALL BRIDGE

49. FOOTBRIDGE IN THE CASTELVECCHIO MUSEUM

49

10. "Tunnel" on the Banca Popolare di Verona

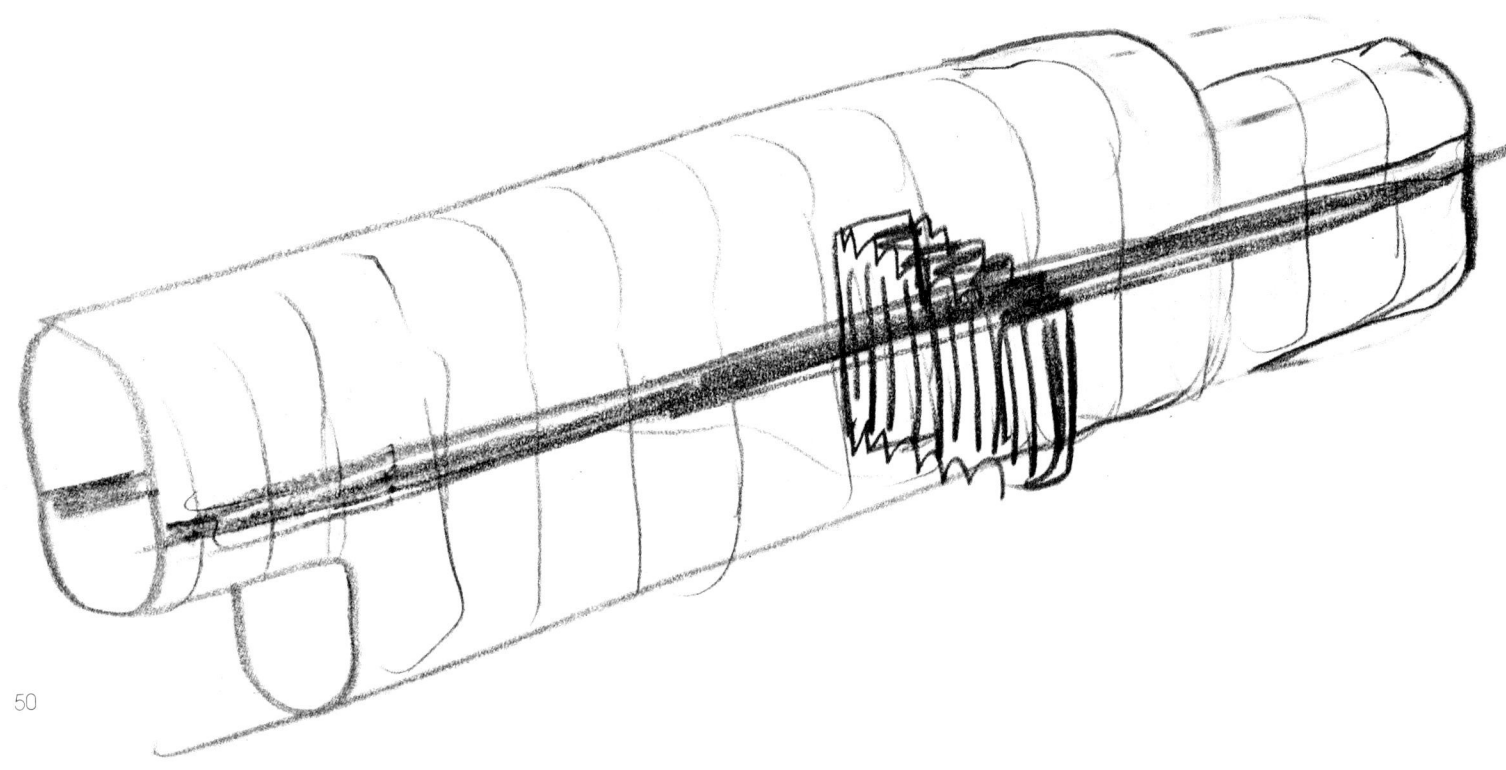

50. Sketch for the "tunnel" on the court frontage of the Banca Popolare di Verona. Pencil on tracing paper

▷
51. Detail of the "tunnel"
52. Sketch of the whole for an initial version. Pencil and crayons on tracing paper
53. Sketches nearing the final version. Pencil and crayons on tracing paper, ink and crayons on onionskin
54. Sketch nearing the final version. Pencil on tracing paper
55. Ingress of "tunnel" on main building

51

52

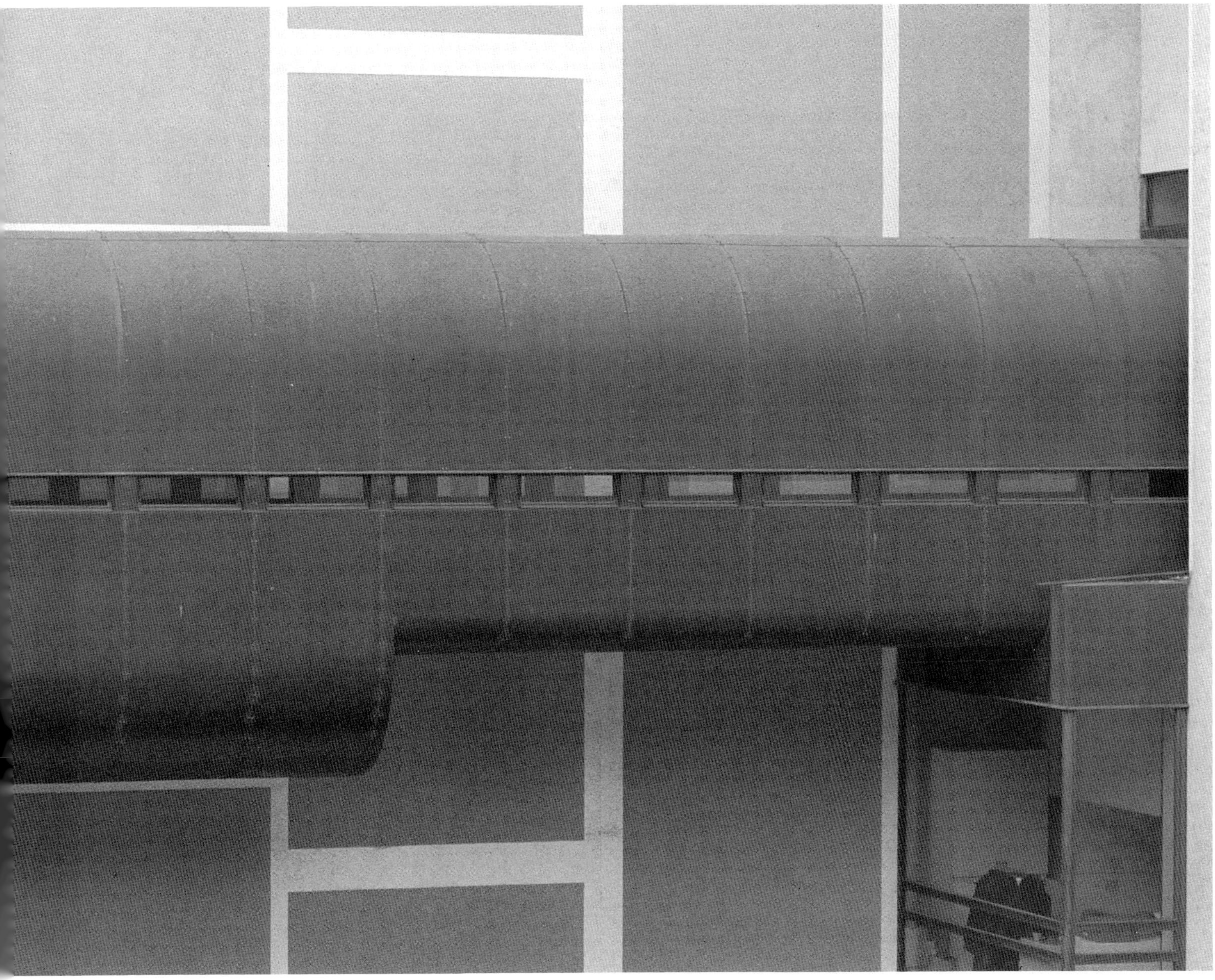

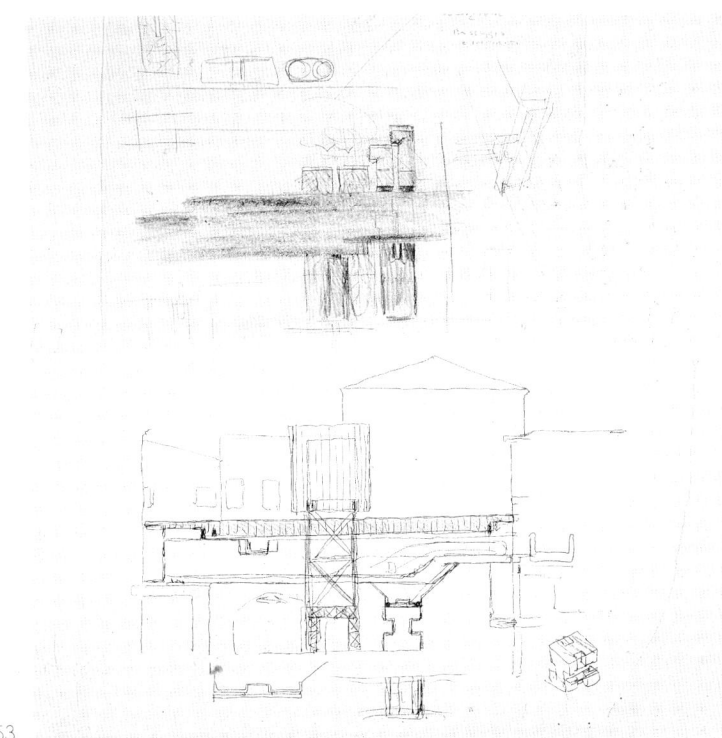

◁
56. Detail of a step on the staircase in Palazzo Abatellis, Palermo

11. Staircase in Palazzo Abatellis

58

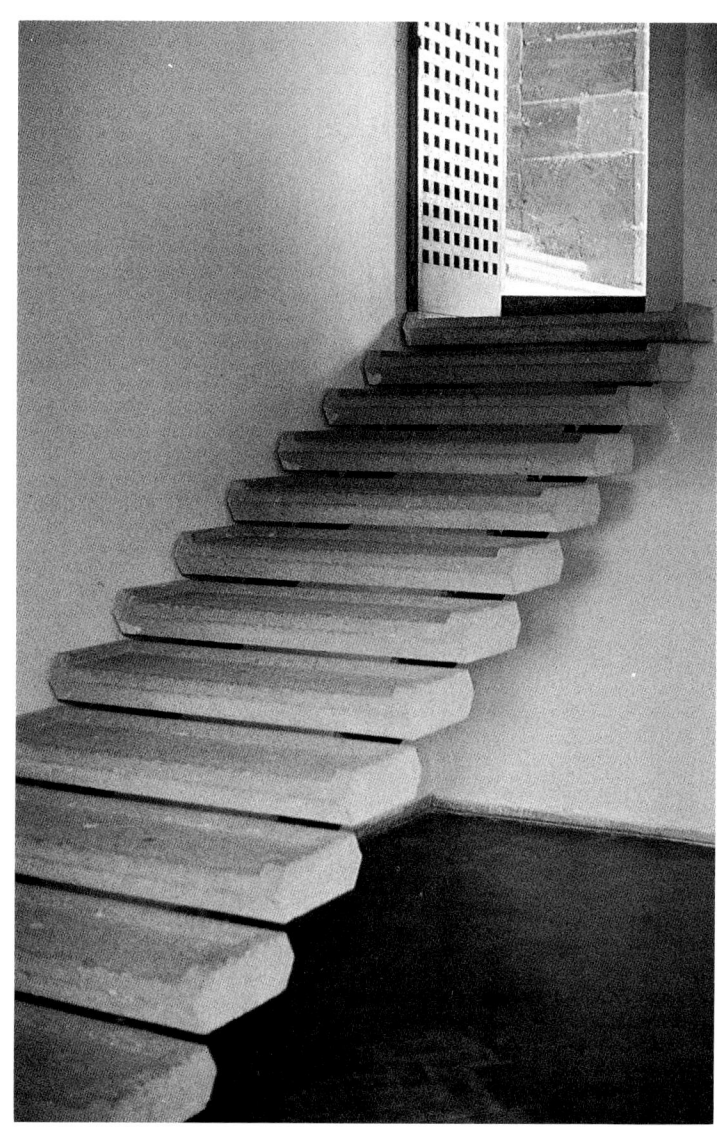

58. Mezzanine exit on the ancient staircase

57. The staircase

57

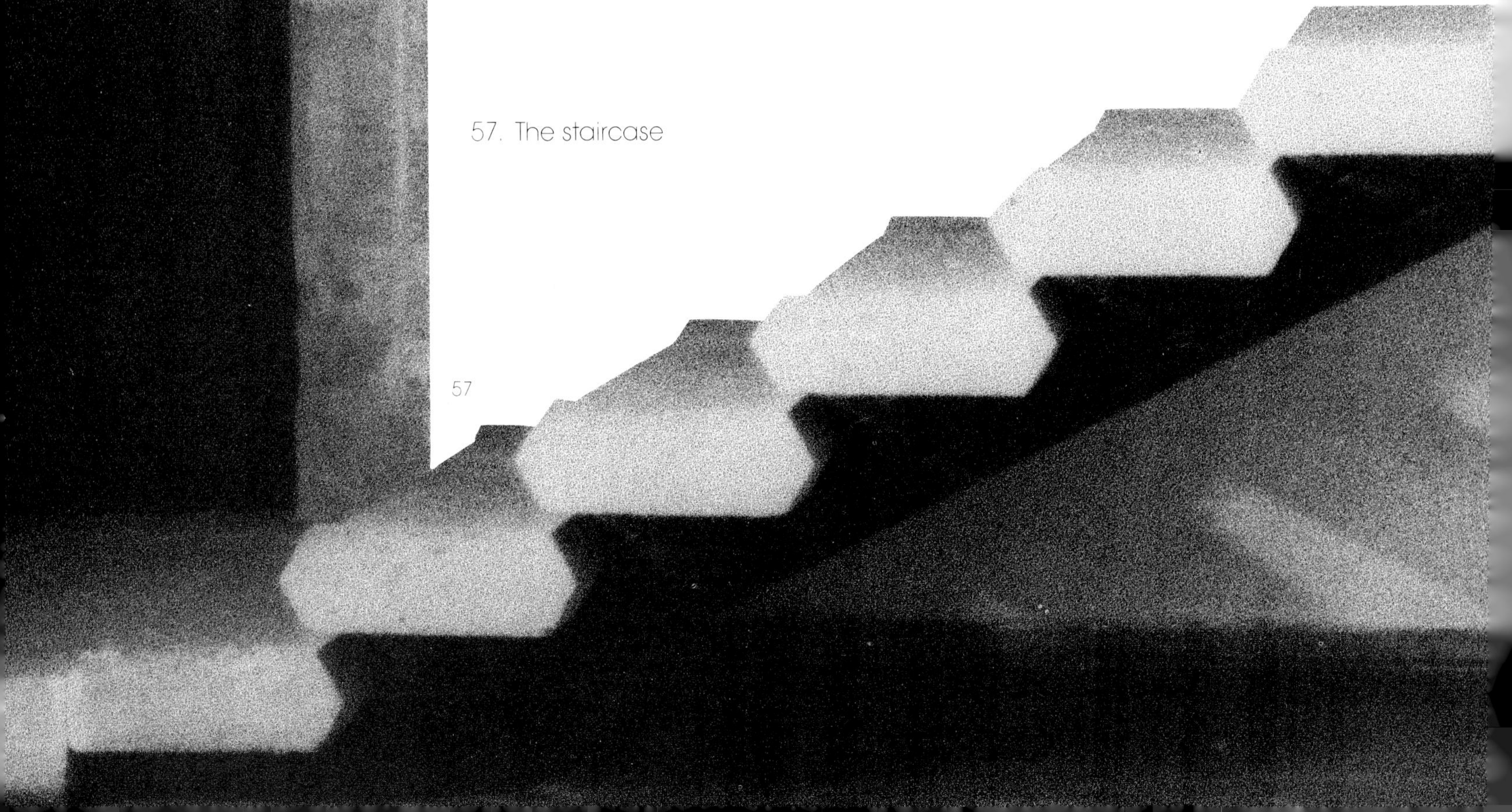

59. Detail of the steps and the load-bearing structure

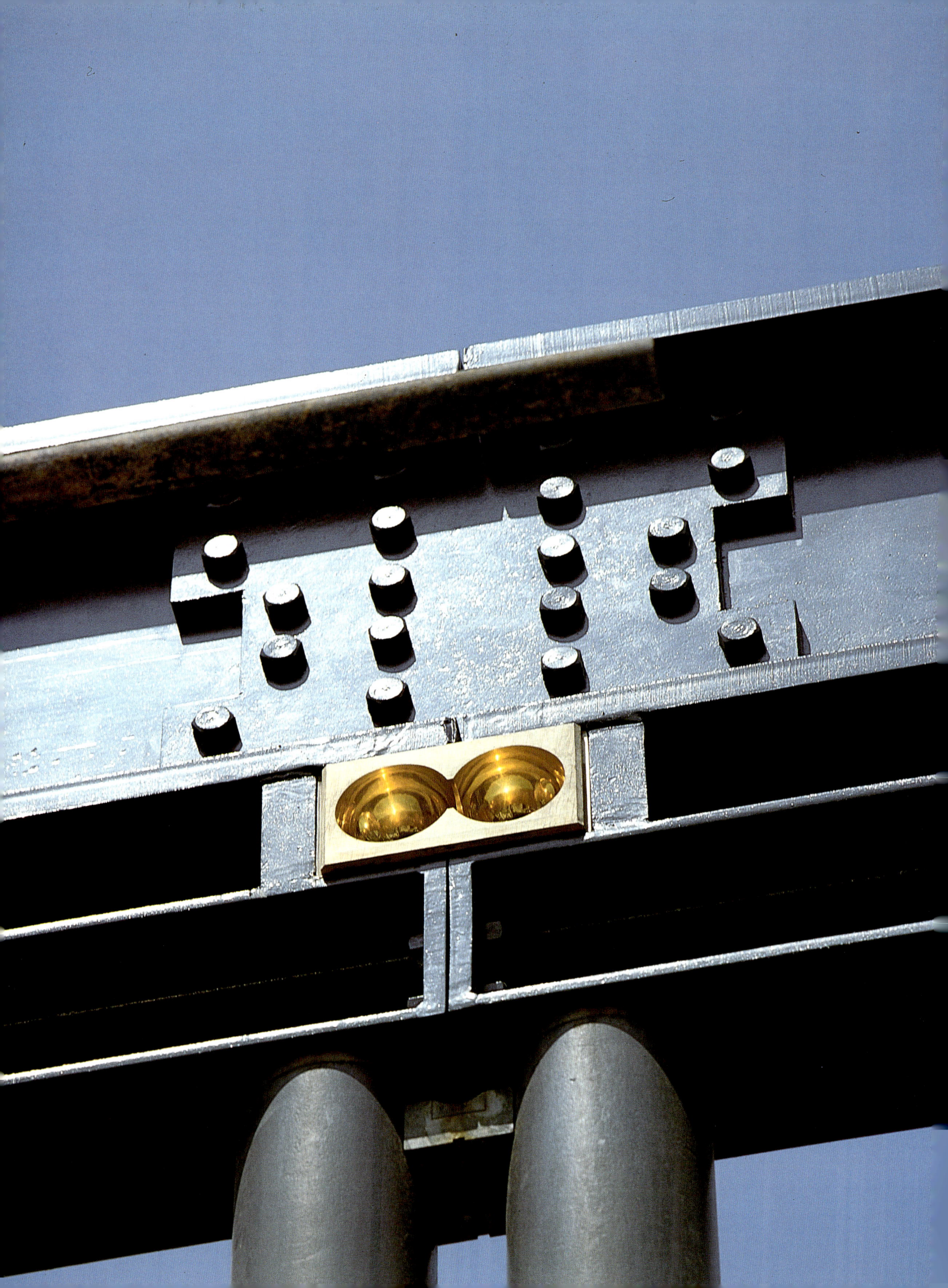

12. Trabeation on the Banca Popolare di Verona

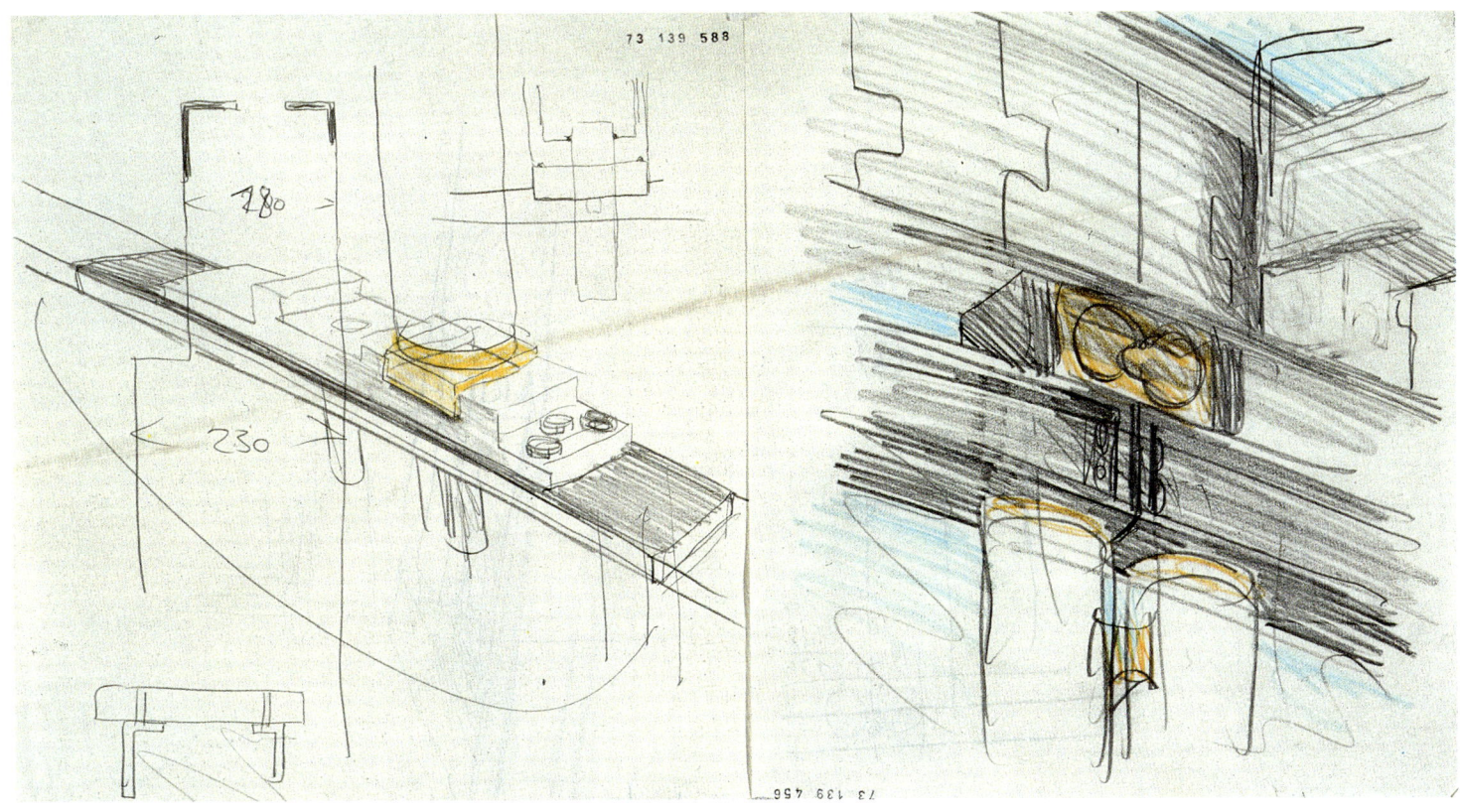

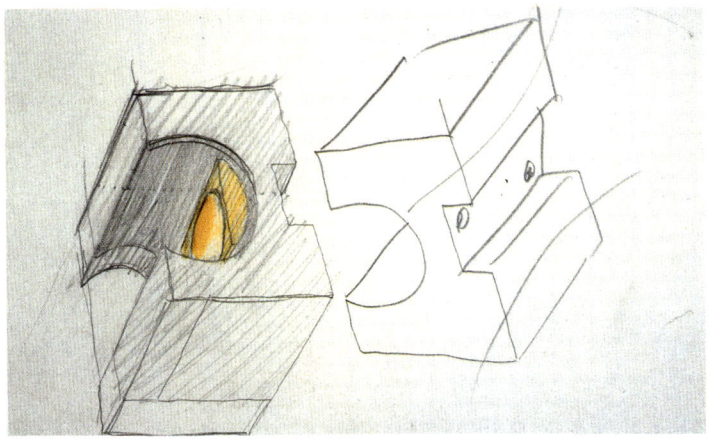

60. Detail of connectors for colonettes and of the trabeation: loggia on the Banca Popolare di Verona

61. Sketches for the base of the colonettes and for the trabeation. Pencil and crayons on paper

62. General study. Pencil and crayons on Bristol board

63. SKETCH FOR THE CONNECTOR BETWEEN TWO ROUND PILLARS, INTERIOR OF THE BANCA POPOLARE DI VERONA. PENCIL AND CRAYONS ON TRACING PAPER

64. DETAIL OF THE TWO PILLARS AND THEIR CONNECTOR

65. The loggia seen from the exterior

66. Sketch of the initial hypothesis for the connectors of the colonettes. Pencil and crayons on tracing paper

67. Detail of the base of the colonettes

68. SKETCHES FOR A MULLIONED WINDOW ON PALAZZO STERI, PALERMO. PENCIL AND CRAYONS ON TRACING PAPER

13. Staircase in the Muraro house

69. Detail of the staircase in the Muraro house, Venice

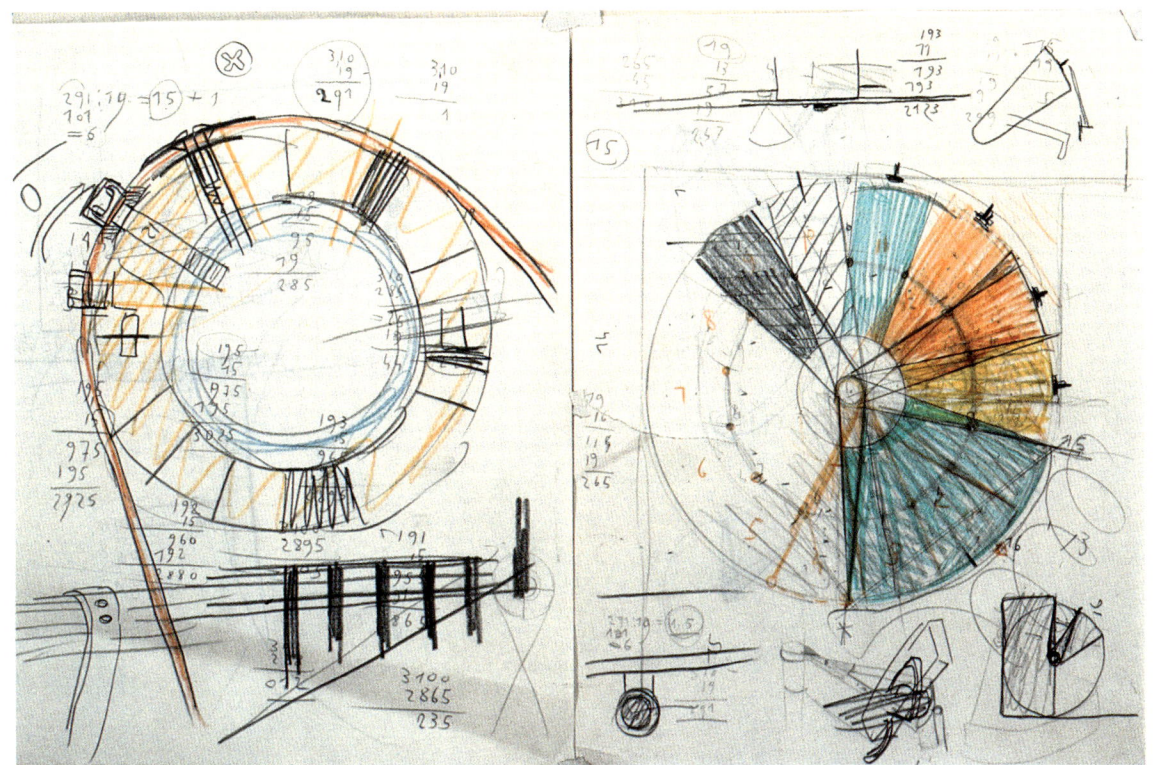

70. Structural detail of the staircase

71. Working drawing of the step. Crayons on heliographic print

72. Detail of the cage enclosing the spiral staircase

73. The staircase seen from above

74. Sketches for the central support, left, and for the staircase as a whole. Pencil and crayons on paper

14. Unpublished table

75

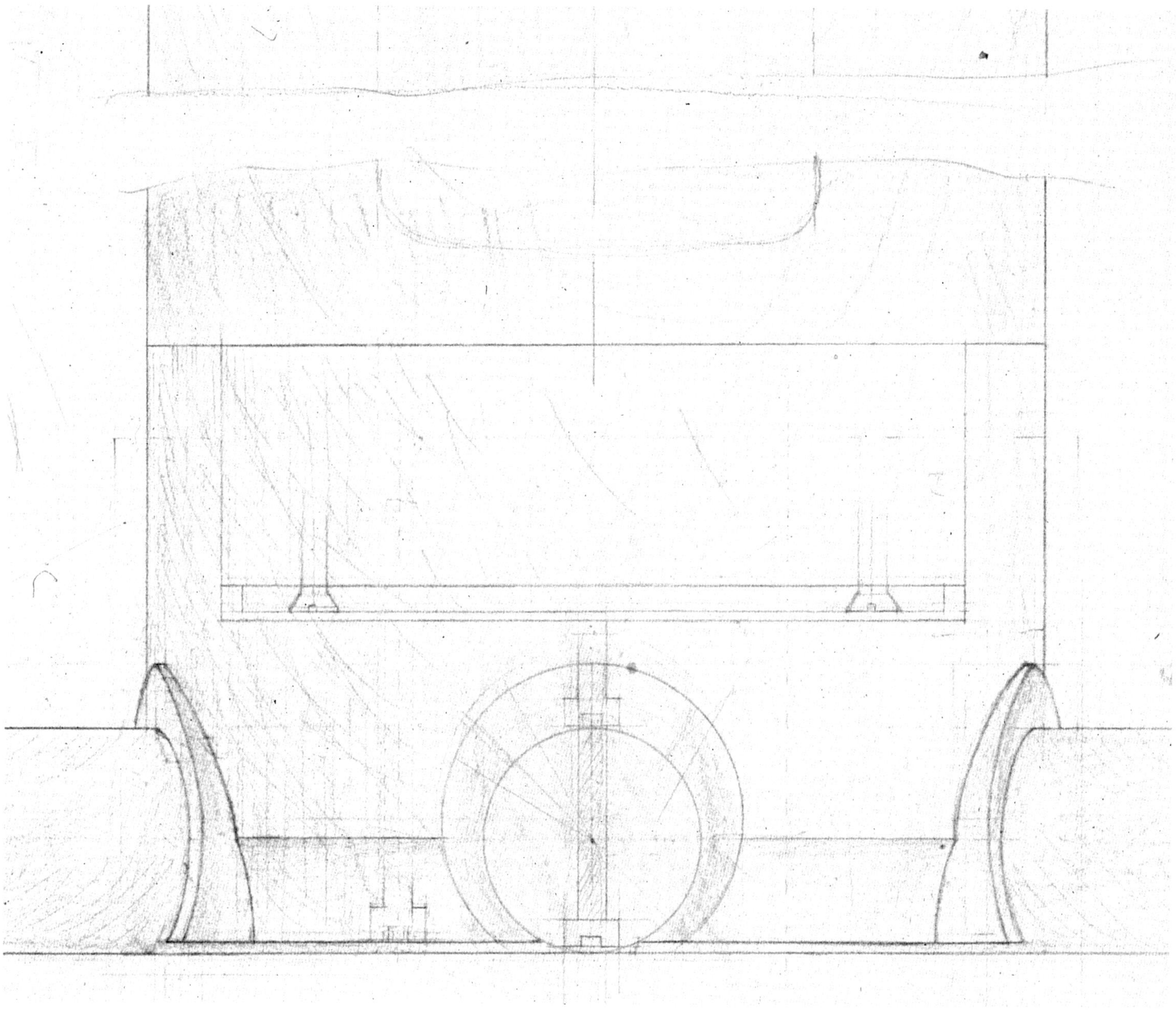

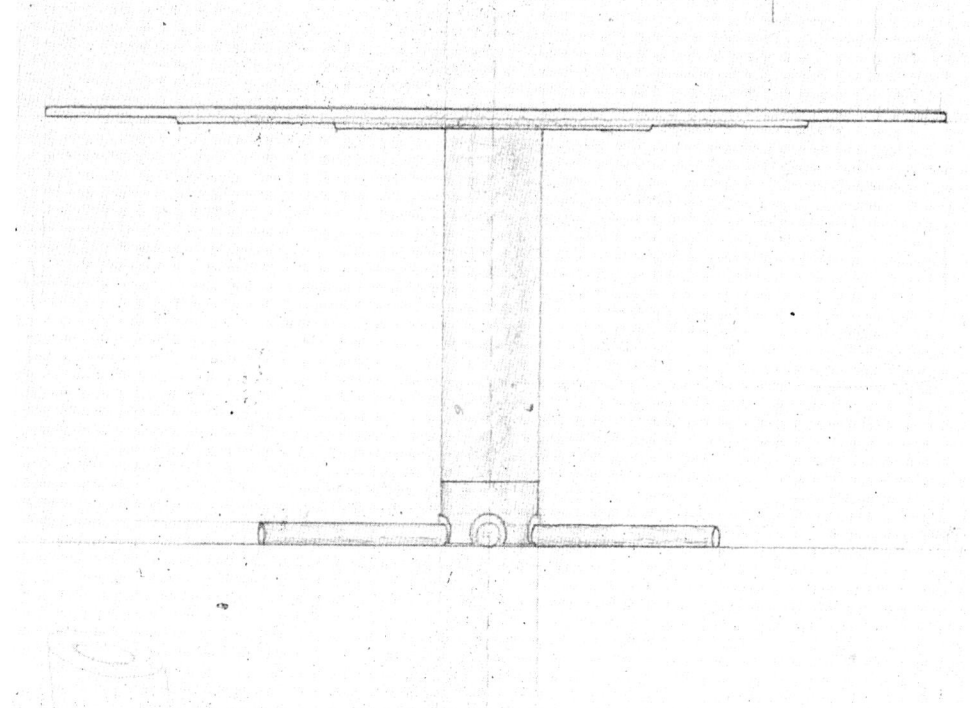

75. Study for the insertion of base elements in the shaft of the table. Pencil and crayons on Bristol board

76. Elevation of the table. Pencil and crayons on Bristol board

76

FIXED JOINT—HINGED JOINT

The point where constituent parts interlock, the nodal element of the structure, juncture, change of level, intersection: the fixed joint lends complexity to a work, it operates three-dimensionally and is the "divertissement" of planning.

It comes into its own where the scale is small, and differing materials meet or overlap with no loss of identity.

The hinged joint also signifies release of forms in an architectural organism, the point from which spaces radiate outward.

Hinging is a constant theme. Whether expressed or concealed, it is the mechanism regulating mysterious and unusual openings or sumptuous detailing.

15. Metal staircase in the Banca Popolare di Verona
16. Candelabrum in the Brion chapel
17. "Toledo" bed
18. Protective barrier at Brescia
19. Door on the Brion chapel
INSTANCES EXTRA-DOSSIER

15. Metal staircase in the Banca Popolare di Verona

77. Detail of a fixed joint in the structure of the metal staircase, Banca Popolare di Verona

78. Sketch for the fixed joint. Pencil and crayons on paper

▷
79, 80, 81, 82, 83. Details of fixed joints

84. A ramp seen from above

82

83

84

85. Sketch for a fixed joint. Pencil on paper

86. Study for the base of the structure at ground level. Pencil on paper

85

86

87

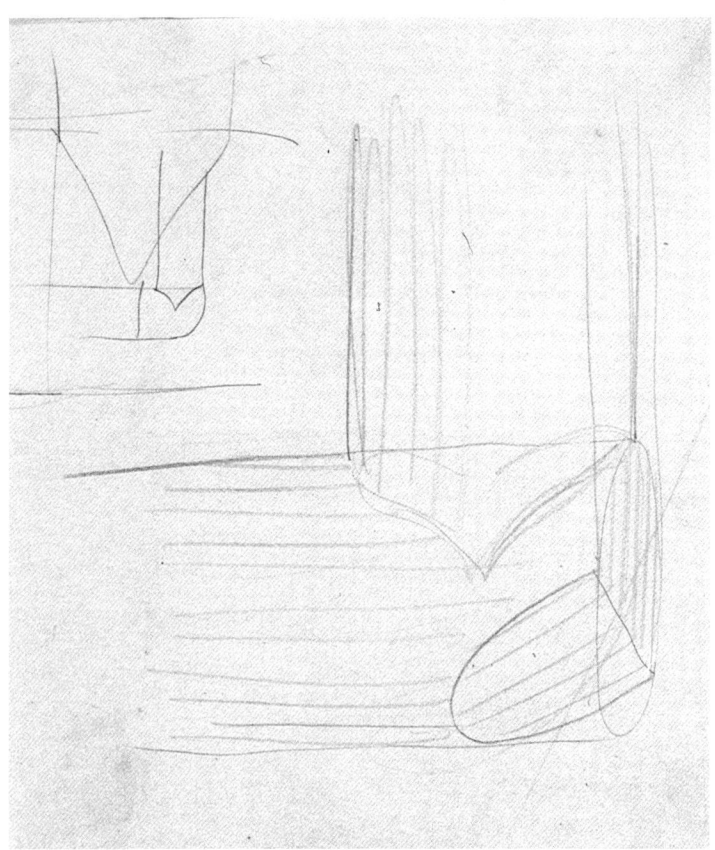

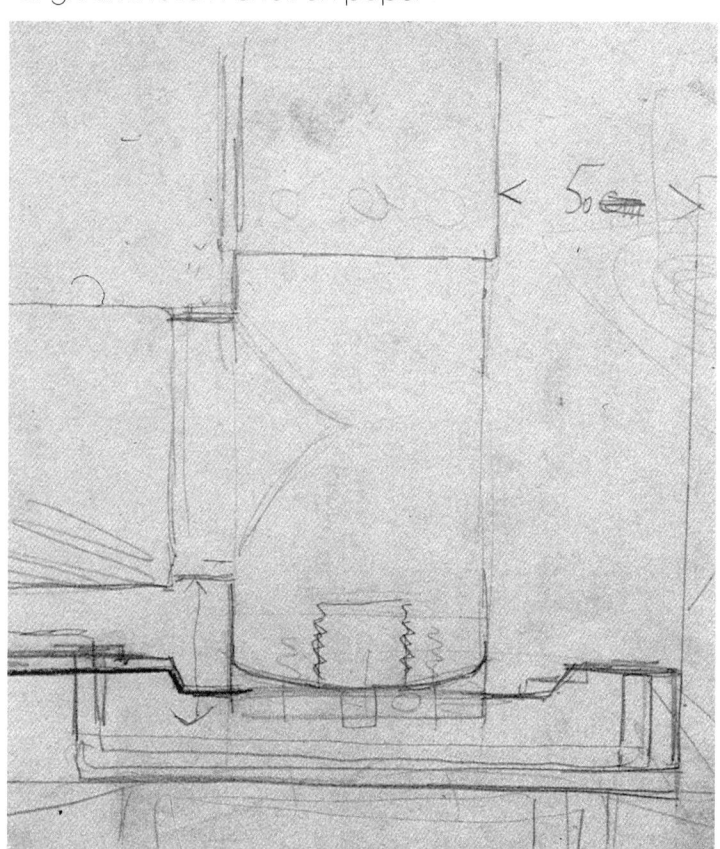

87. Constructional sketches for the structure and for the step. Pencil on tracing paper

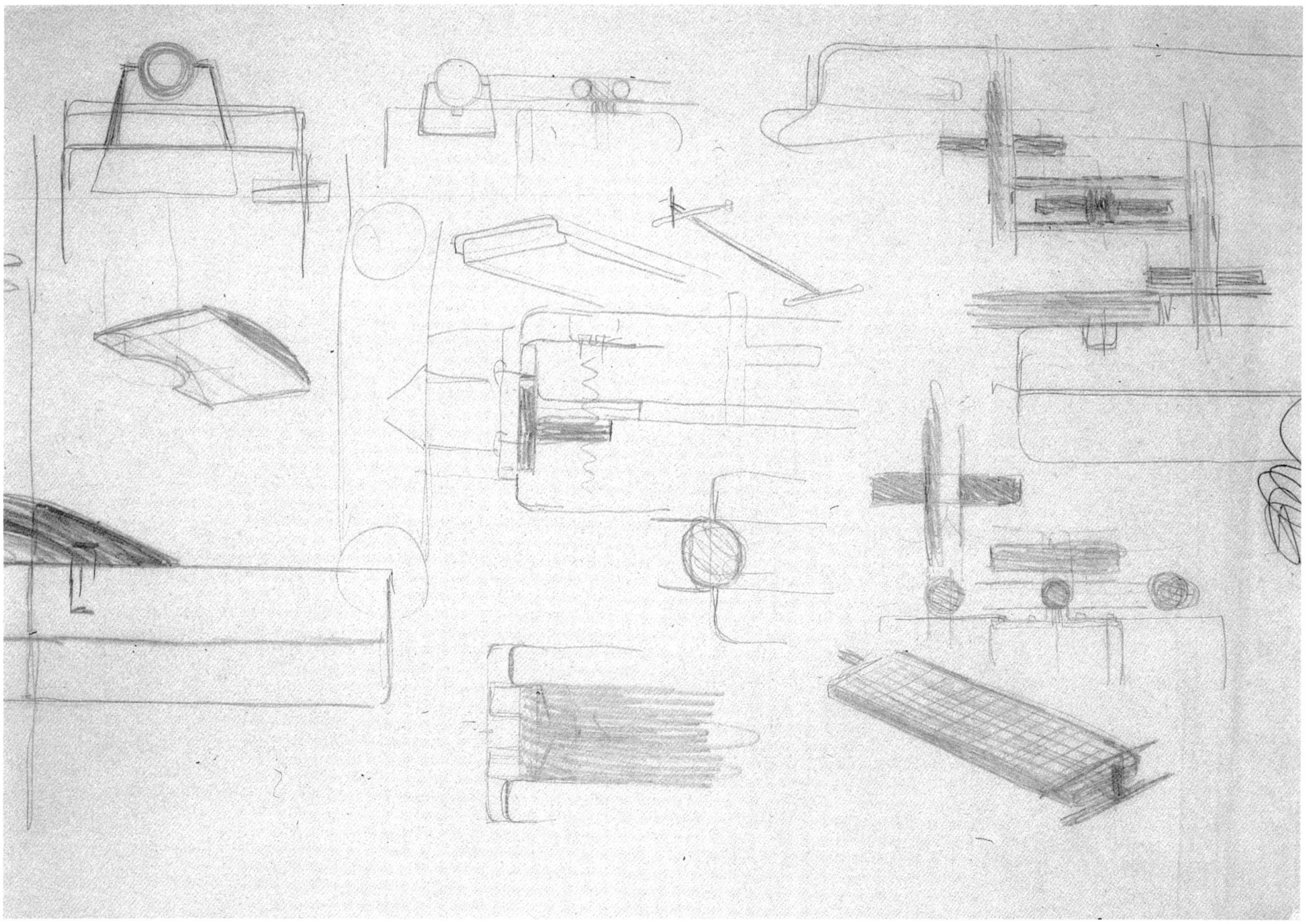

88. Detail of the plan of the building, highlighting the staircase. Pencil and crayons on Bristol board

89. Plan of the staircase. First version. Pencil and crayons on Bristol board

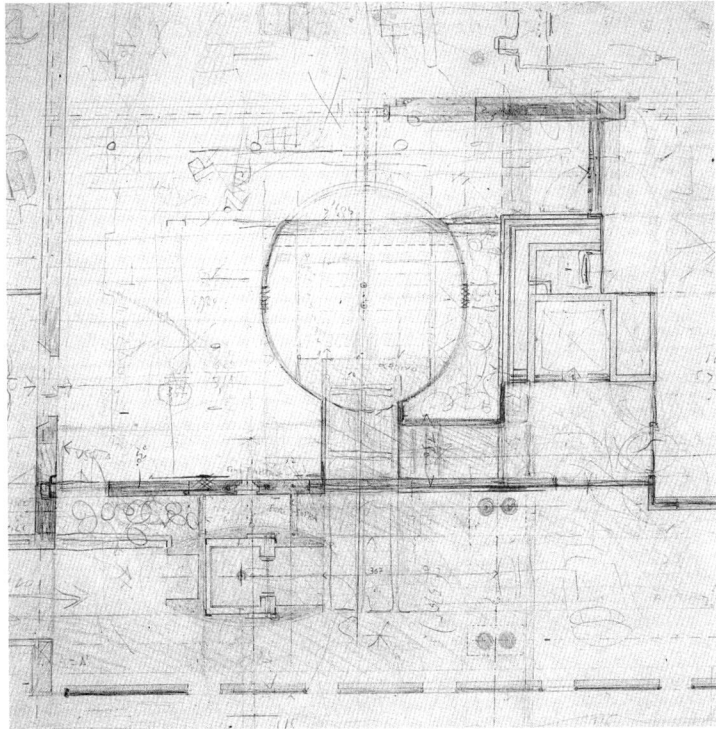

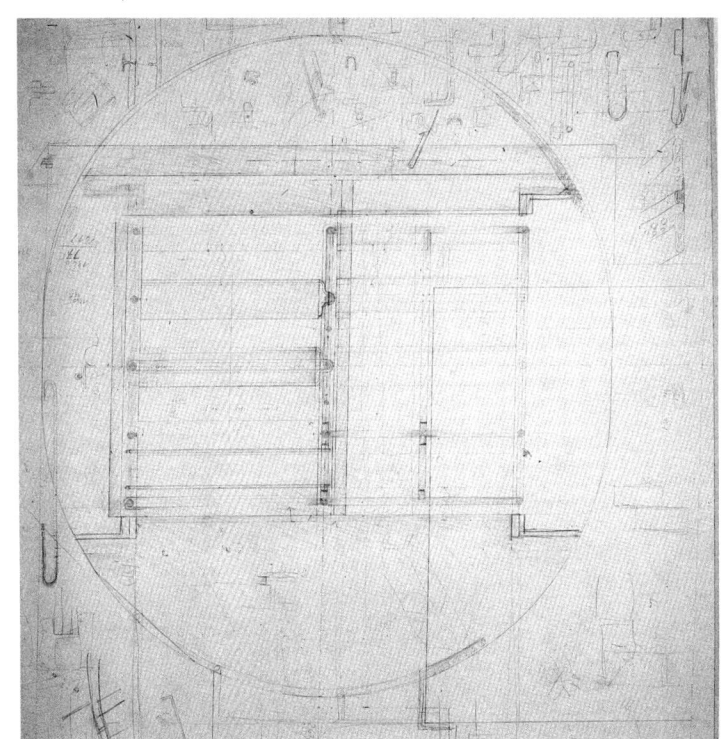

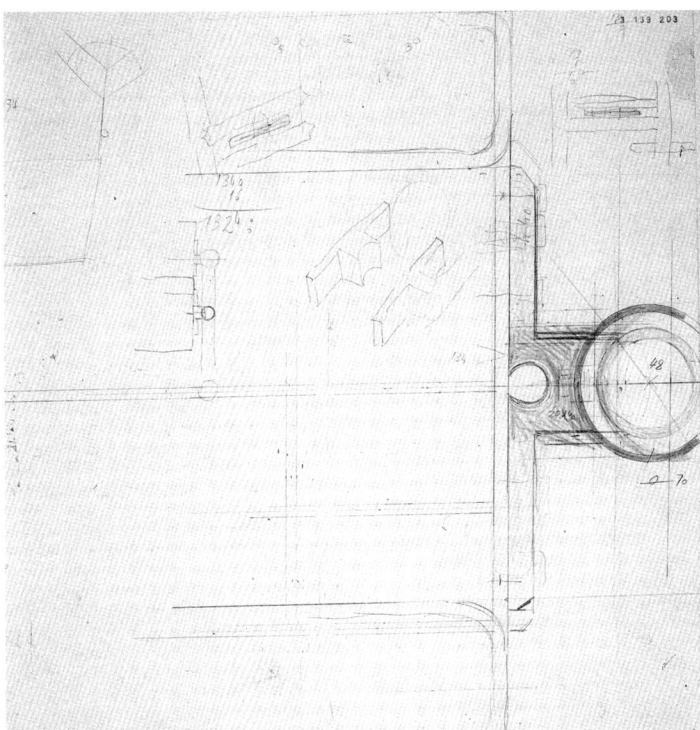

90. Transversal section of the staircase. First version. Pencil and crayons on Bristol board

91. Full-scale study for the step. Final solution. Pencil and crayons on Bristol board

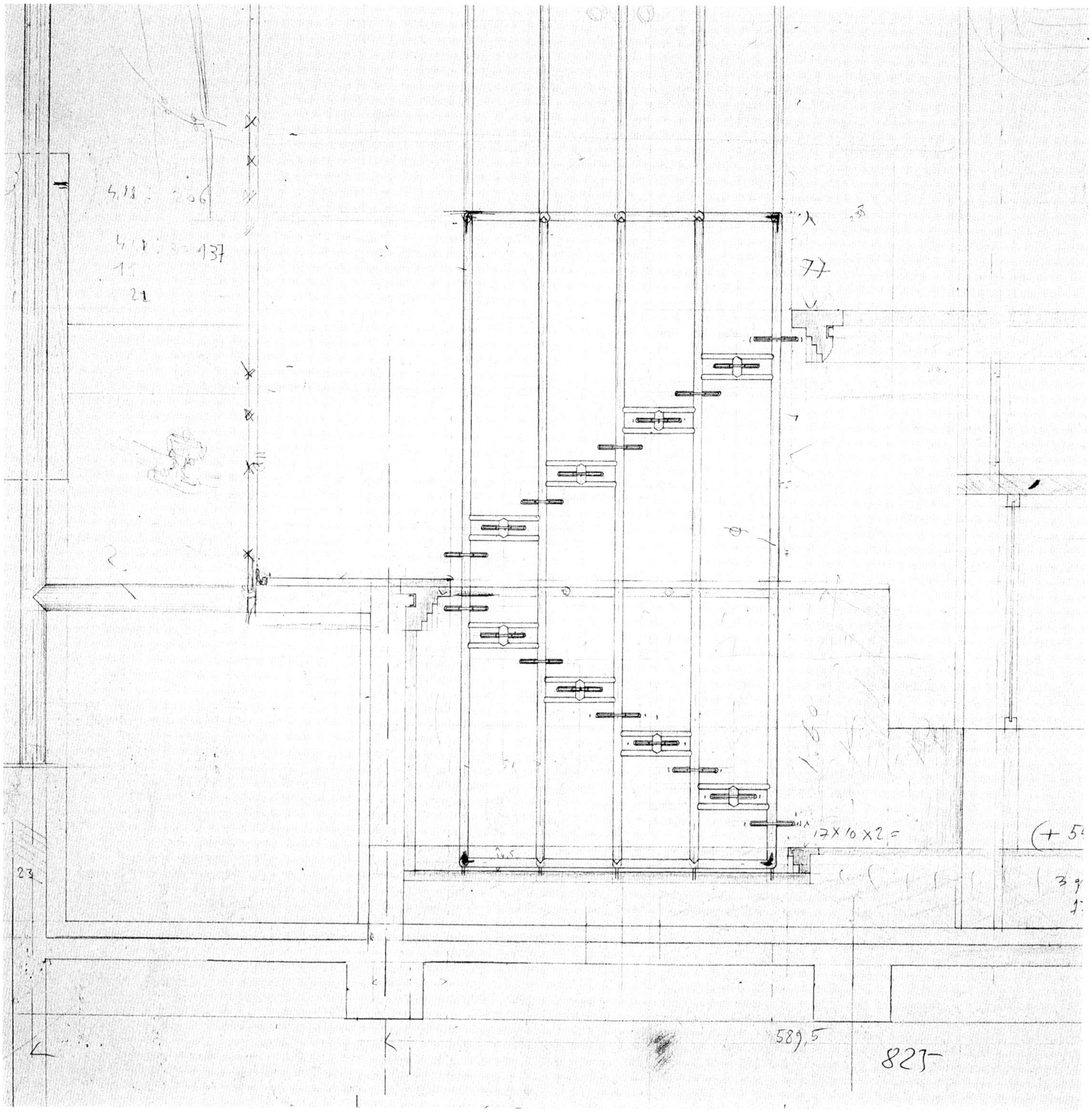

92

93

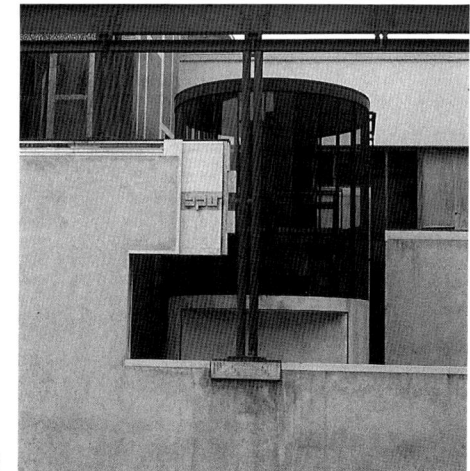

92. Longitudinal section of the staircase. First version. Pencil and crayons on Bristol board

93. External view of the staircase

16. Candelabrum in the Brion chapel

94. First sketch for the candelabrum in the chapel of the Brion cemetery, S. Vito di Altivole. Ink on paper

95

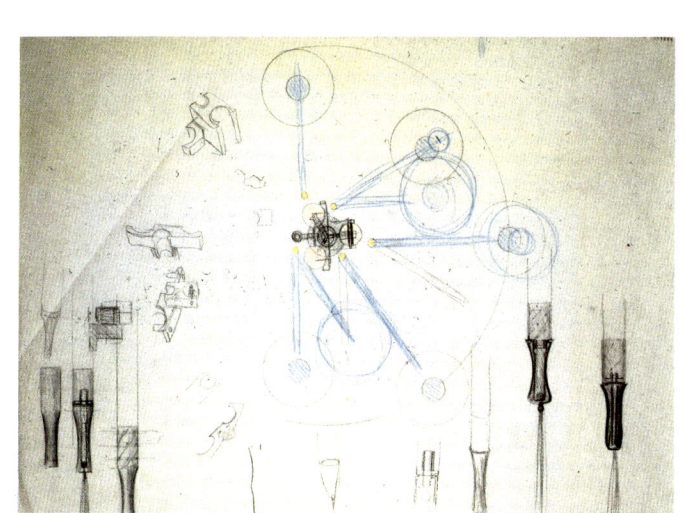

95. Study for detailing of the candelabrum. Pencil and crayons on Bristol board

96. Sketch for the candleholders and the terminal elements. Pencil and crayons on tracing paper

96

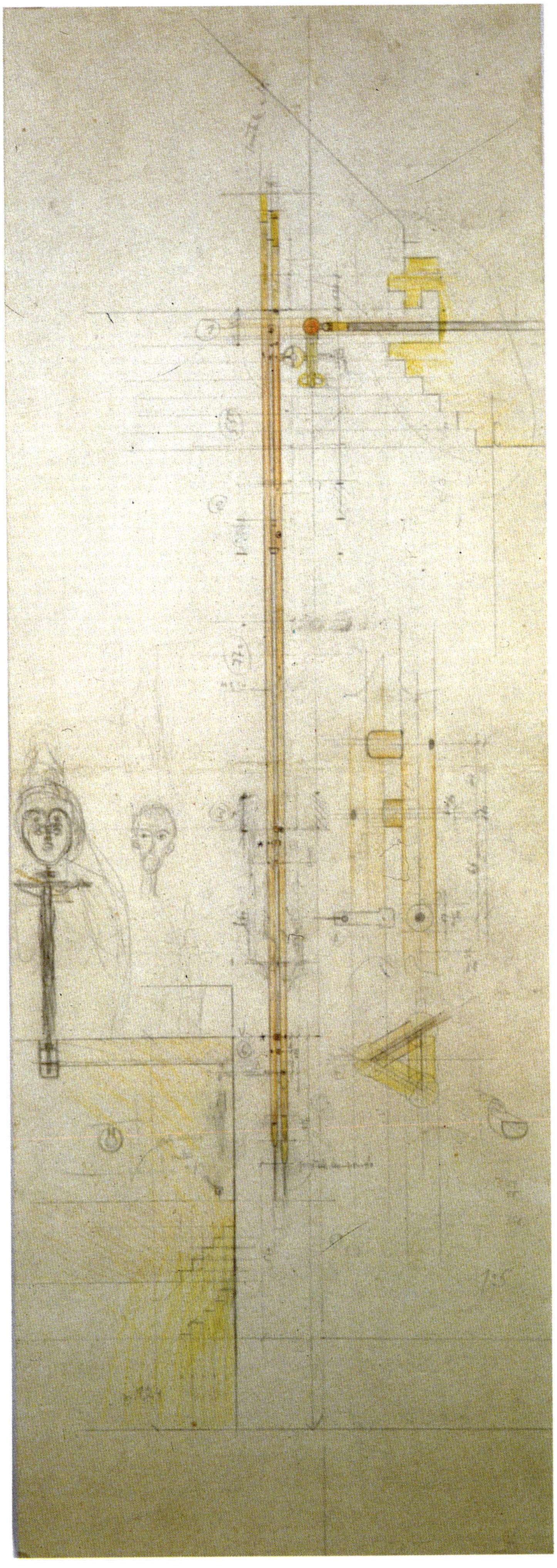

97. Study for the candelabrum. Pencil and crayons on Bristol board

98. Sketch for the couplings between arms and shaft. Pencil and crayons on tracing paper

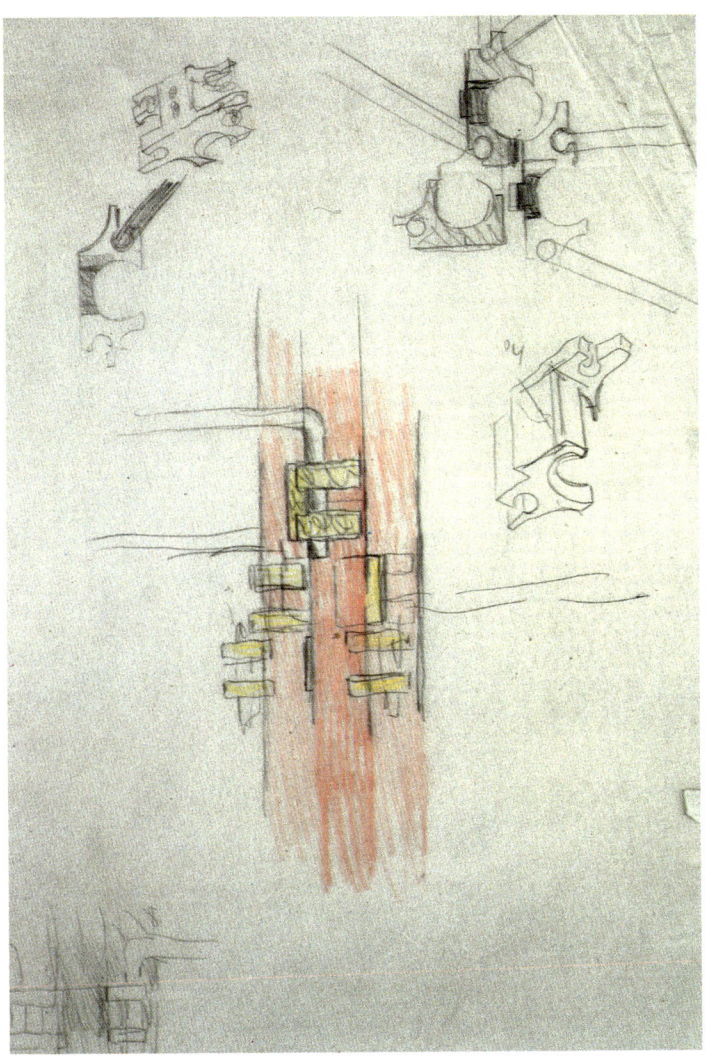

98

▷
99. The candelabrum
100. Hinging element of the shaft
101. Coupling of arms to the shaft

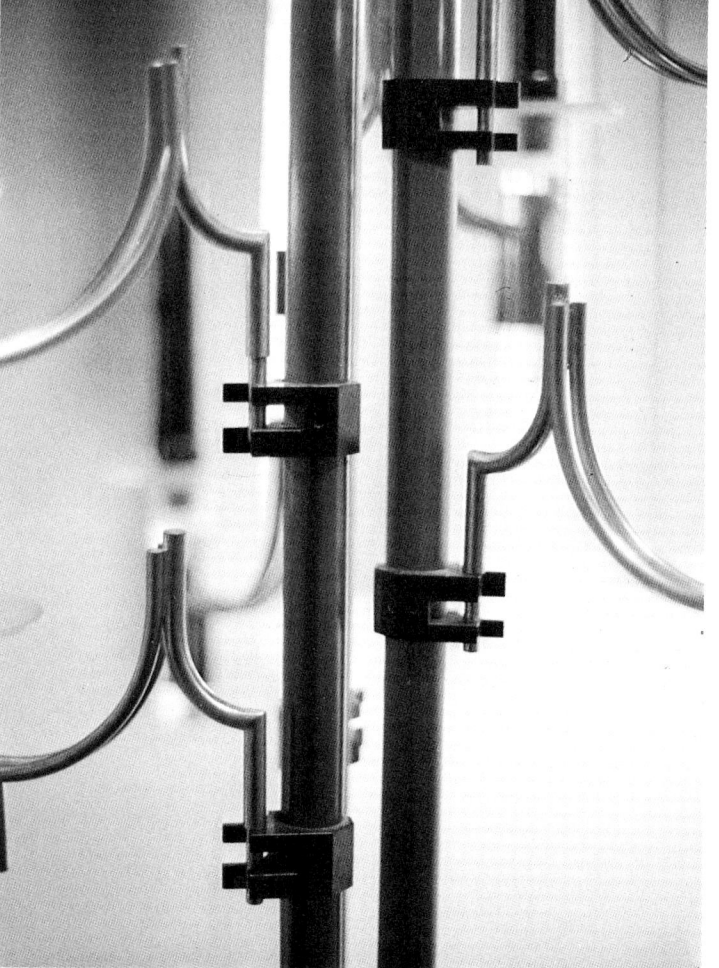

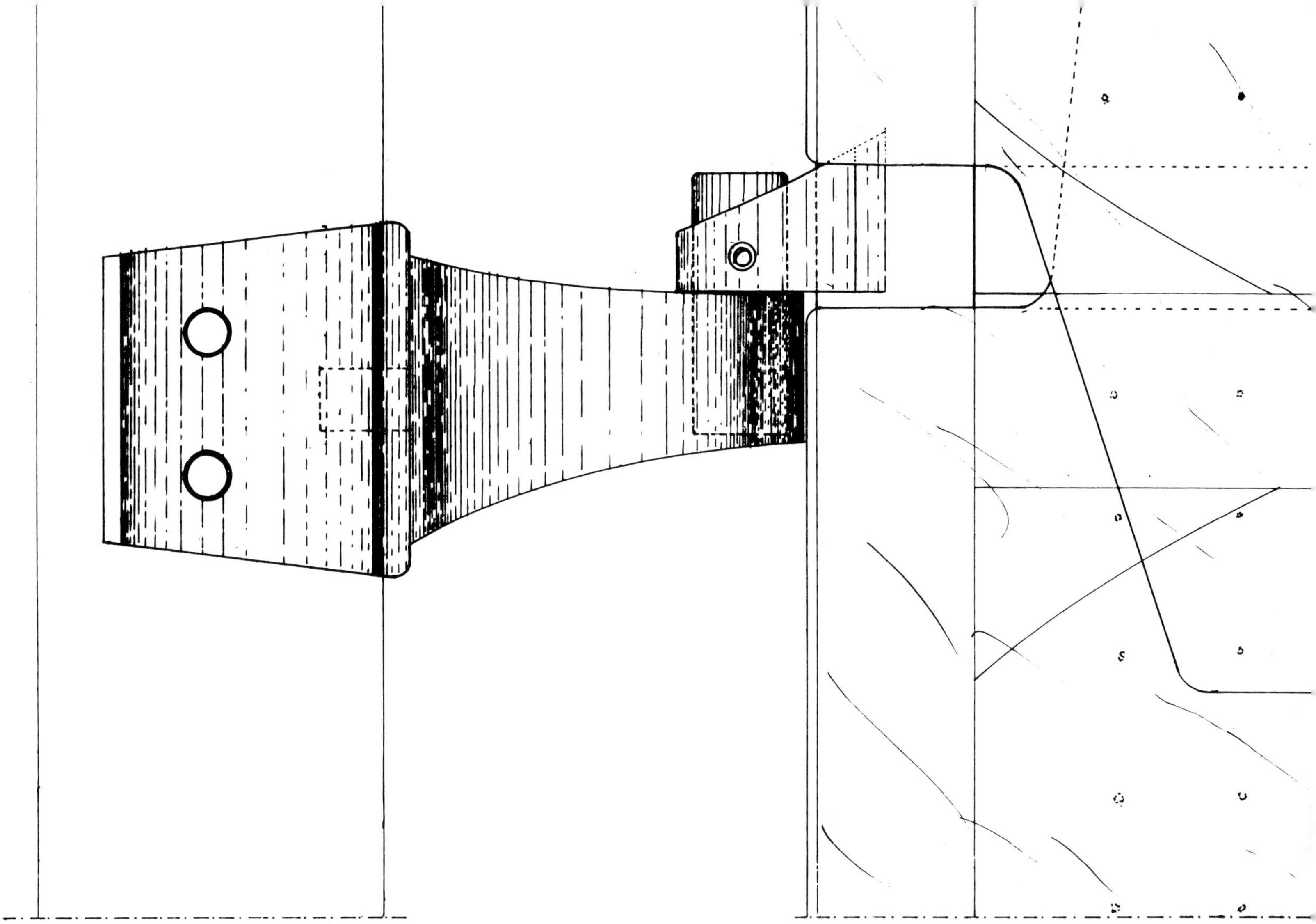

102

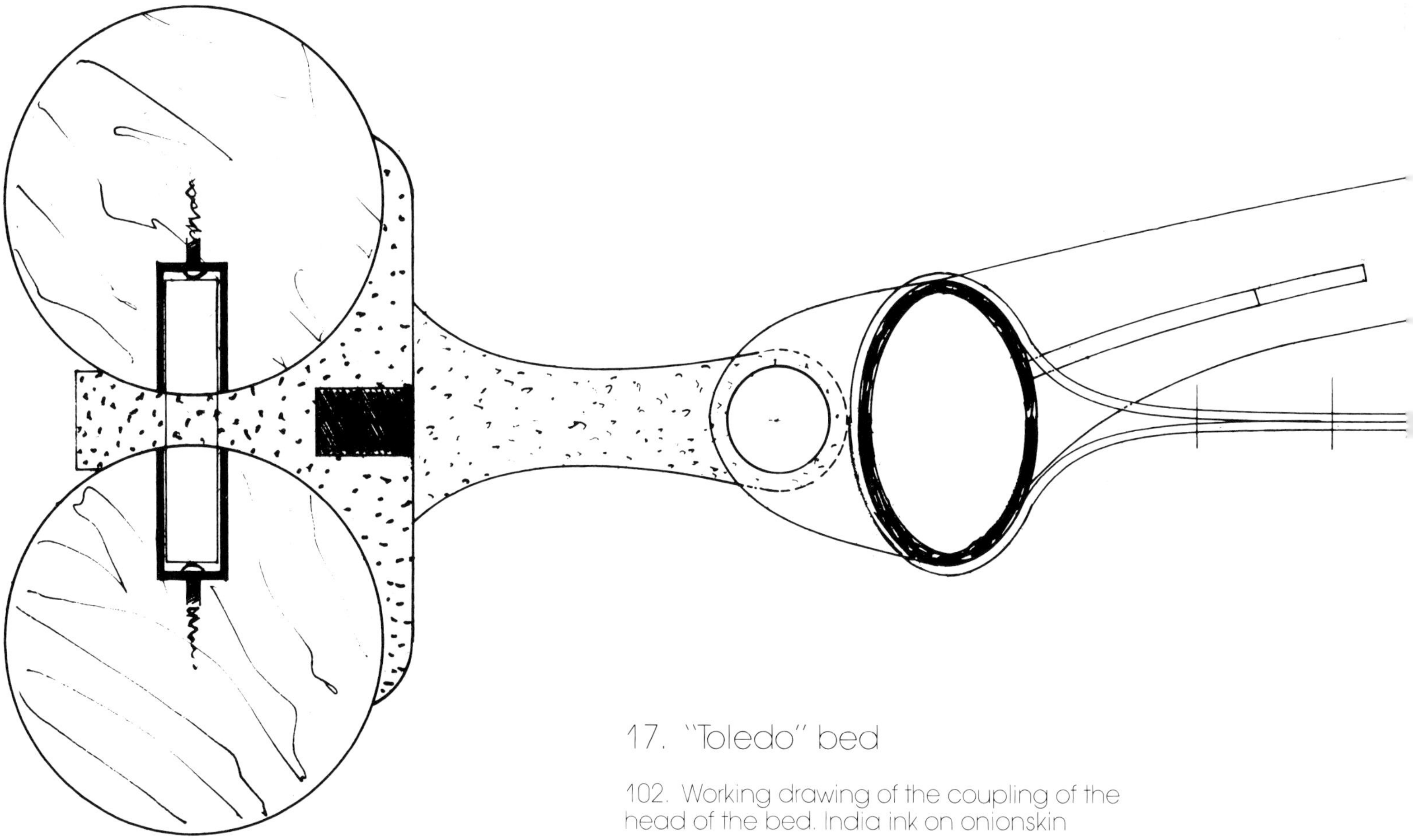

17. "Toledo" bed

102. Working drawing of the coupling of the head of the bed. India ink on onionskin

103

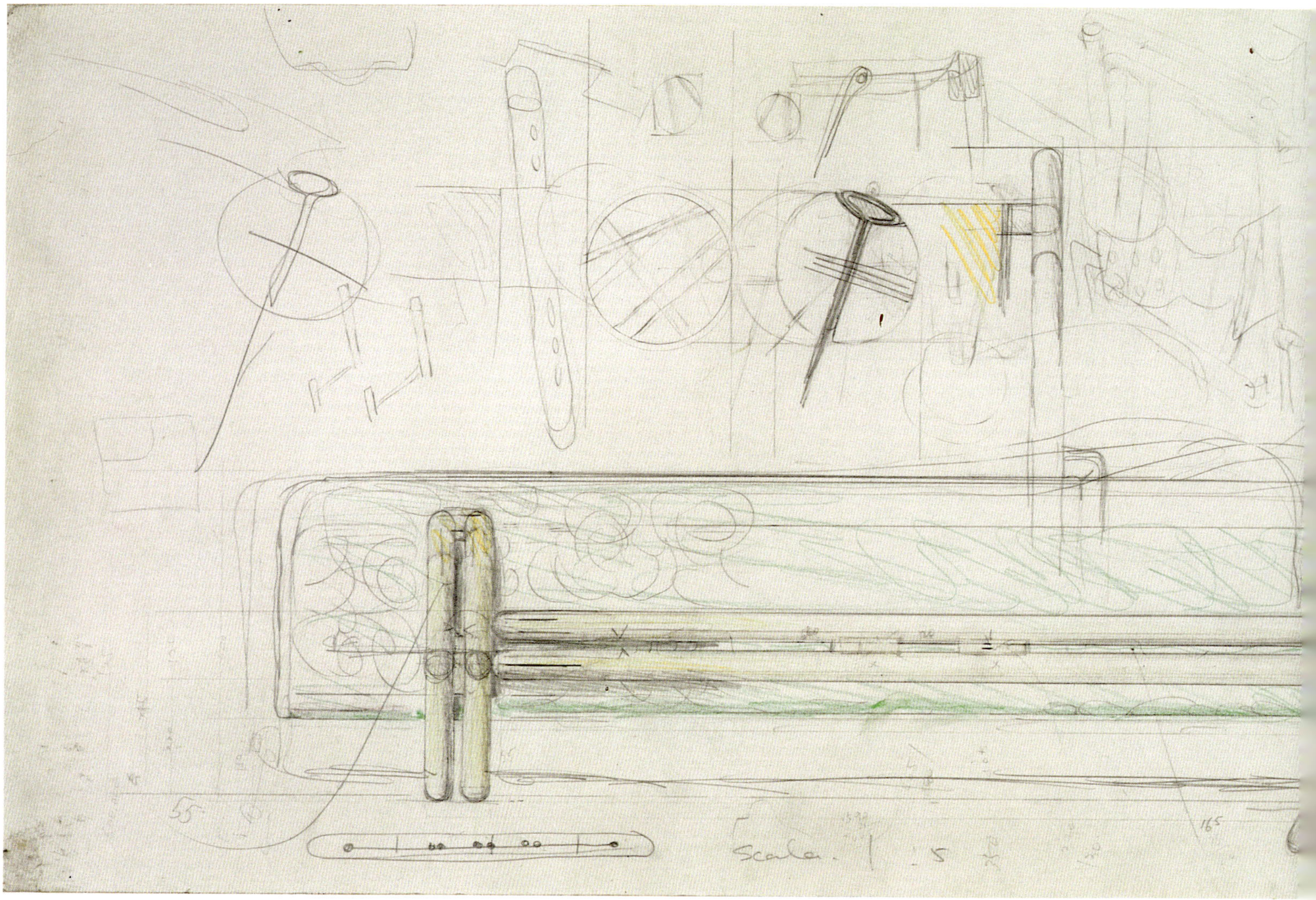

103. Study for the bed. Pencil and crayons on Bristol board

104. Study for the head of the bed. Pencil and crayons on Bristol board

105. Working drawing for the head of the bed. India ink and adhesives on onionskin

104

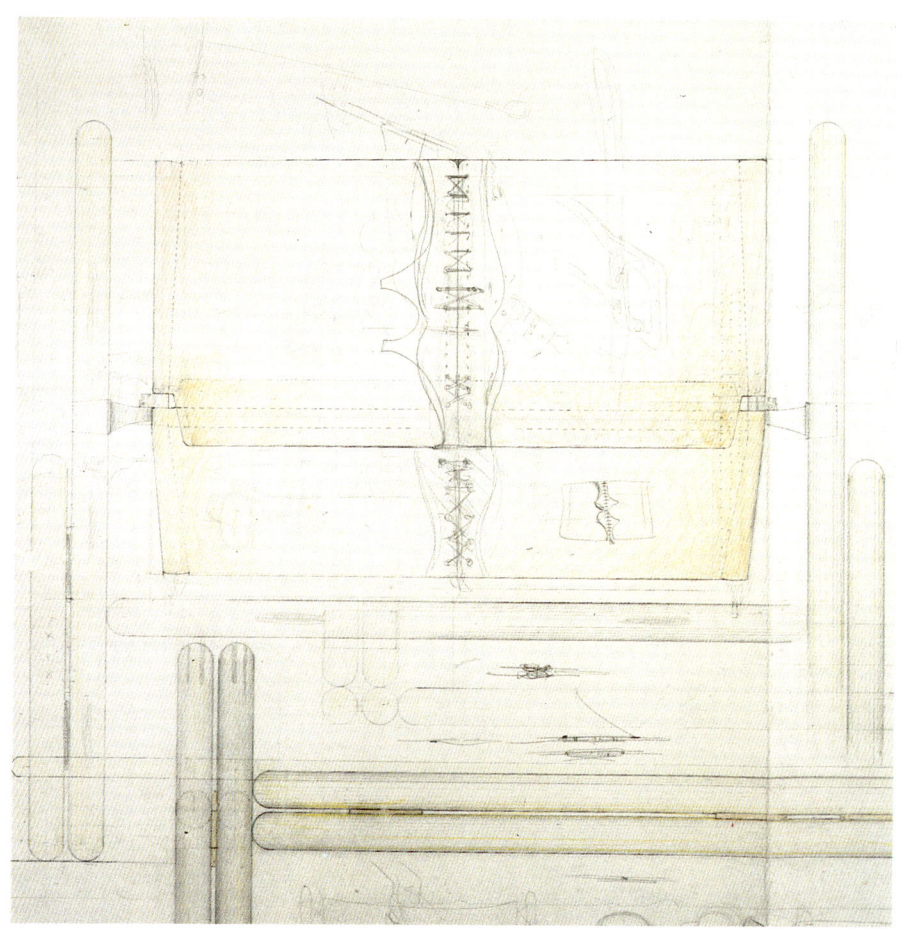

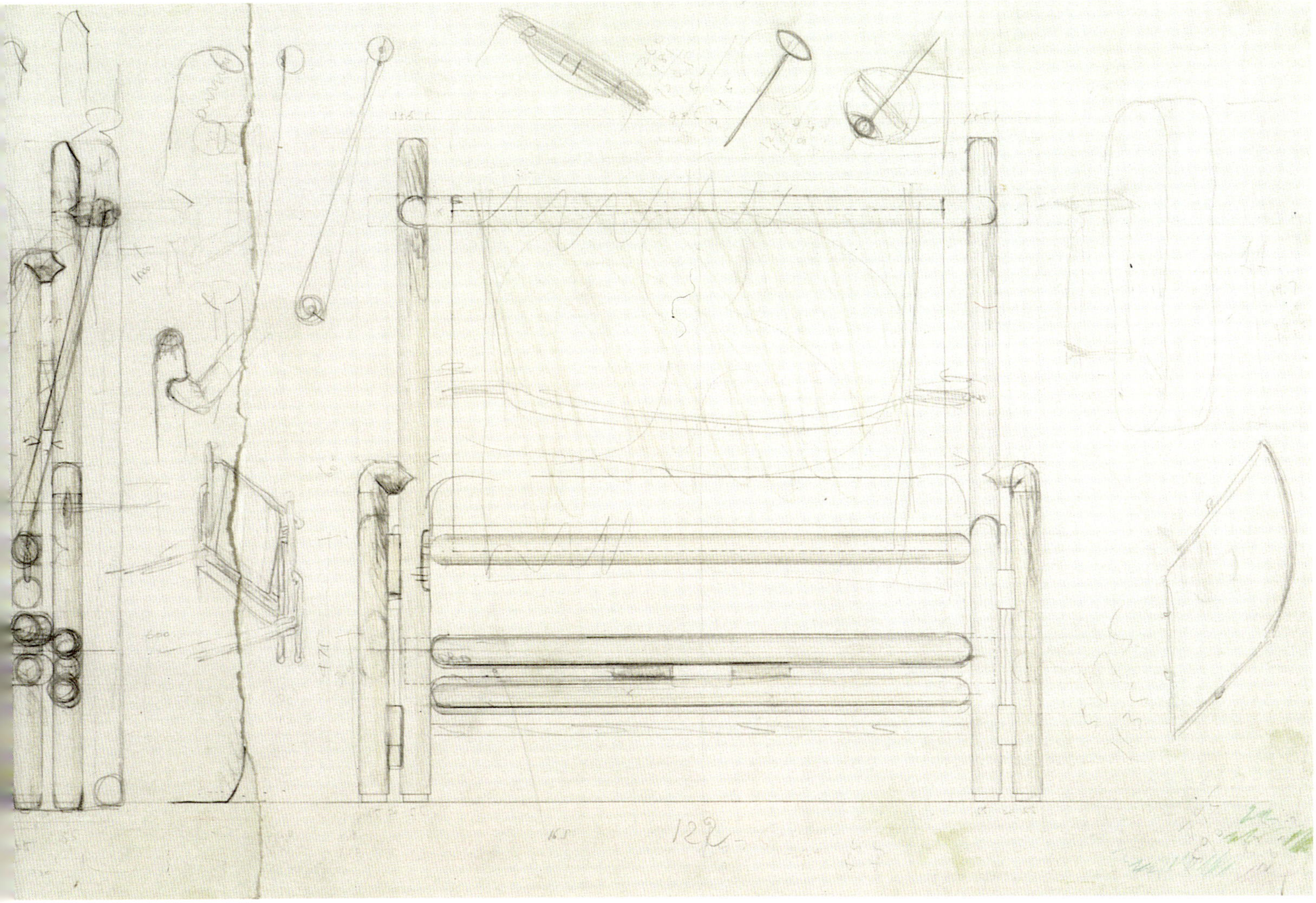

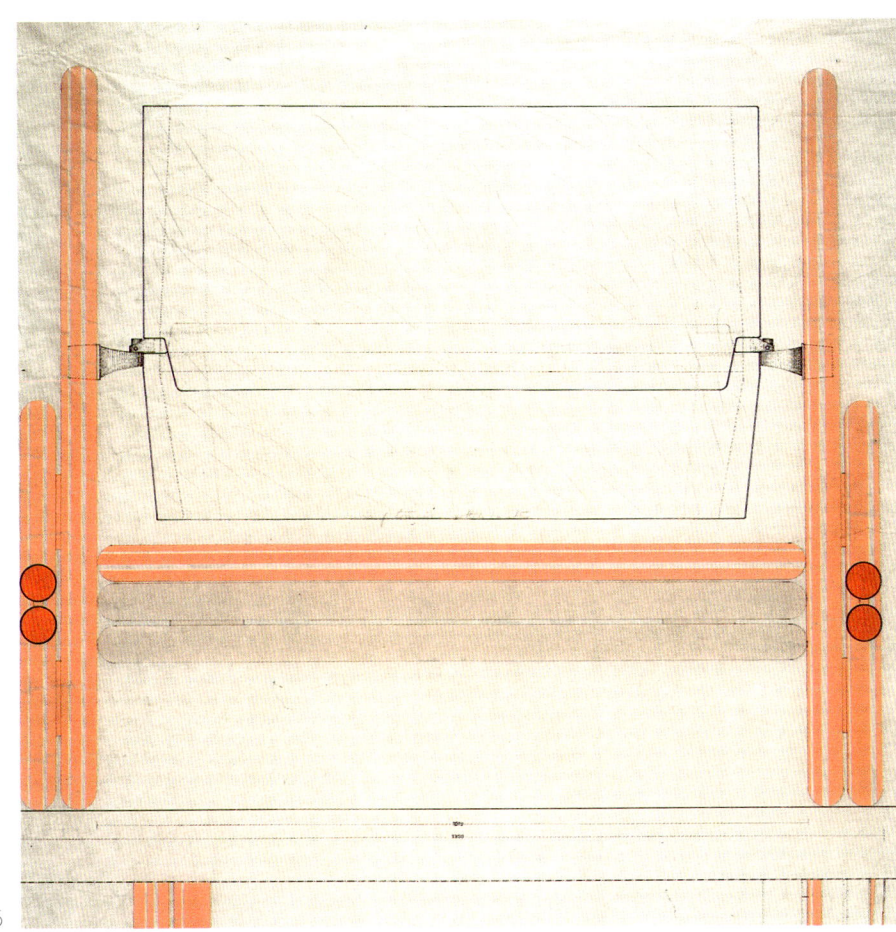

105

106

107

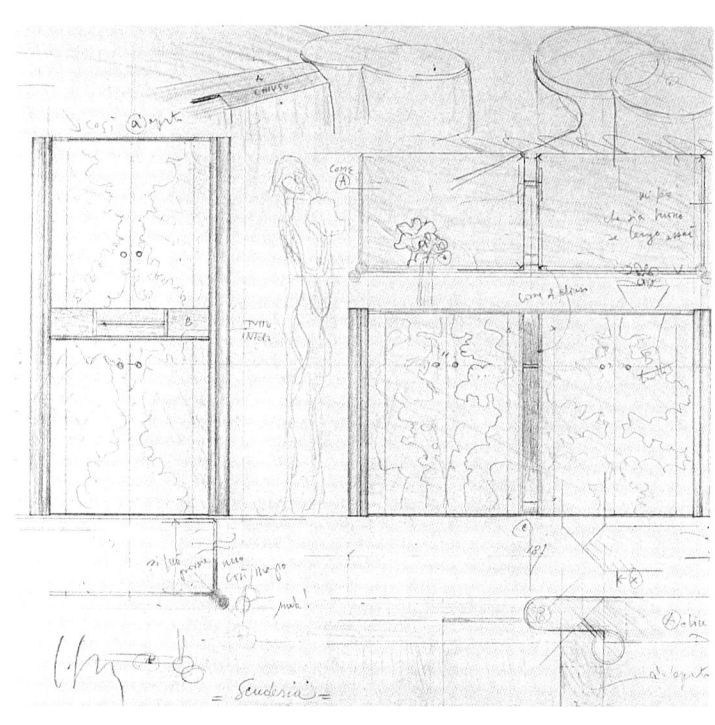

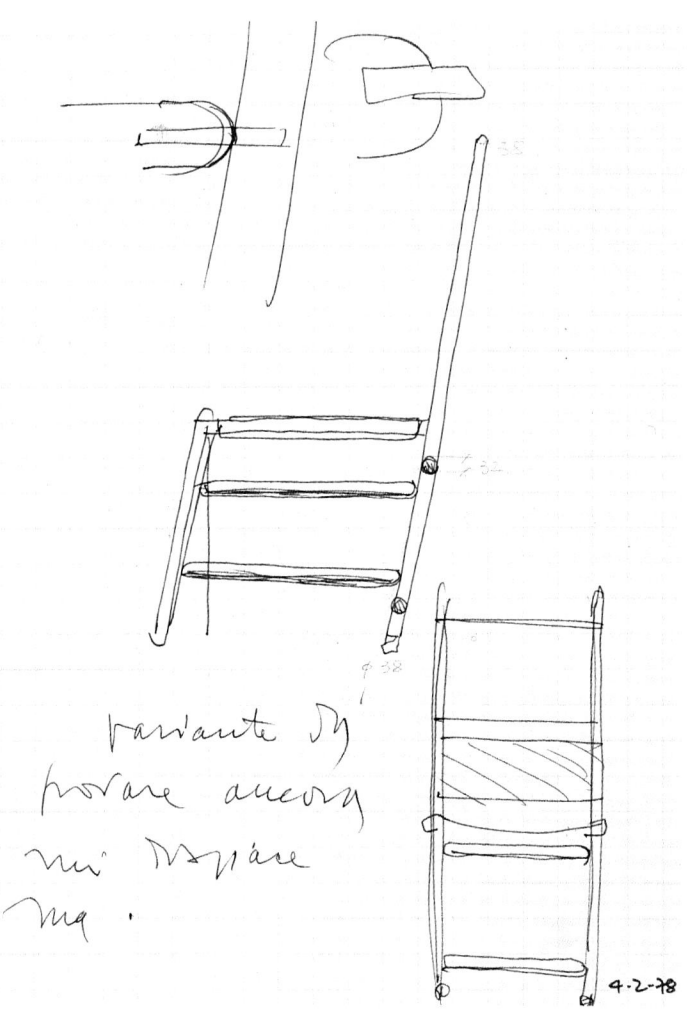

106. STUDY FOR THE "SCUDERIA" TABLE. PENCIL AND CRAYONS ON BRISTOL BOARD

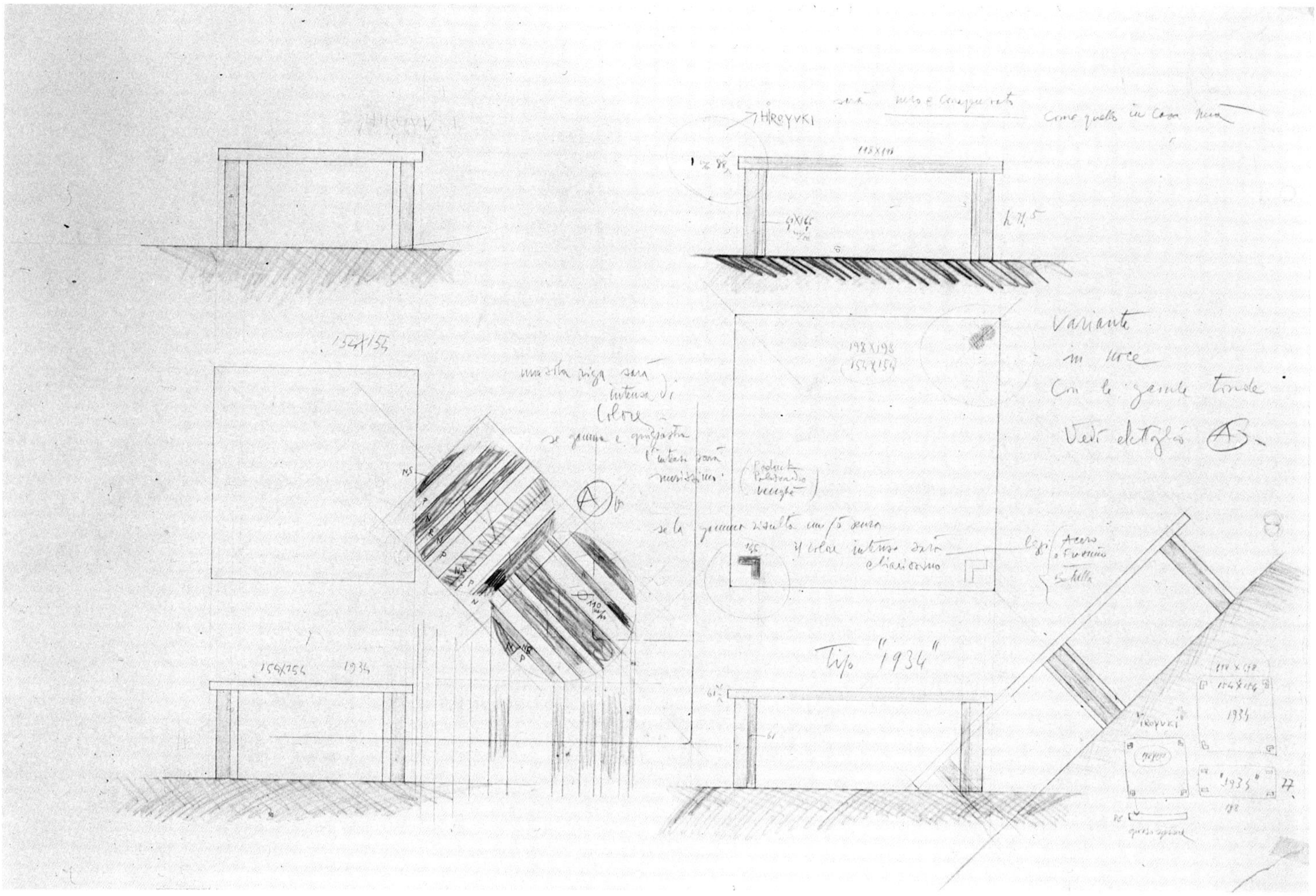

107. STUDY FOR THE "SCUDERIA" CUPBOARD. PENCIL ON BRISTOL BOARD

108. SKETCH FOR THE "KENTUCKY" CHAIR. INK ON SQUARED PAPER

18. Protective barrier at Brescia

109. Detail of the protective barrier before the commemorative monument in Piazza della Loggia, Brescia

▷
110. Elevation detail of the barrier. Pencil and crayons on Bristol board

111. Sketch for the distancers of the bars. Pencil and crayons on onionskin

112. Study for the vertical metal element. Pencil and crayons on Bristol board

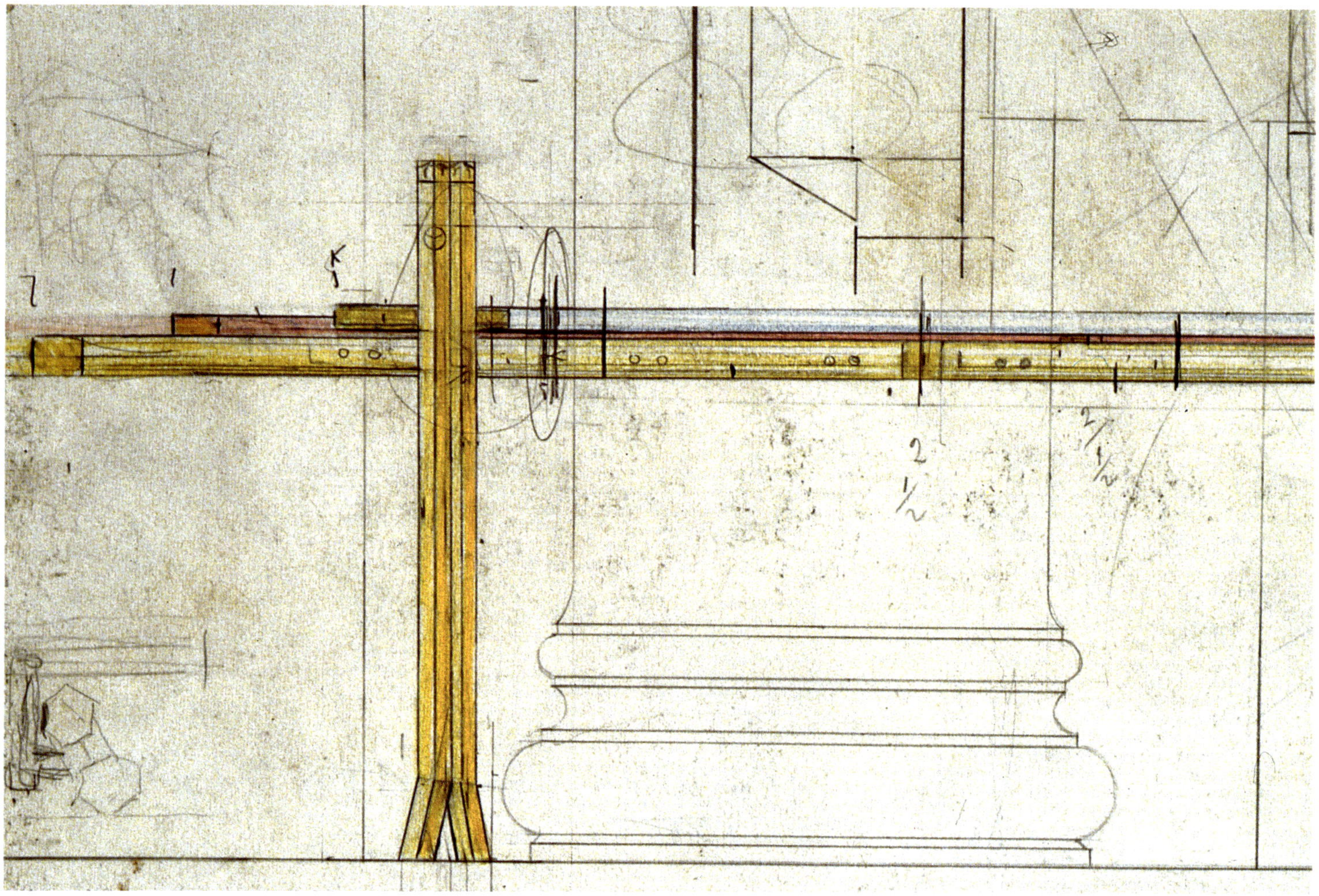

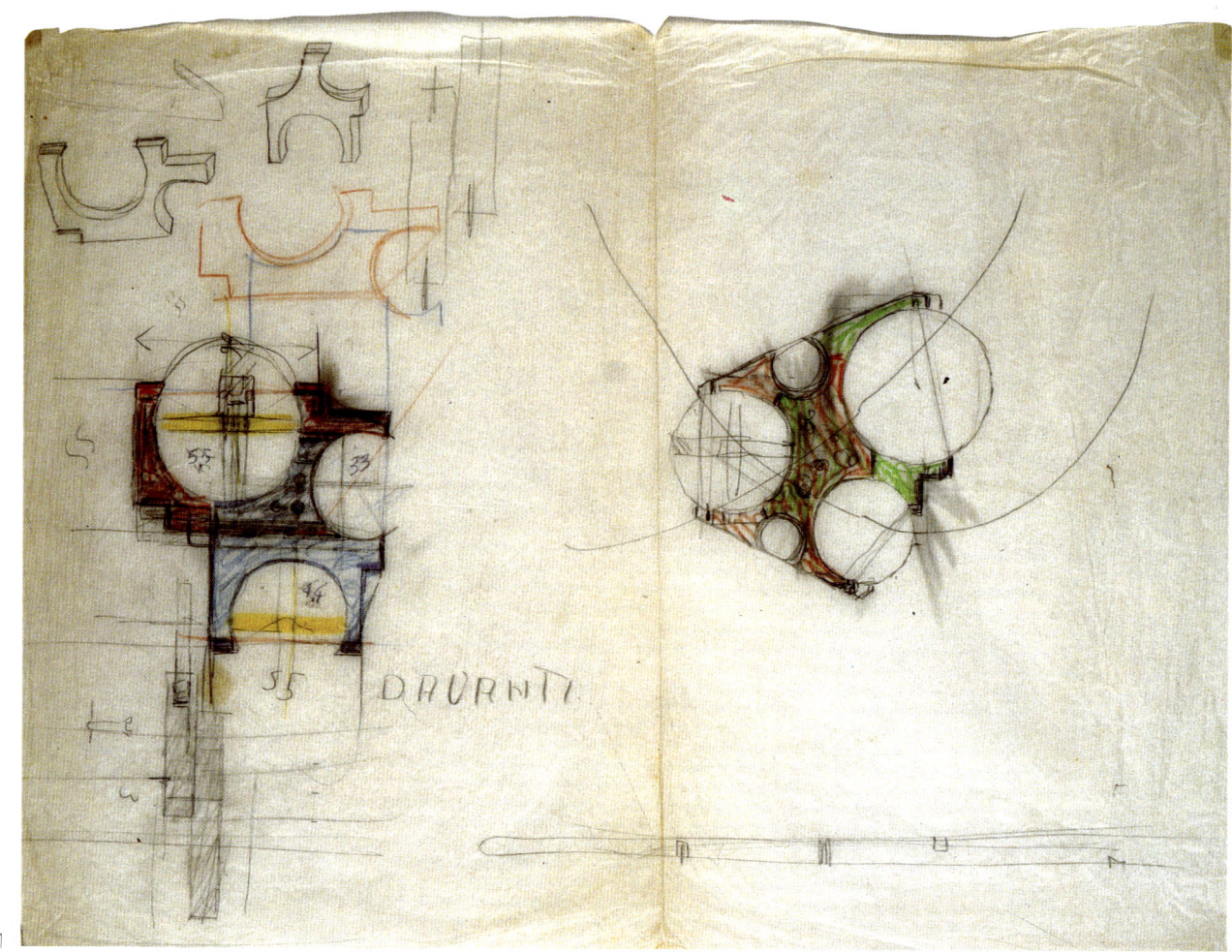

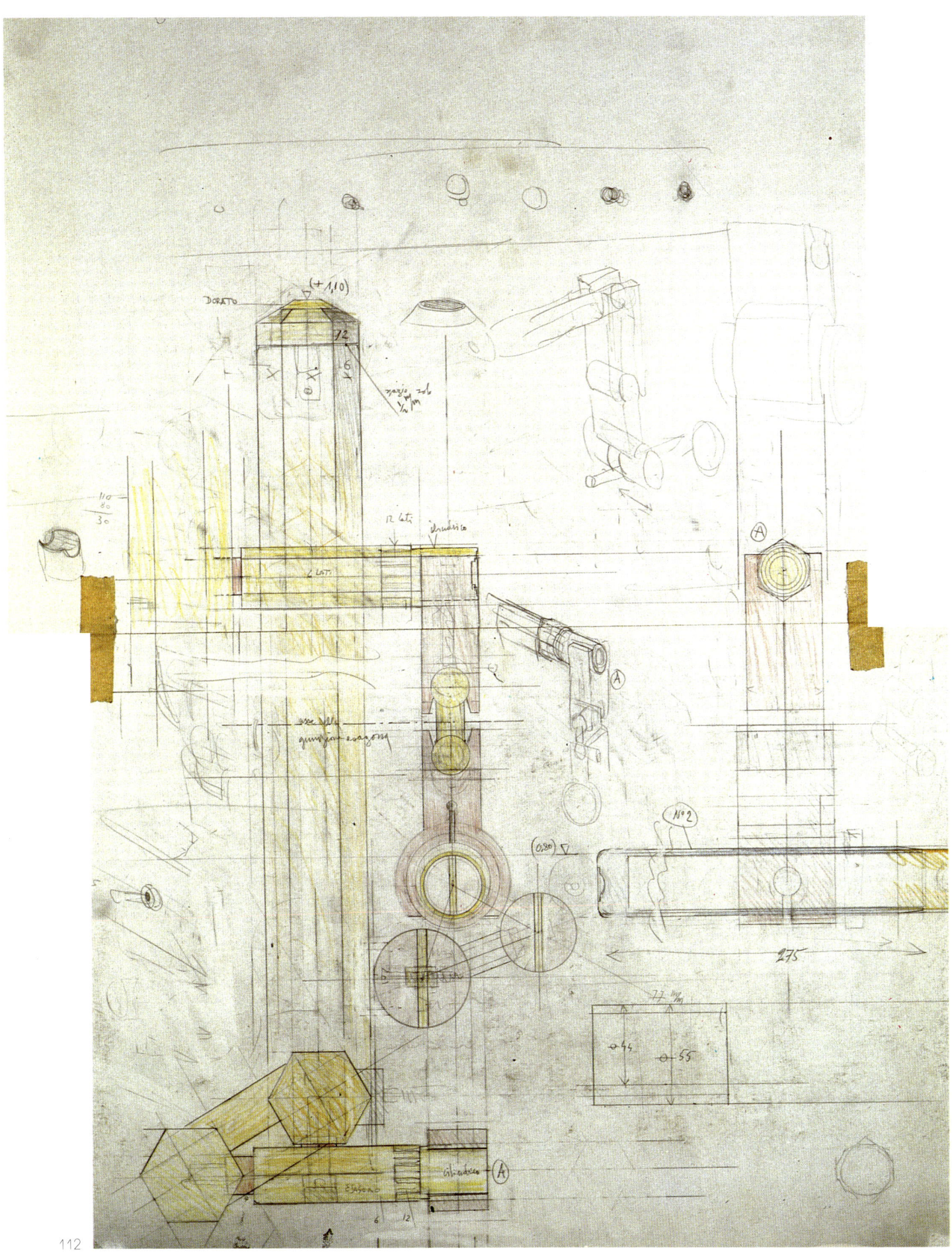

113. The barrier

114. DETAIL OF A BARRIER IN THE CASTELVECCHIO MUSEUM, VERONA

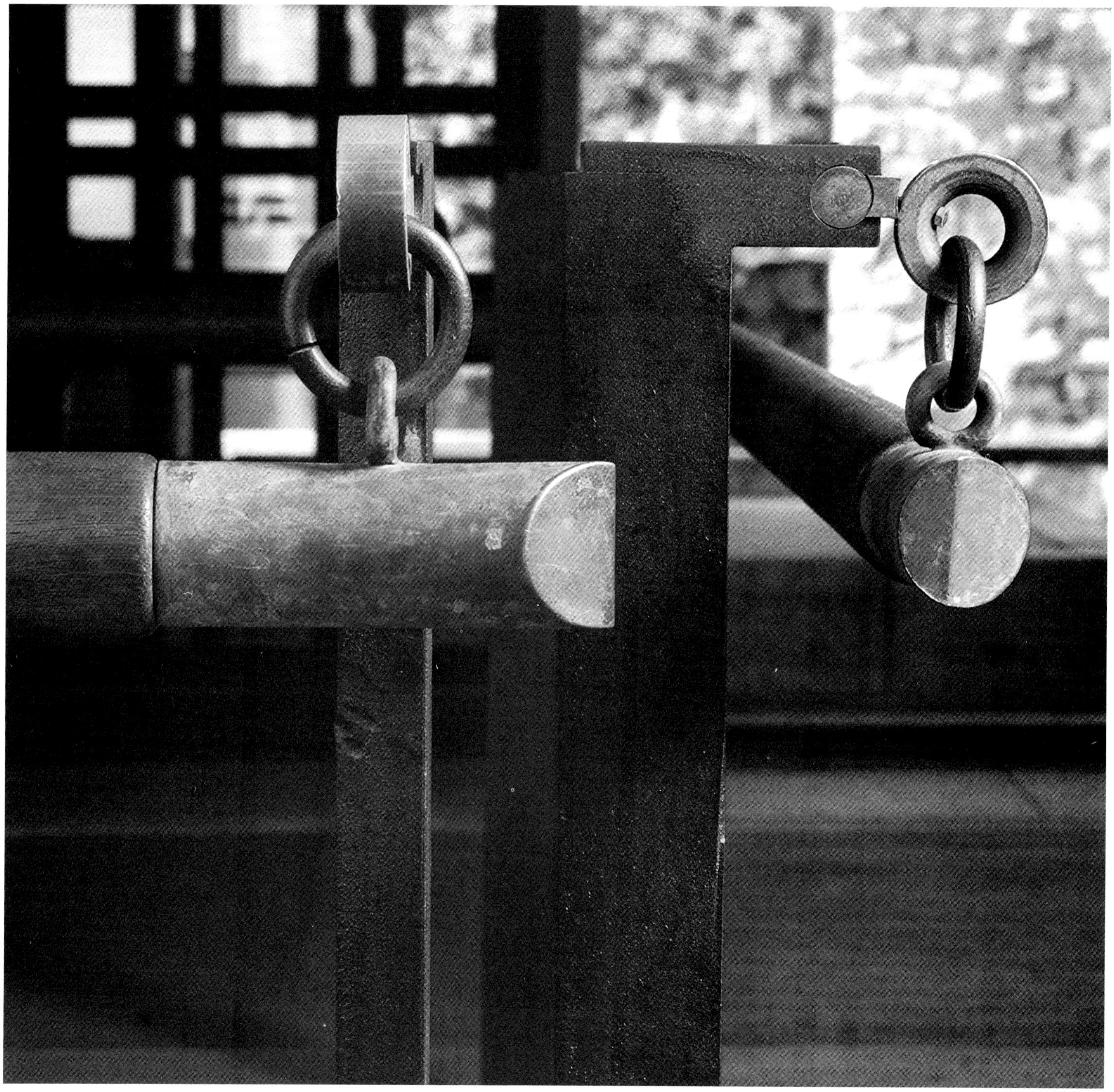

19. Door on the Brion chapel

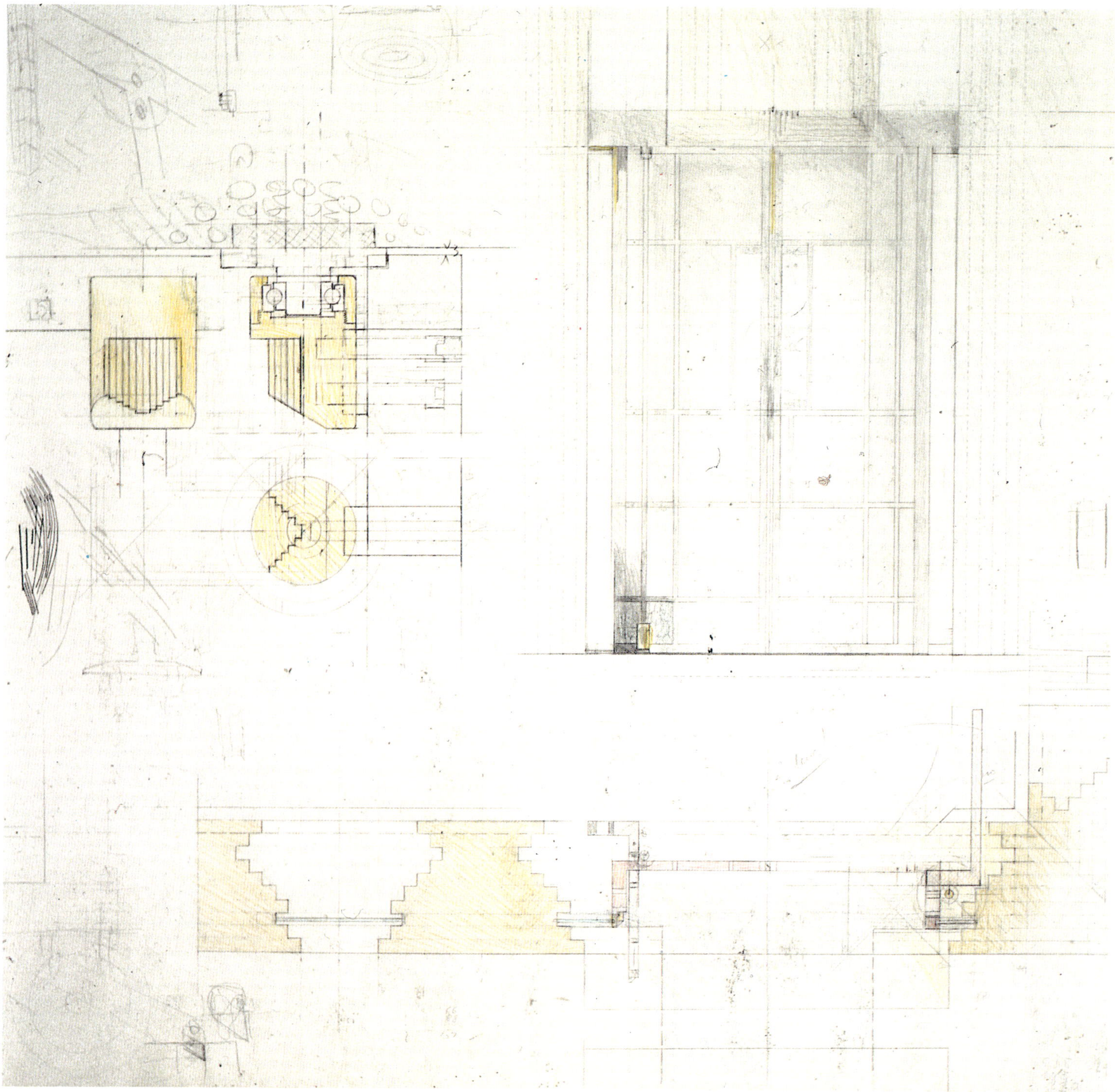

116

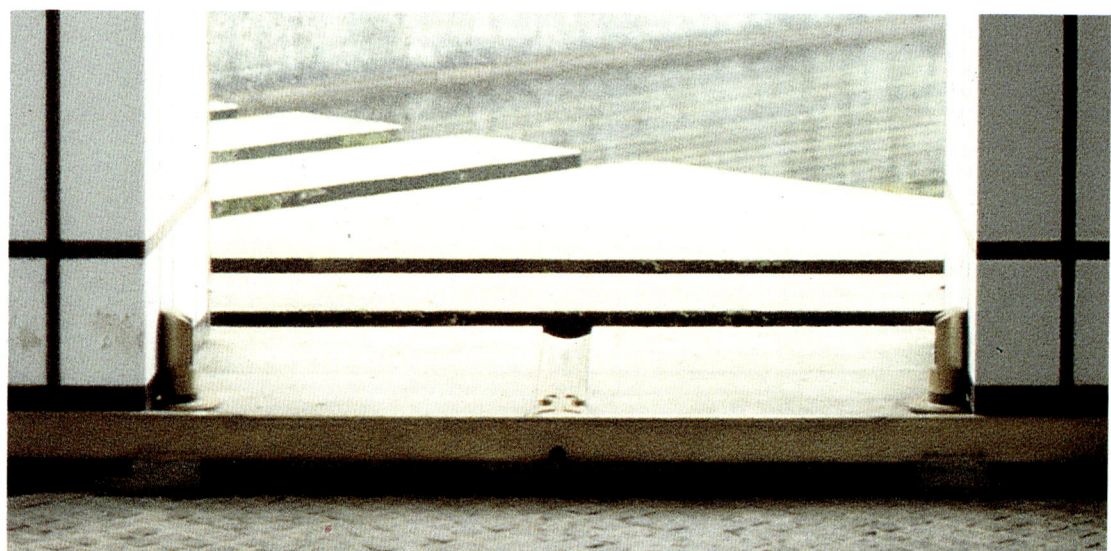

116. Study for the door and the hinge. Pencil and crayons on Bristol board

117. Detail of the hinge and bottom rail

117

◁
115. Hinge of the door on the chapel in the Brion cemetery, S. Vito di Altivole

121.

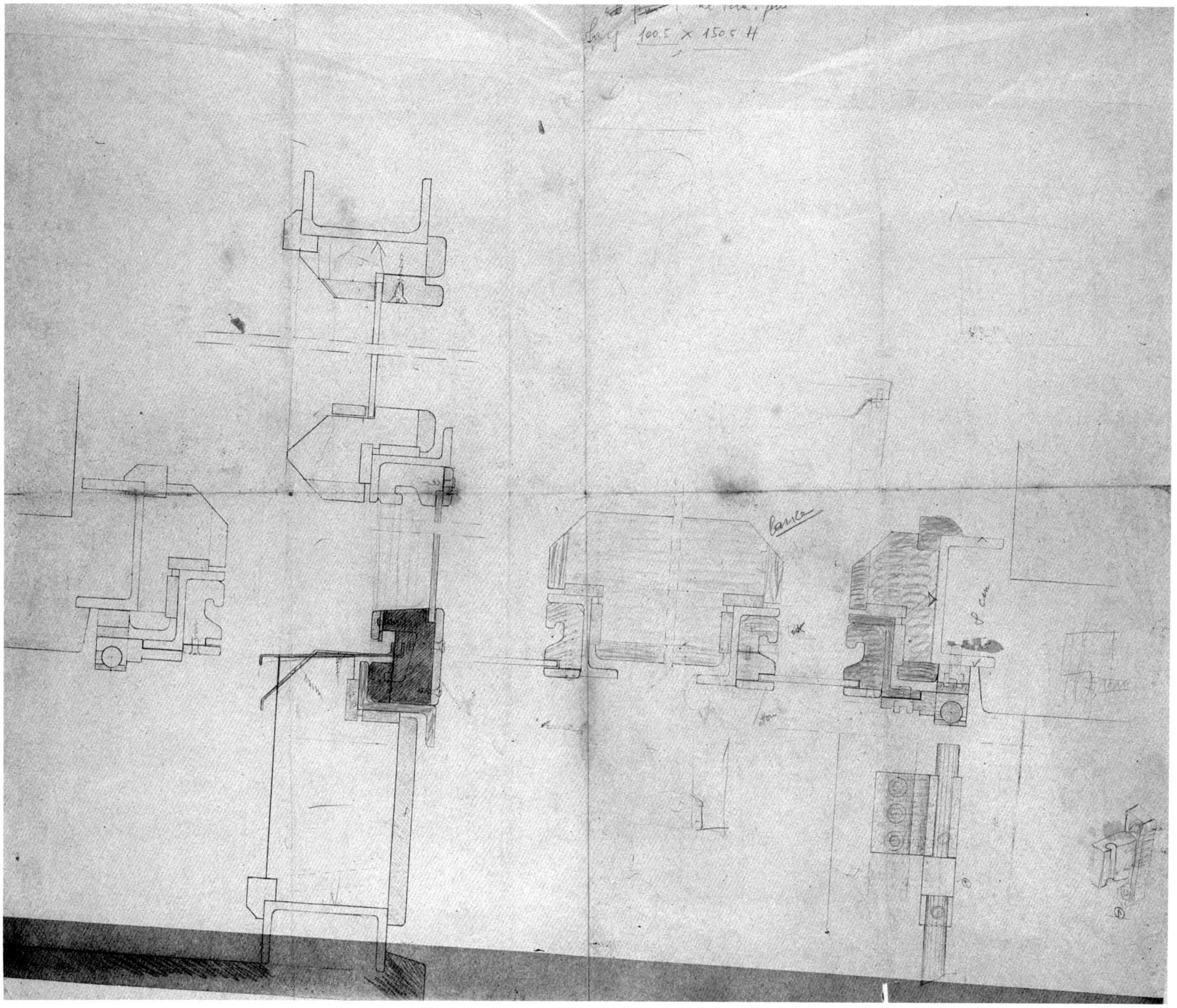

122.

◁
118. DOOR ON PALAZZO ABATELLIS, PALERMO

119. UPPER HINGE

120. LOWER HINGE

121. WORKING DRAWING OF THE FRAME TO THE WINDOW ON THE STAIRCASE IN THE QUERINI STAMPALIA FOUNDATION, VENICE. CRAYONS ON HELIOGRAPHIC PRINT

122. DETAIL OF THE HINGE

CLOSURE—APERTURE

A break in the continuity of a surface constitutes a barrier, but for air, light or water it is a carefully gauged passage.

A vestige of shade or a fissure, then fragmentation of a solid, almost to suggest absence of weight, ultimately, a translucent or transparent part: an entire wall that swivels or slides, a grating, a grille or a gate.

In a wider sense, a door or a window, a simple, geometrically shaped opening articulating the solid it breaks into. An opening that screens itself with a mimetic plane or, vice versa, abruptly and uncompromisingly proclaims its diversity.

20. Grille on the Banca Popolare di Verona
21. Gate on the Brion cemetery
22. Window on the Olivetti store
23. Gate on the Gavina store
24. Main entrance to Palazzo Steri
25. Gate, Querini Stampalia Foundation

INSTANCES EXTRA-DOSSIER

20. Grille on the Banca Popolare di Verona

123

124

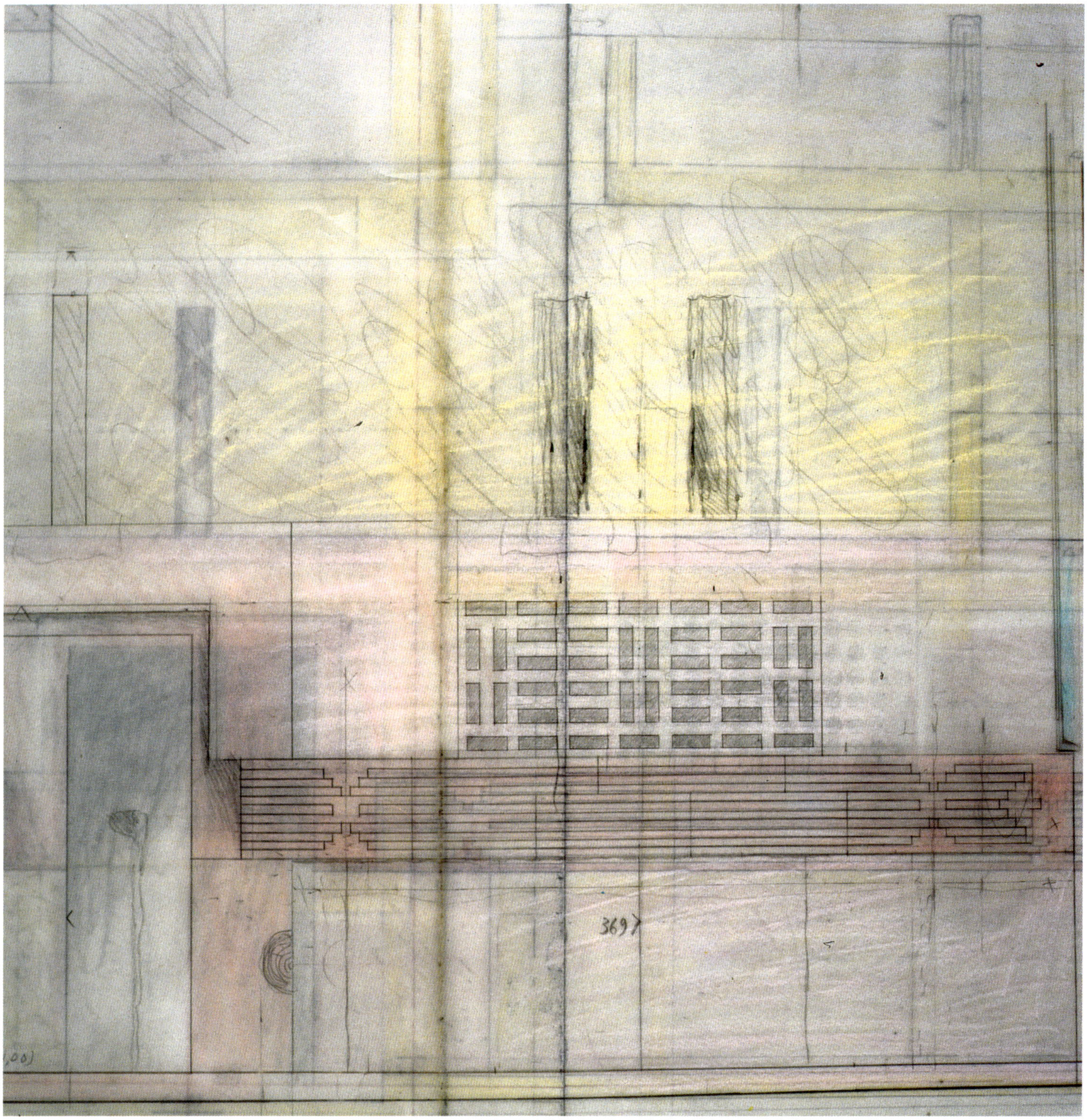

123. Study for the grille and the small windows on the façade of the Banca Popolare di Verona. Pencil and crayons on acetate

124. Study for the grille. Pencil and crayons on Bristol board

125. The grille, exterior

126. The grille, interior

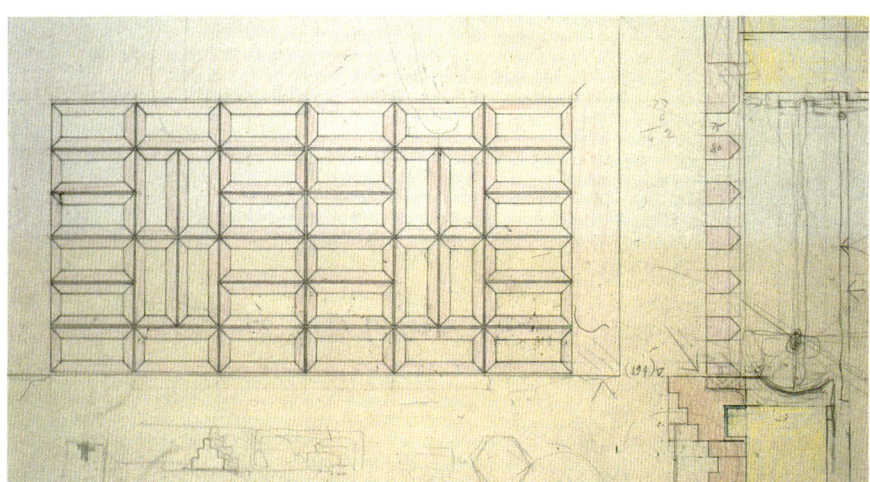

125

126

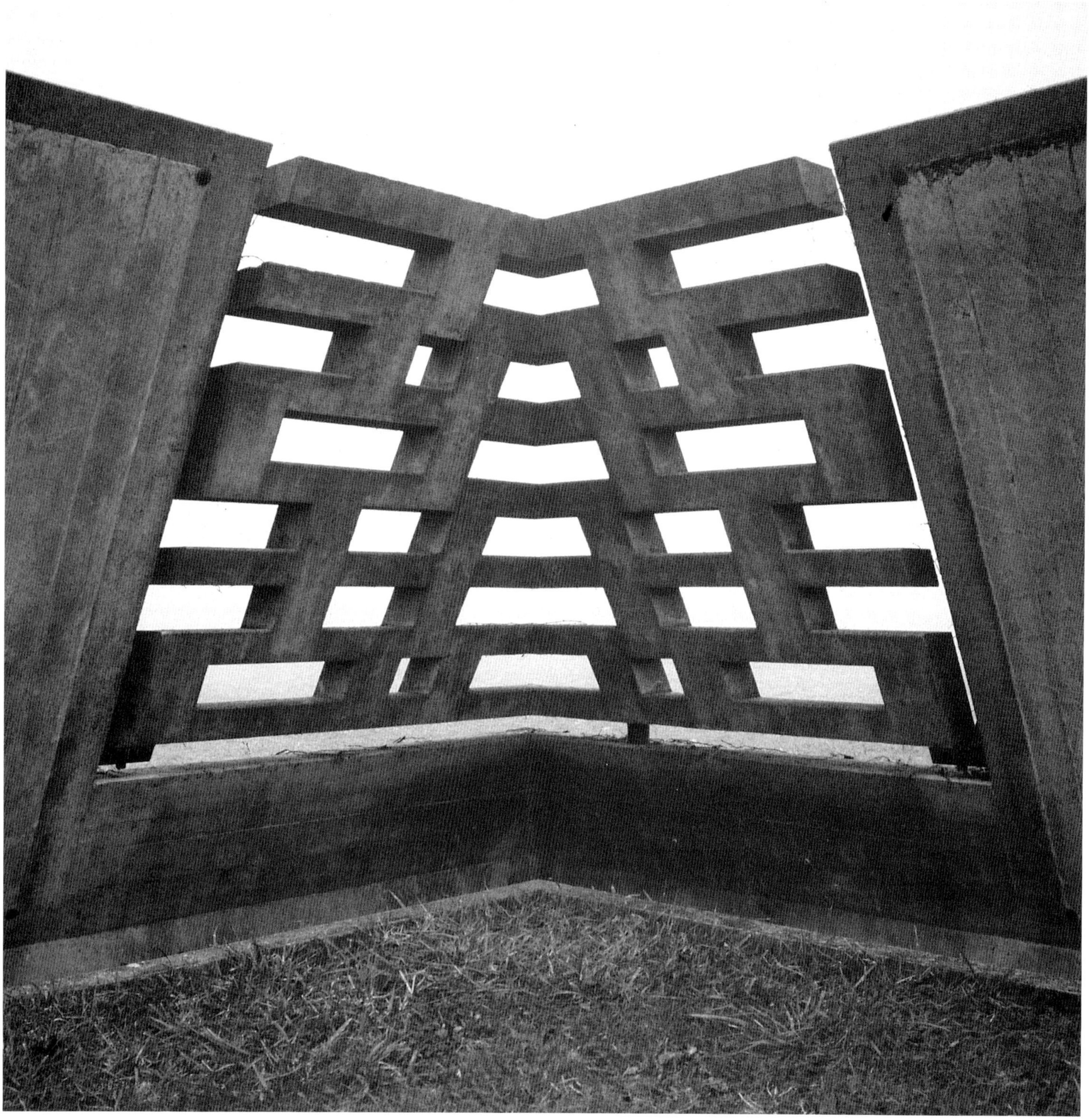

127

127, 128. GRILLE IN THE ENCLOSURE WALLS OF THE BRION CEMETERY, S. VITO DI ALTIVOLE, SEEN FROM INSIDE THE CEMETERY

128

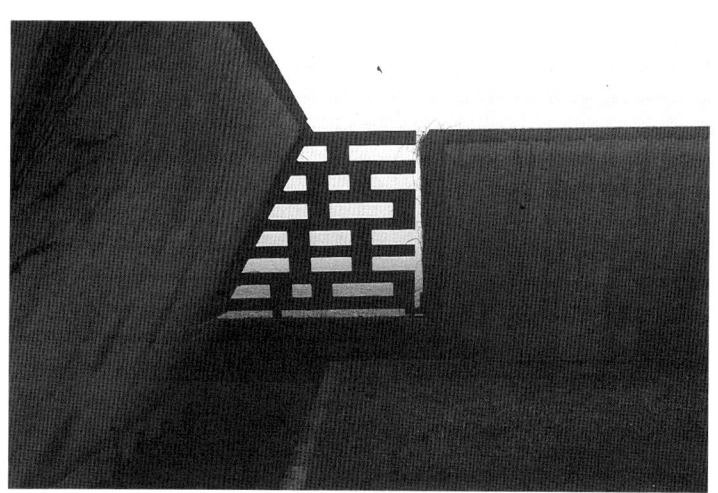

21. Gate on the Brion cemetery

129. Sketches for the sliding gate at the entrance to the Brion cemetery, S. Vito di Altivole. Pencil on paper

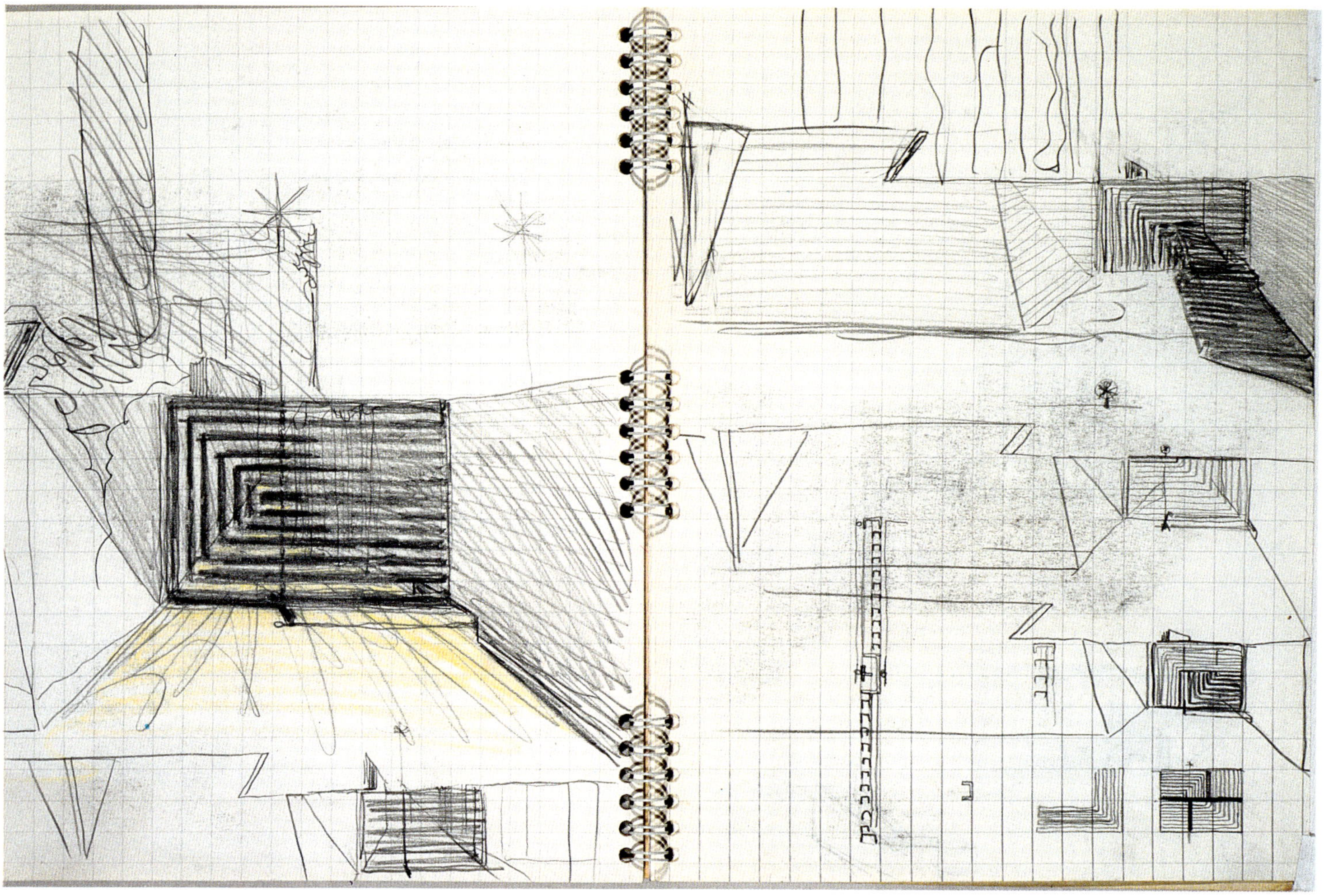

130. Sketches for the gate.
Pencil and crayons on
squared paper

131. The gate seen from the interior

132. Detail of the carriage

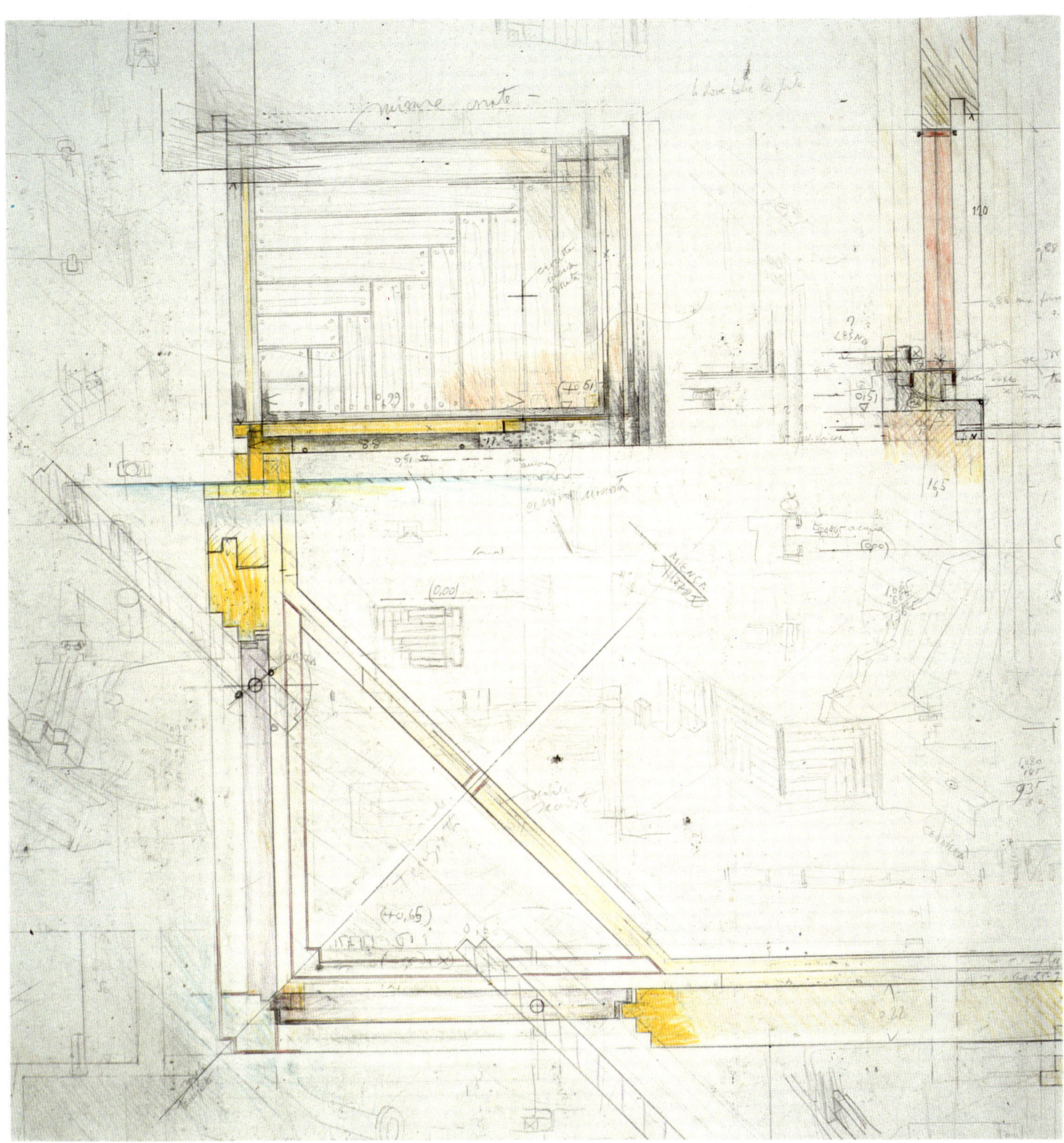

133. STUDY FOR THE LOW GATED APERTURES BEHIND THE ALTAR IN THE CHAPEL
OF THE BRION CEMETERY. PENCIL AND CRAYONS ON BRISTOL BOARD

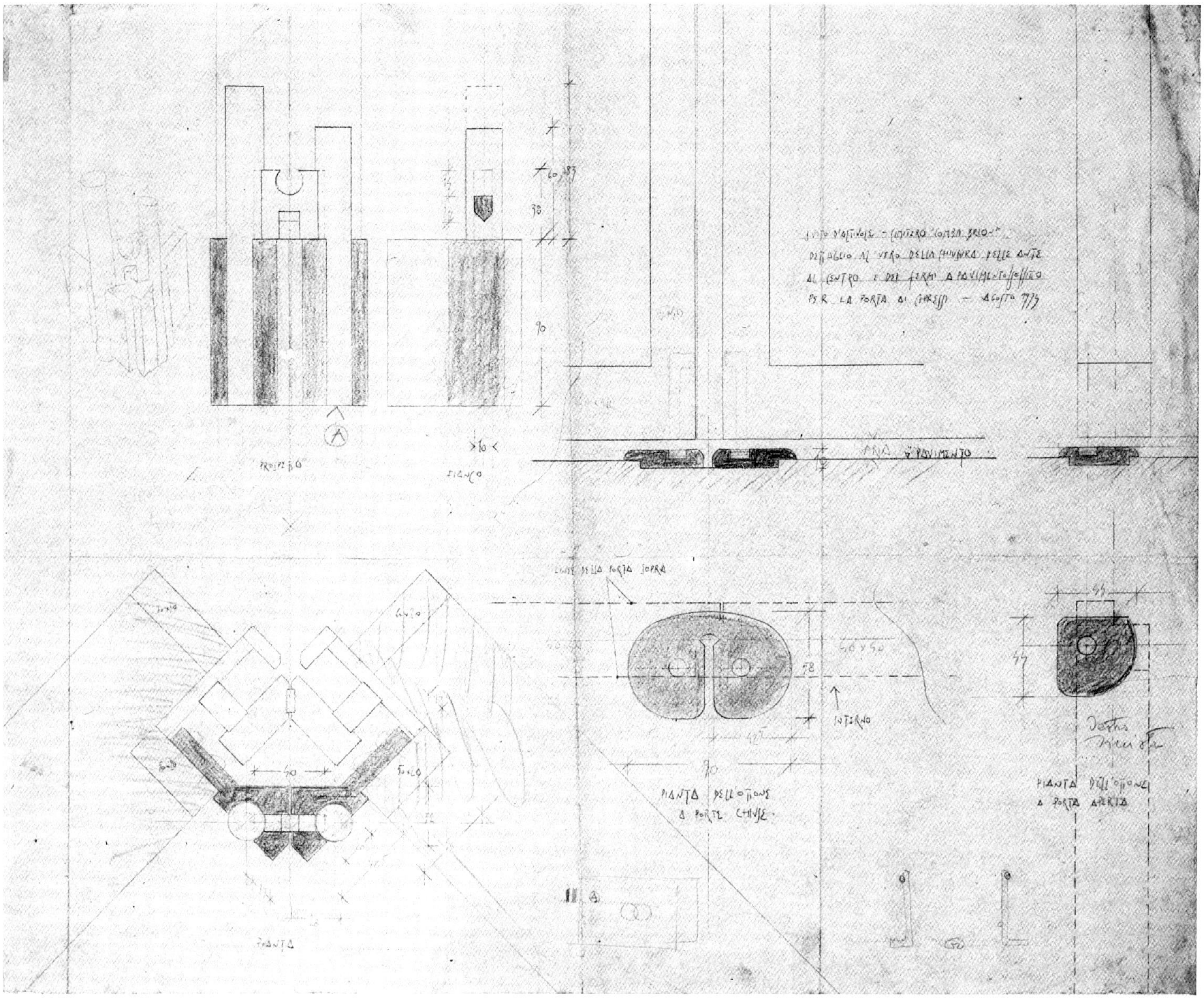

134

134. WORKING DRAWINGS. CLOSURE OF LOW GATED APERTURES AND FLOOR-CEILING CATCHES OF THE CHAPEL DOOR. CRAYONS ON HELIOGRAPHIC PRINT

135. THE CHAPEL WITH LOW GATED APERTURES SEEN FROM THE EXTERIOR

135

22. Window on the Olivetti store

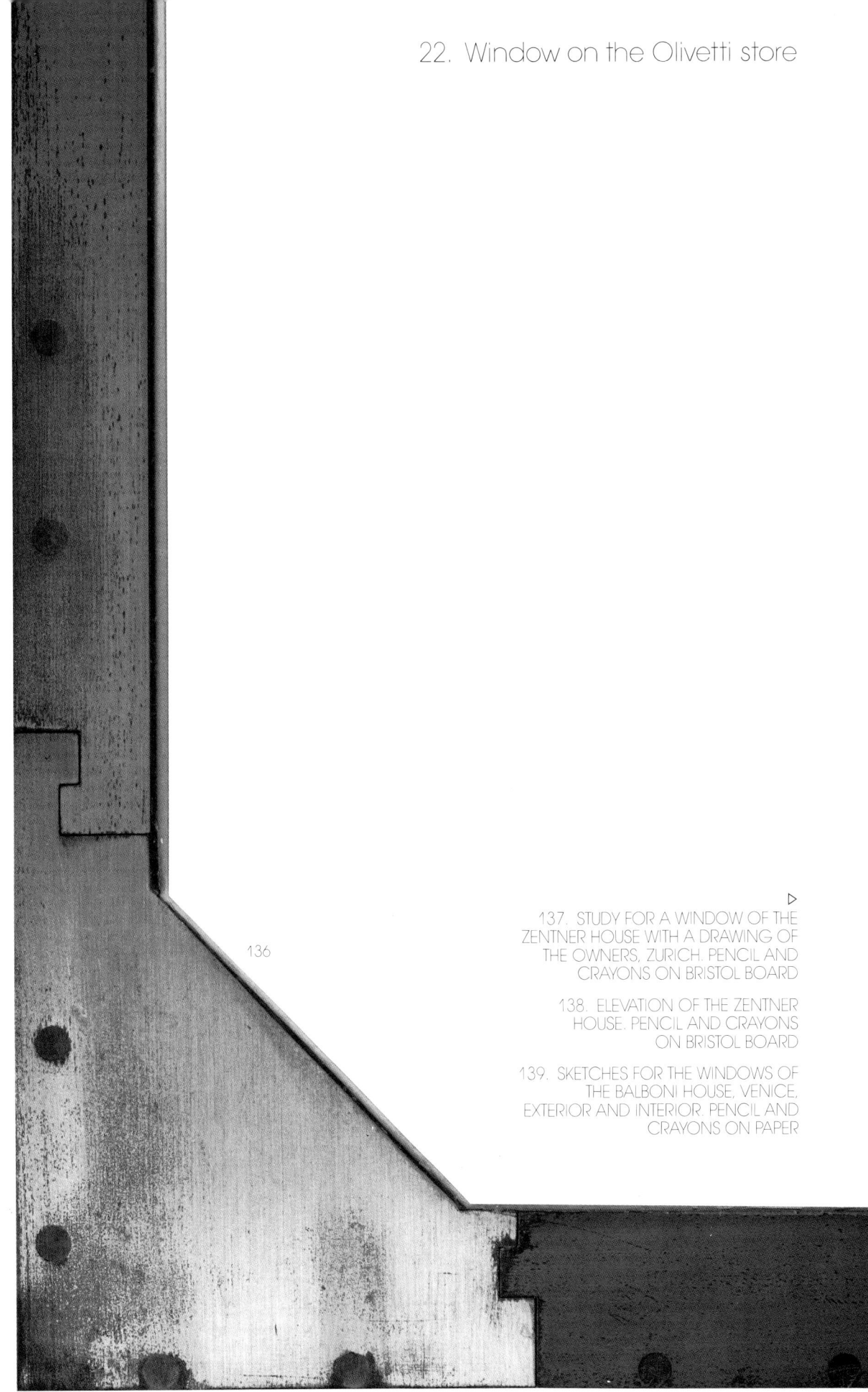

▷
137. STUDY FOR A WINDOW OF THE
ZENTNER HOUSE WITH A DRAWING OF
THE OWNERS, ZURICH. PENCIL AND
CRAYONS ON BRISTOL BOARD

138. ELEVATION OF THE ZENTNER
HOUSE. PENCIL AND CRAYONS
ON BRISTOL BOARD

139. SKETCHES FOR THE WINDOWS OF
THE BALBONI HOUSE, VENICE,
EXTERIOR AND INTERIOR. PENCIL AND
CRAYONS ON PAPER

136. Detail of the frame of the window on the Olivetti store, Venice

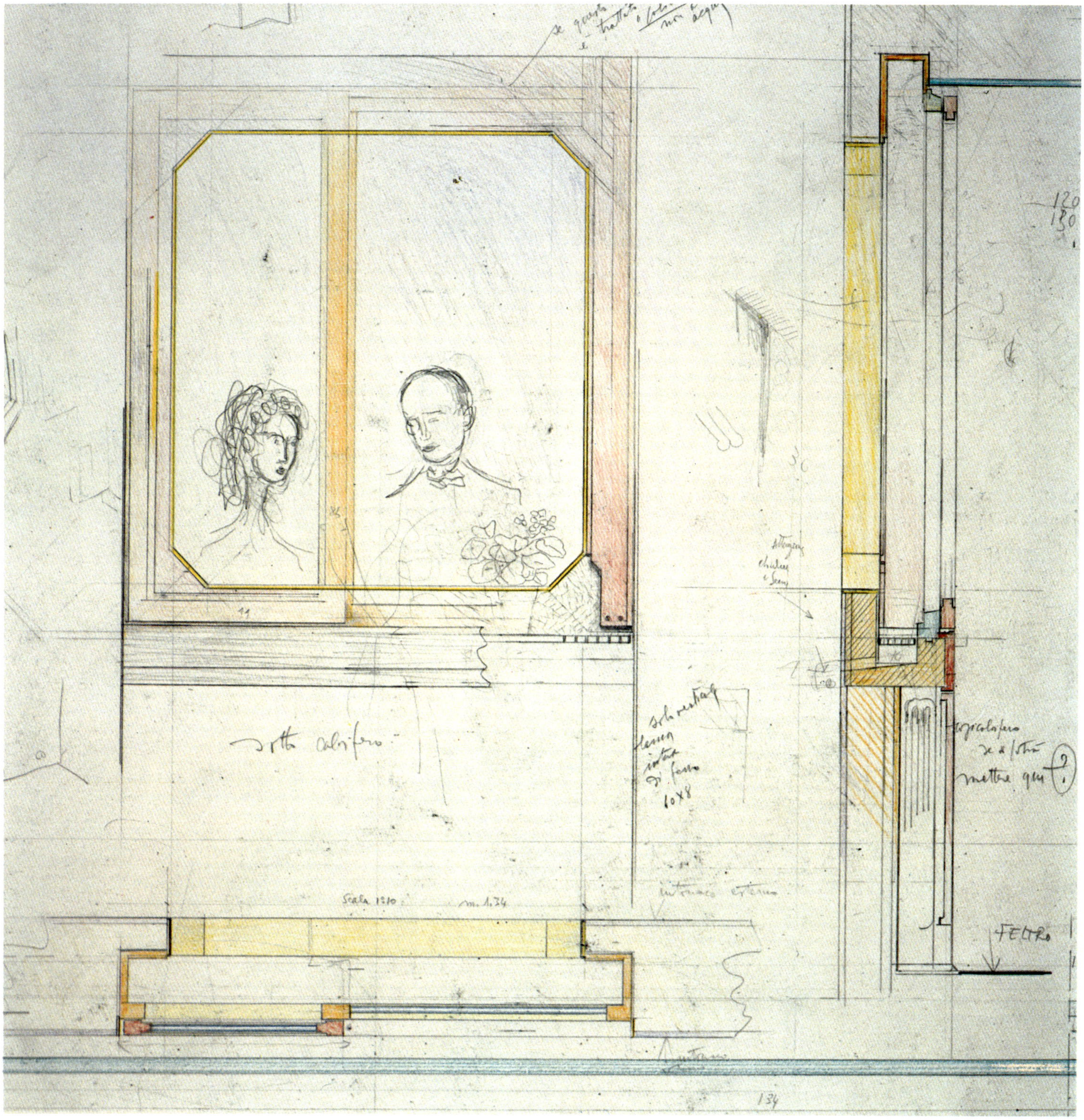

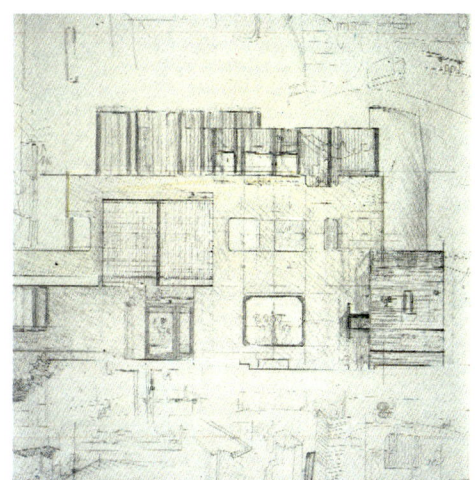

23. Gate on the Gavina store

◁
140. Detail of the gate on the Gavina store, Bologna

141. The gate

142. Detail of the hinge

143, 144. Detailing of the vertical elements

145. First idea for the gate. Pencil and crayons on paper

145

146

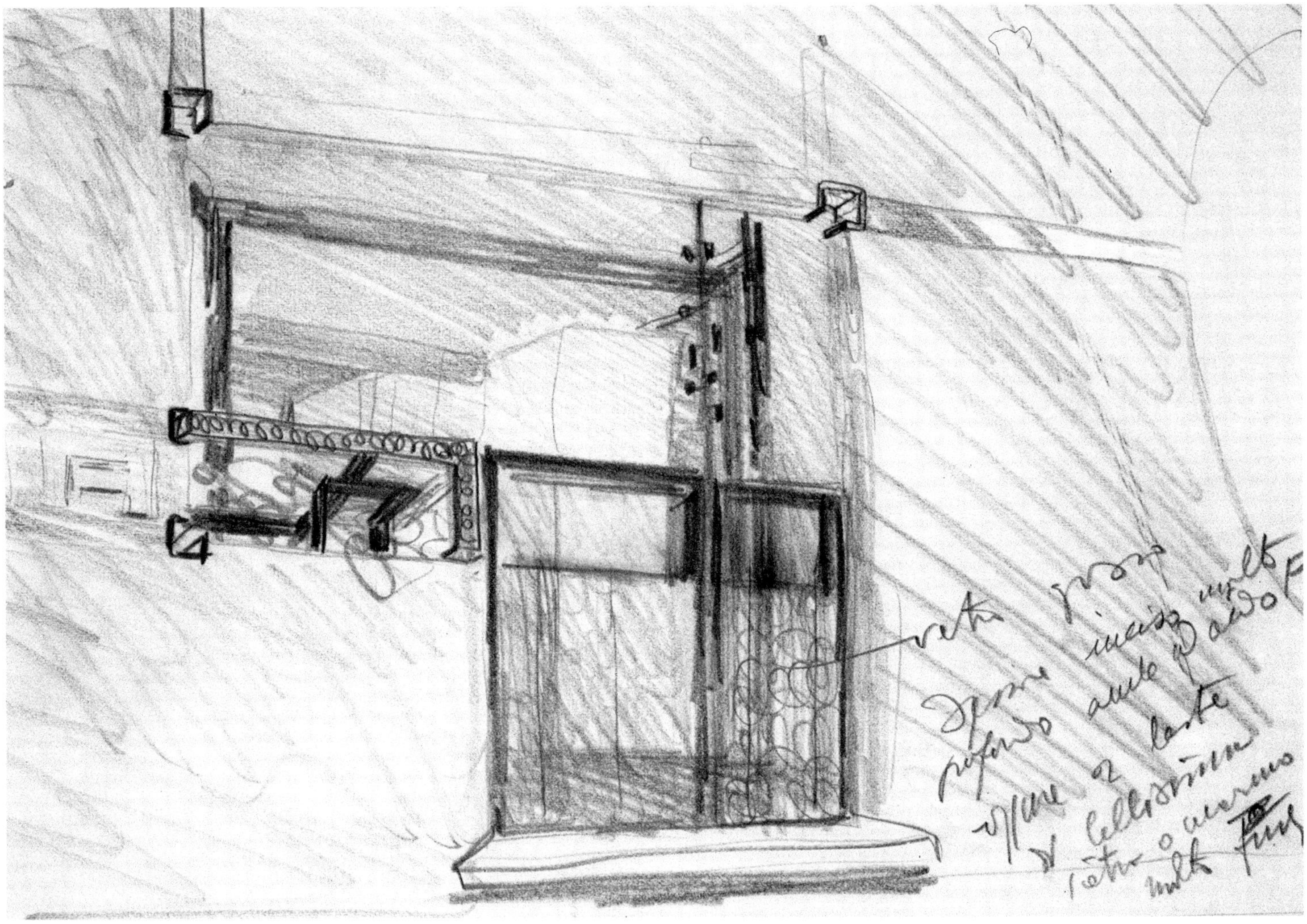

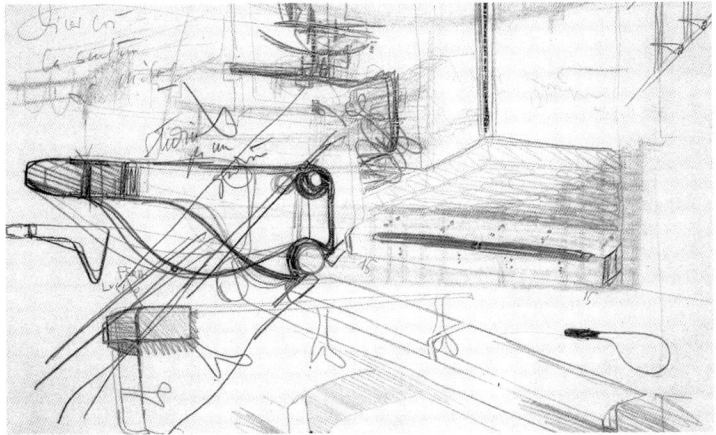

146. Sketches for constructional details and for the movement of the gate. Pencil and crayons on onionskin

147

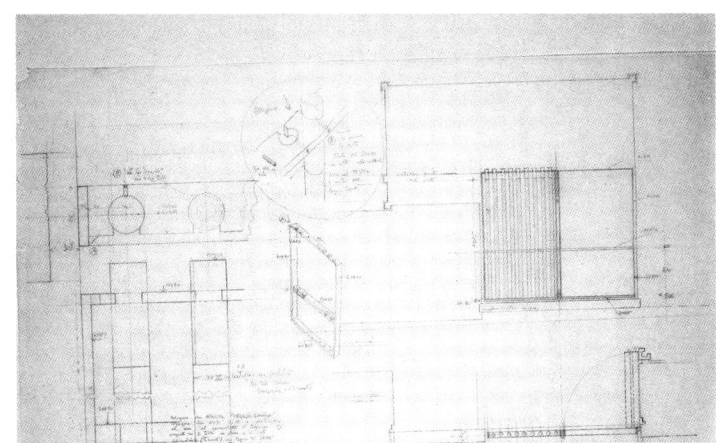

147. Working drawing for the gate. Heliographic print

148

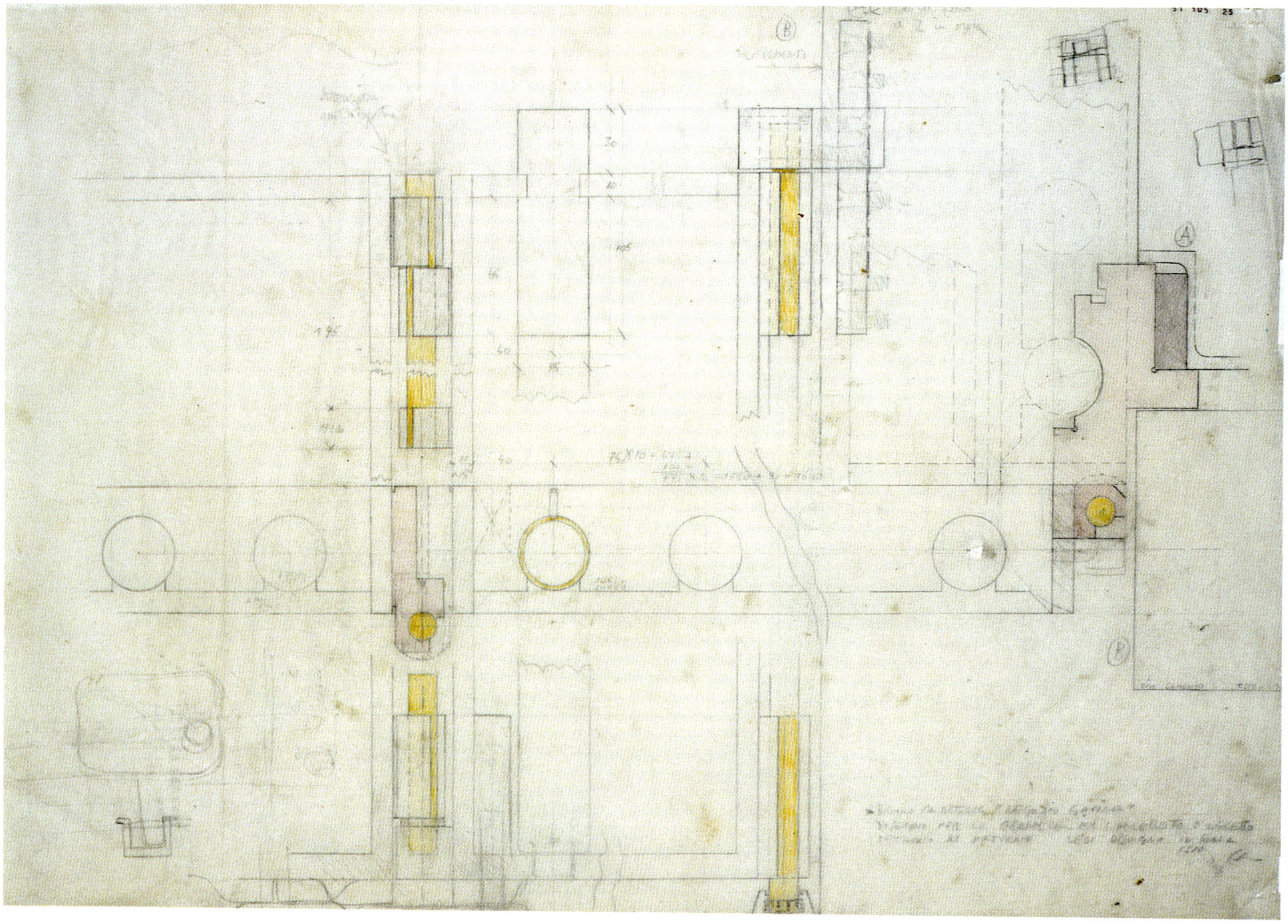

148. Working drawing for the gate. Pencil and crayons on tracing paper

149. Study for the gate. Pencil and crayons on Bristol board

149

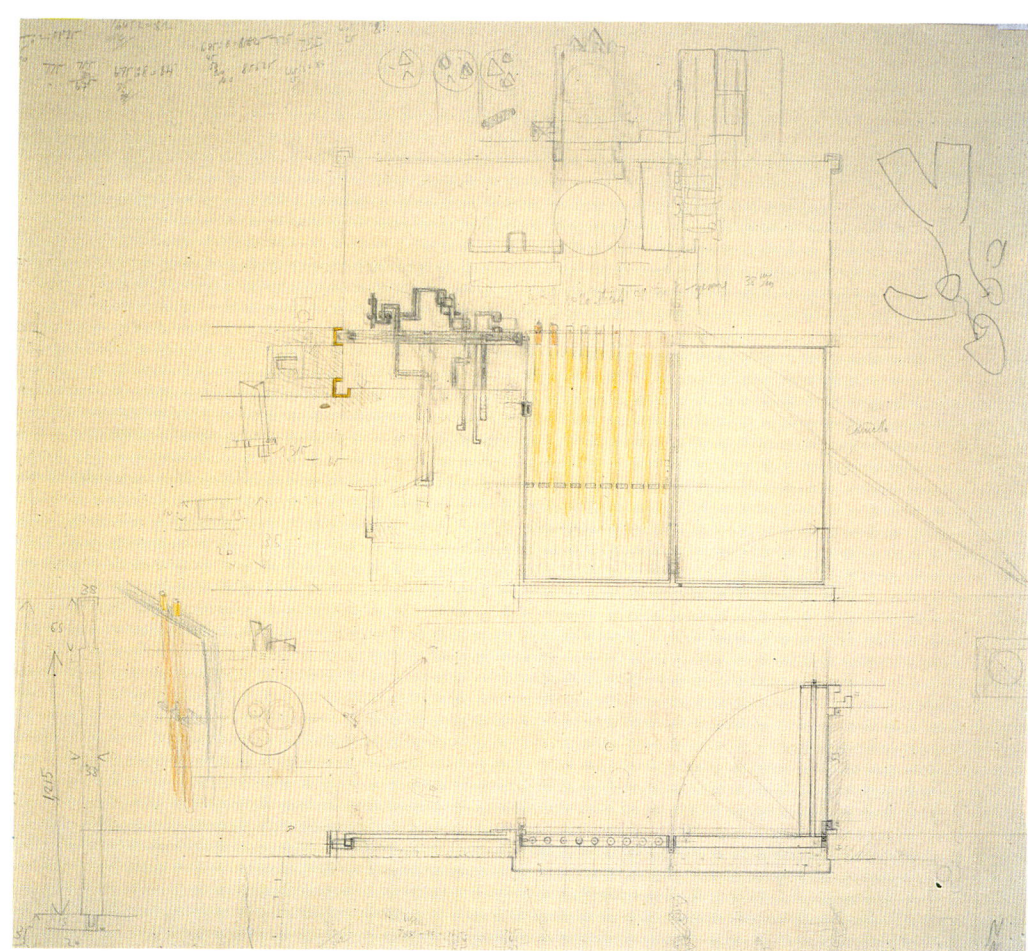

24. Main entrance to Palazzo Steri

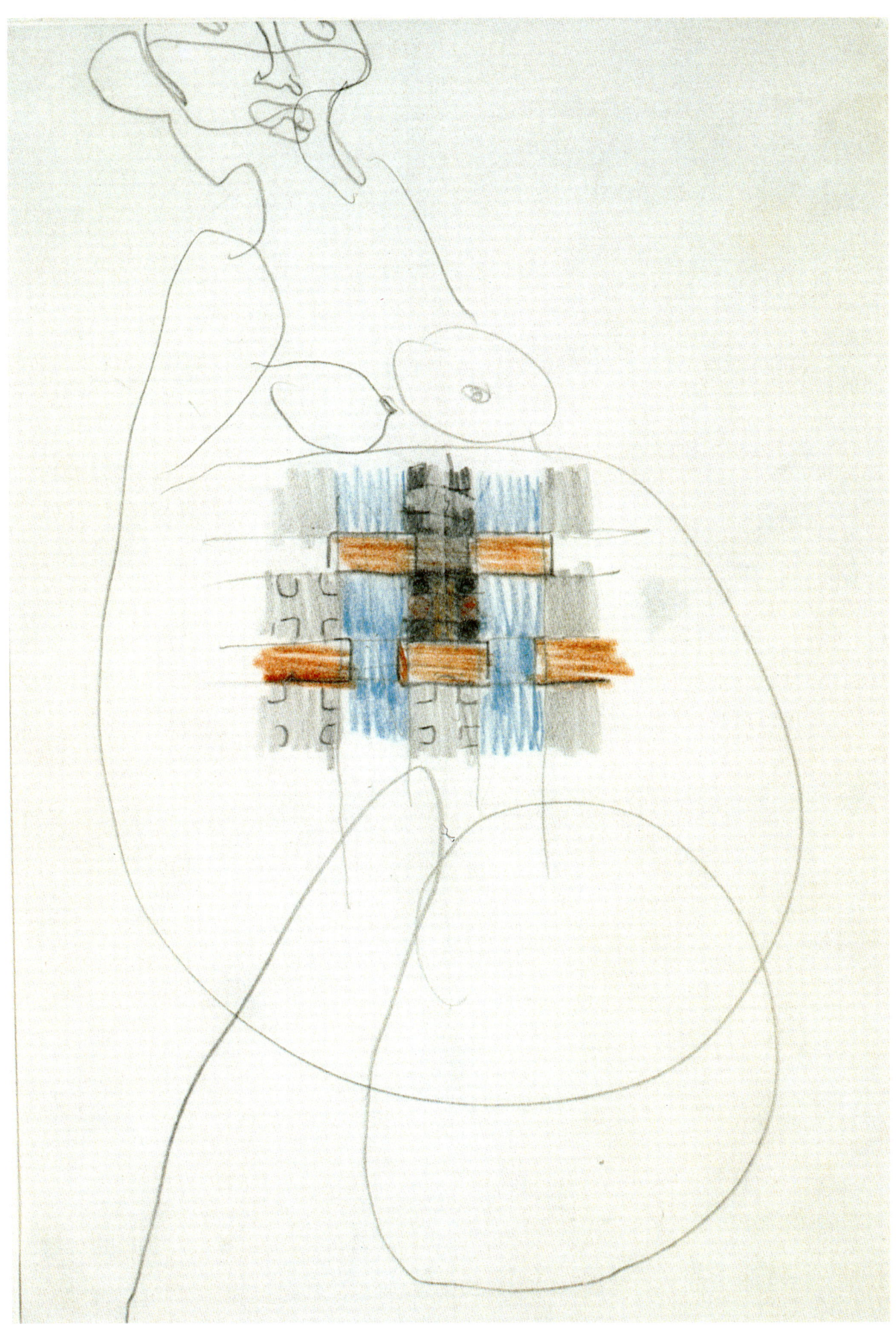

150. Sketch for the main entrance to Palazzo Steri, Palermo. Pencil and crayons on paper

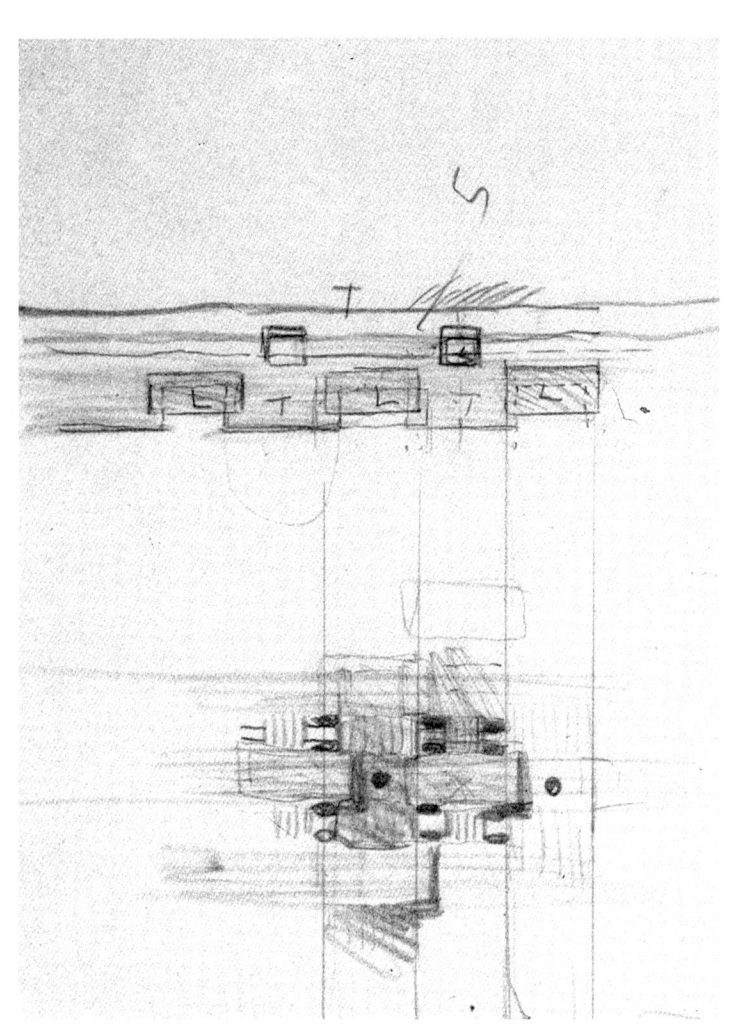

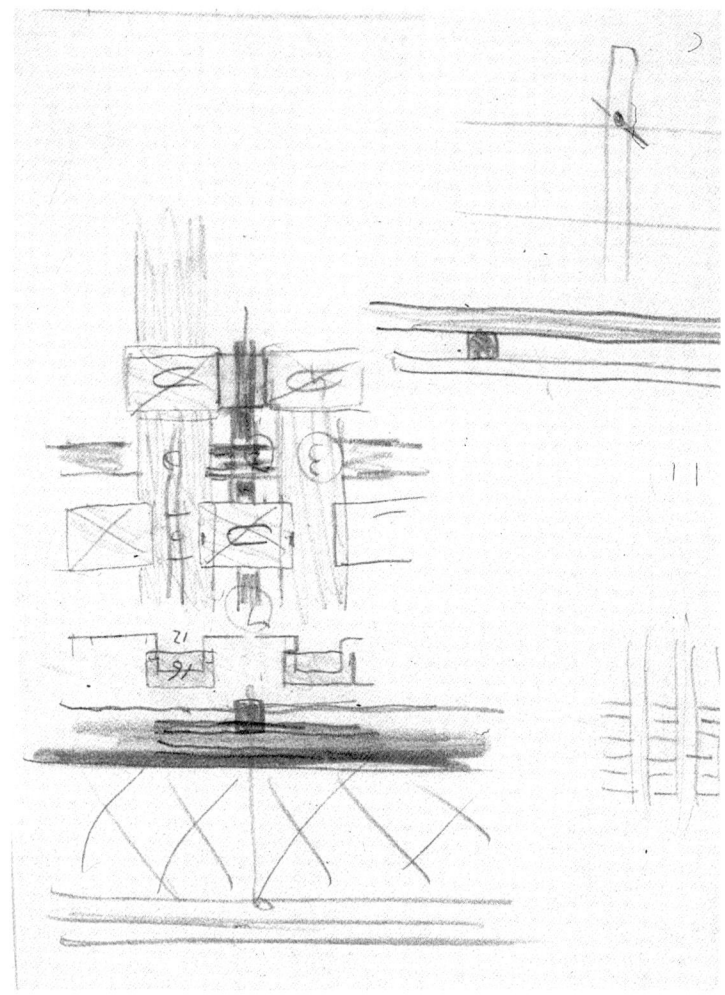

151. Three sketches for the main entrance. Pencil and crayons on paper

152. Sketch for the main entrance. Pencil and crayons on paper

153. Sketch for the main entrance. Pencil on paper

154. SKETCH FOR THE FRAME OF A WINDOW ON PALAZZO STERI. CHARCOAL ON TRACING PAPER

155. SKETCH FOR THE FRAME SEEN FROM THE INTERIOR. PENCIL AND CRAYONS ON TRACING PAPER

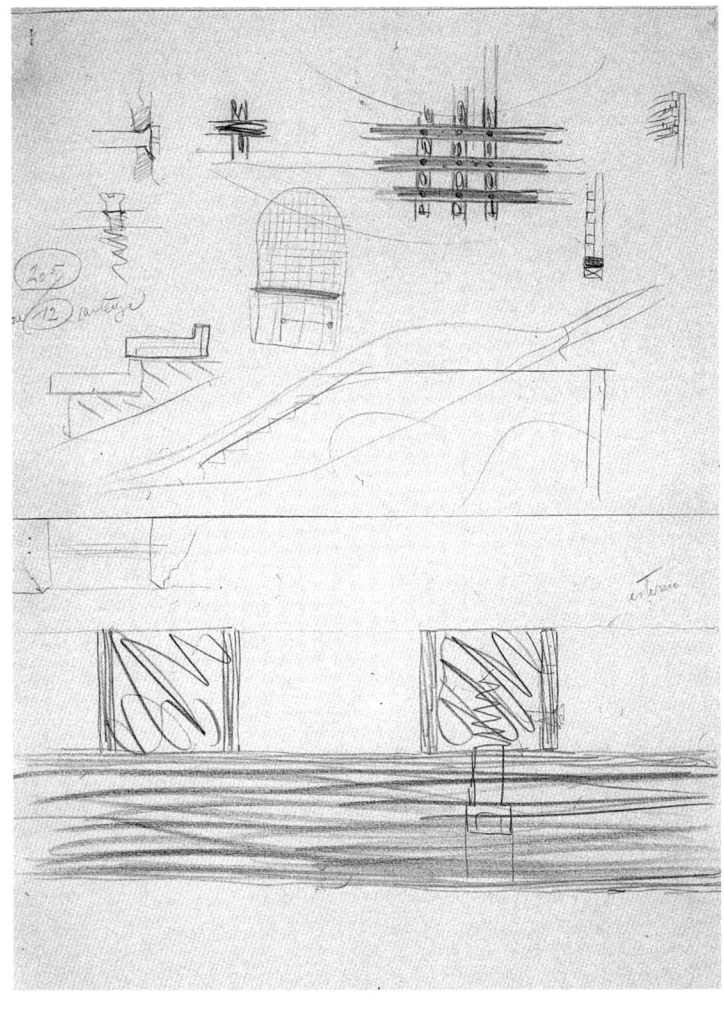

152

153

154

155

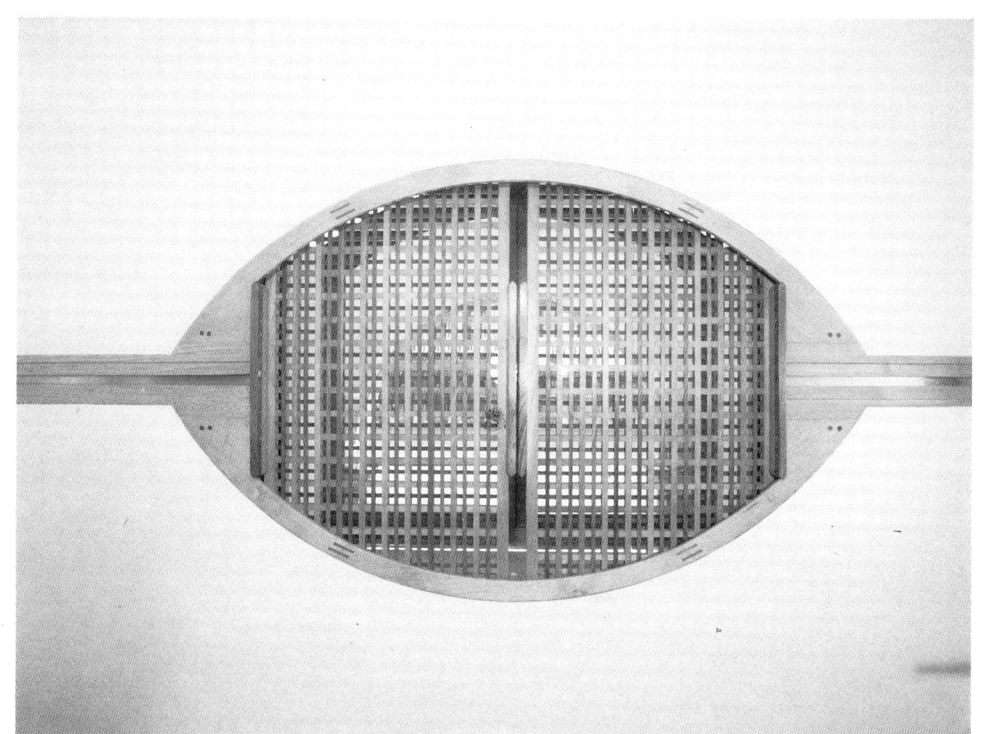

156. FORESHORTENED VIEW OF A WINDOW ON PALAZZO STERI

157. DETAIL OF PALAZZO STERI

158. SHUTTER ON THE OLIVETTI STORE, VENICE

159. RADIATOR SCREEN IN THE OLIVETTI STORE

160. SKETCH FOR A CANOPY ON THE ZENTNER HOUSE, ZURICH. PENCIL AND CRAYONS ON PAPER

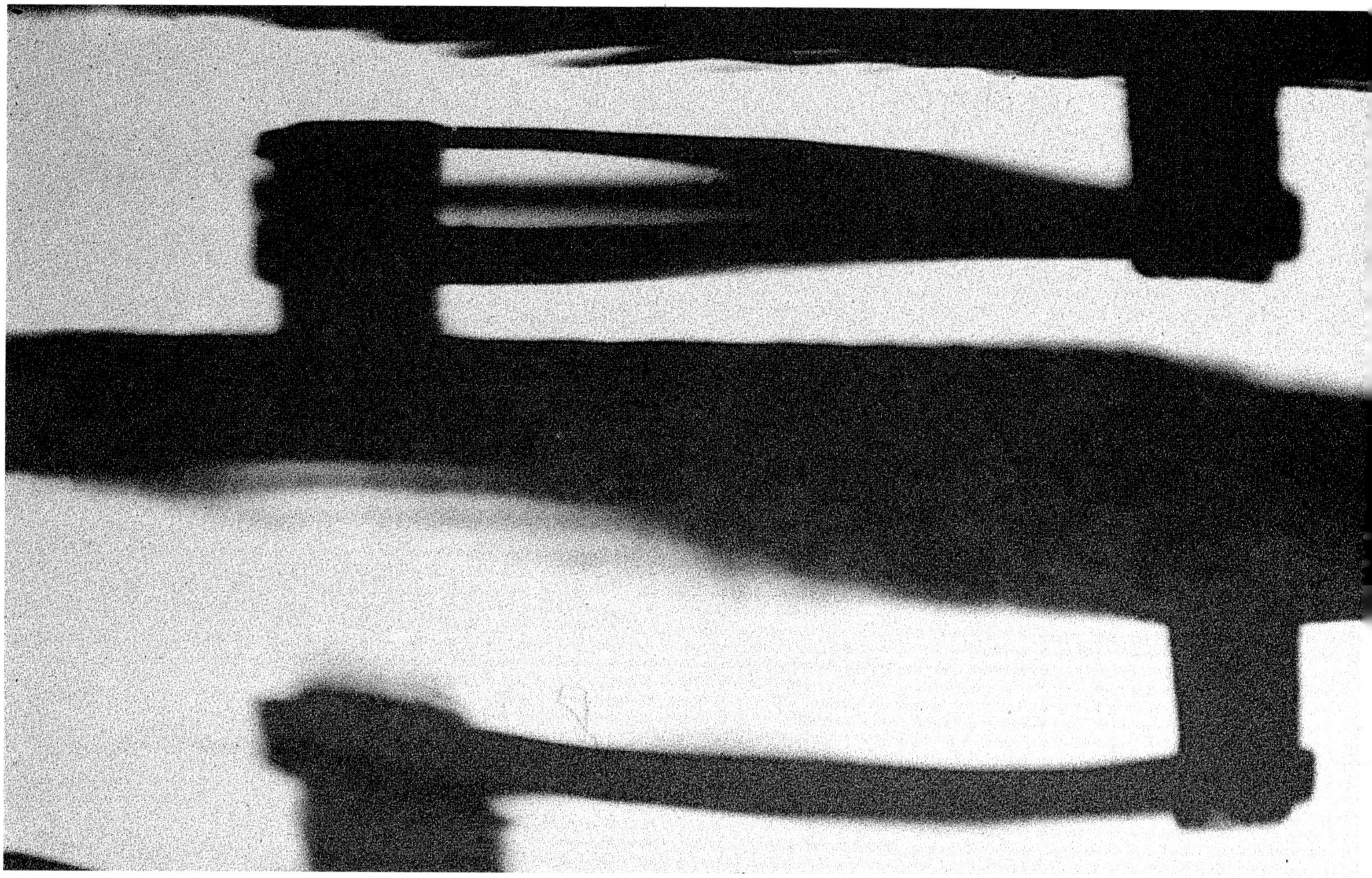
161

162

163

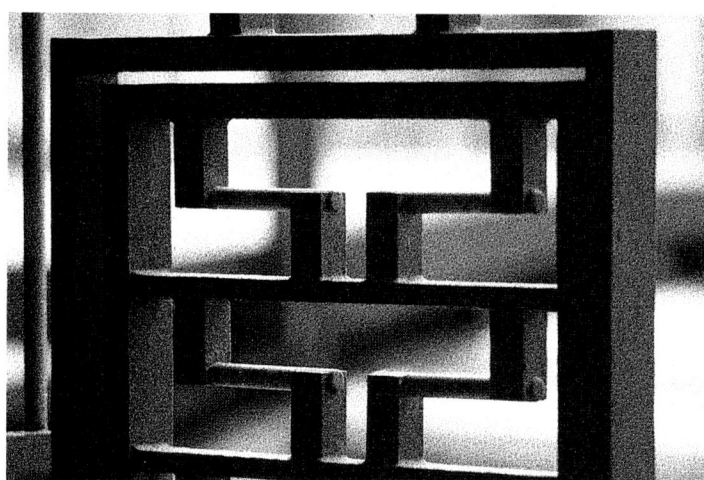

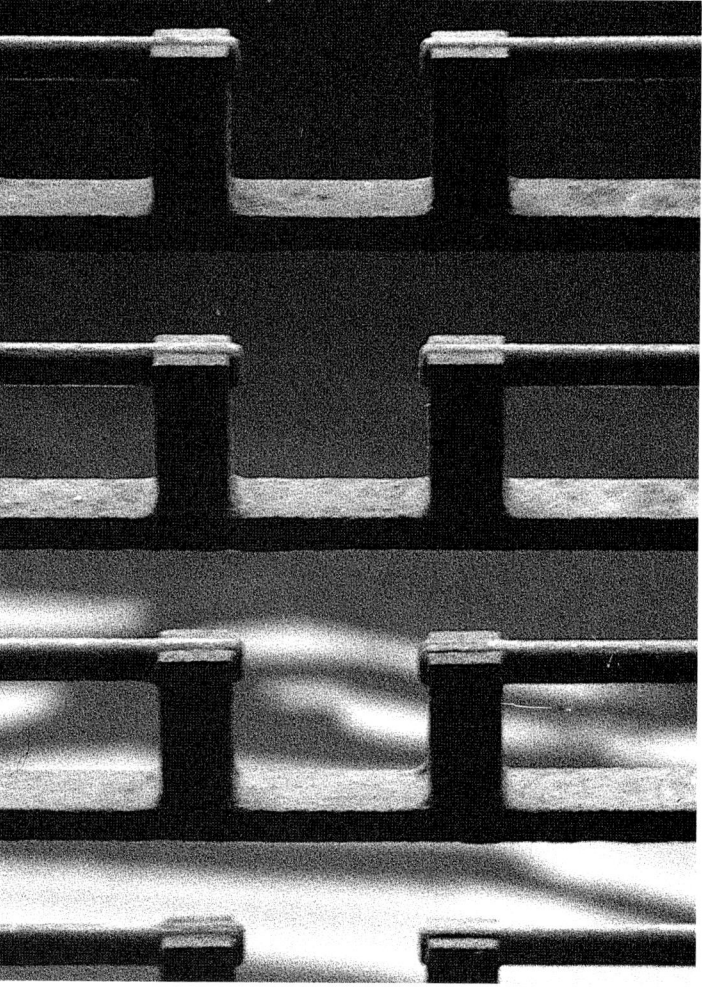

161. Canal water reflections of the gate on the Querini Stampalia Foundation, Venice

162, 163, 164. Detailing on the gate

165. Detail of the gate

25. Gate, Querini Stampalia Foundation

166

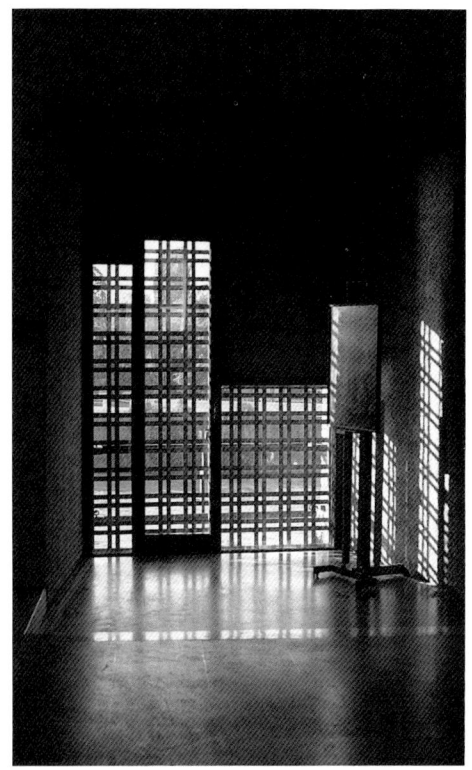

166. GRATING IN THE CASTELVECCHIO MUSEUM, VERONA

167. DETAIL OF THE GRATING

167

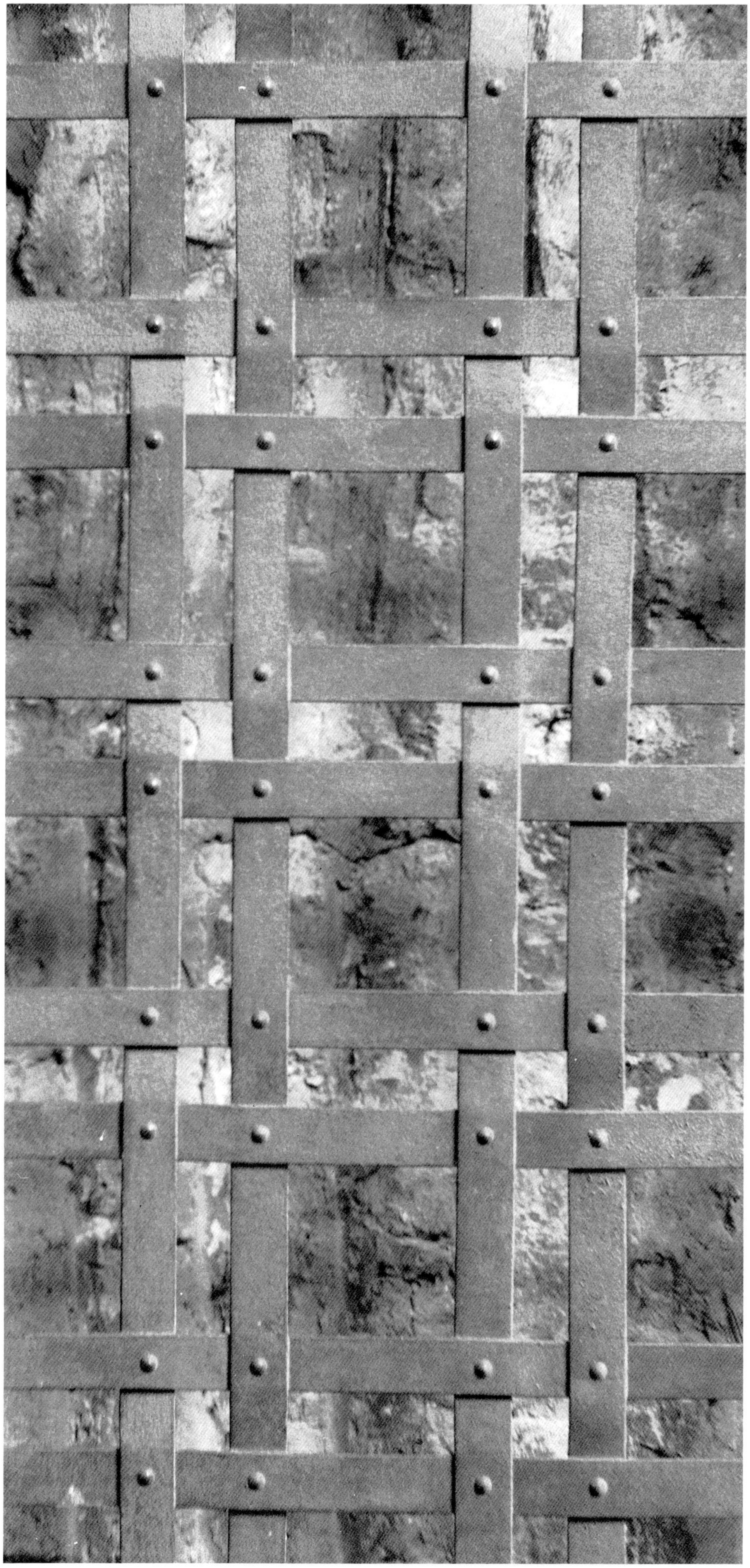

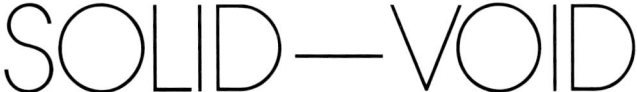
SOLID—VOID

It is not the obvious spatial relationship, but the use of a volume well articulated by its involucre, extending or enclosing, to complement the cavity of its interior.

A portion of expanding space, but stayed by a shell that confines it: it may be a part that breaks through to the front, or is contained by an interior.

Space yielded up by a void, but also space appropriated from a solid: a game of opposites, transposing the meanings of spatial categories that are deliberately complex in their roles, yet straightforward in formal definition. On the plane, this reads as balancing of parts, play of chiaroscuro, modulation of rhythms, relating of multiple symmetries and concealed alignments. Nothing here is casual. Every factor has a purpose and represents a new departure.

26. Sacellum in the Castelvecchio Museum
27. Volumes on the Ottolenghi house
28. Skylights
29. Frontage of the condominium at Vicenza
30. Fronts of the Banca Popolare di Verona
INSTANCES EXTRA-DOSSIER

26. Sacellum in the Castelvecchio Museum

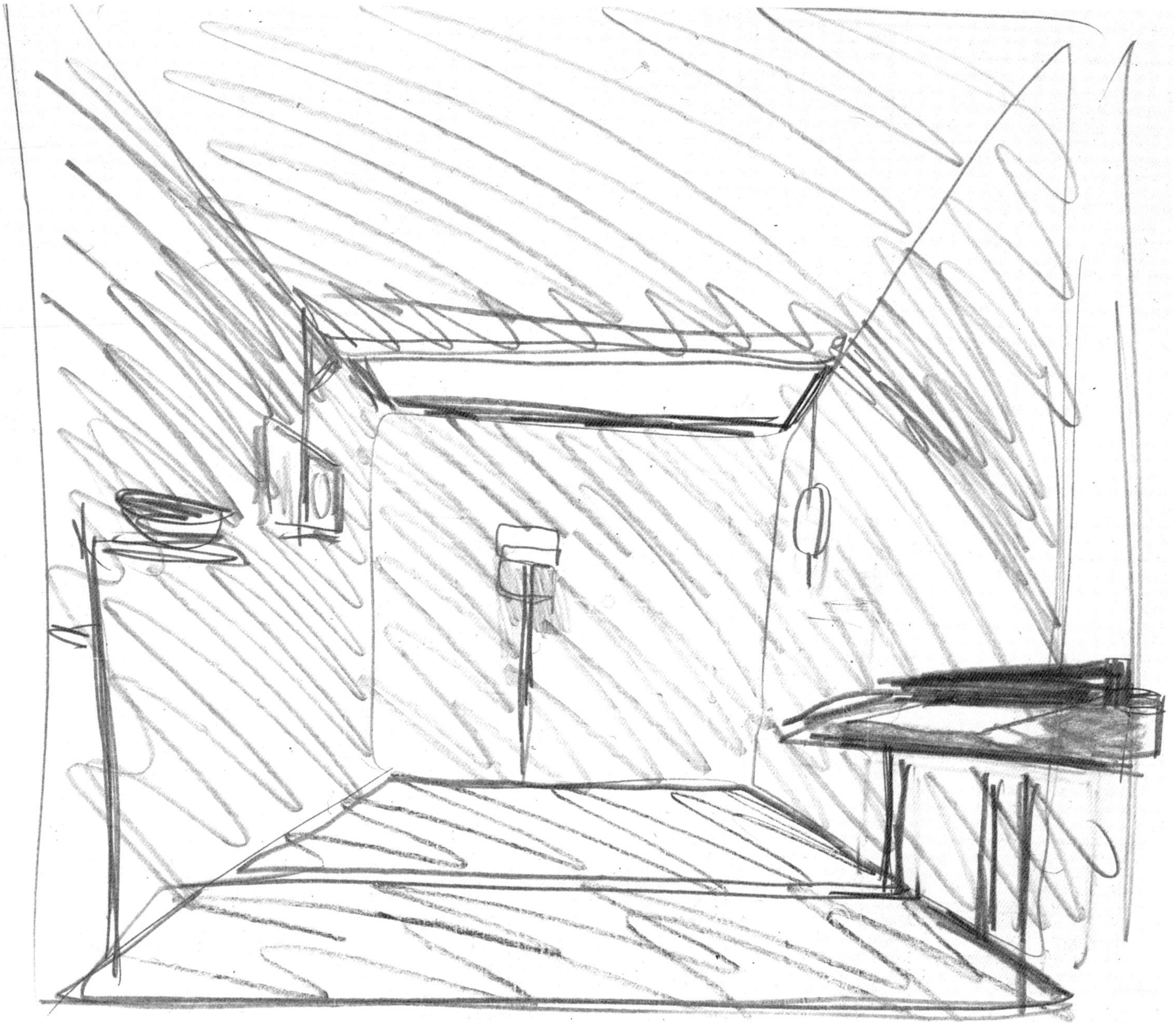

168

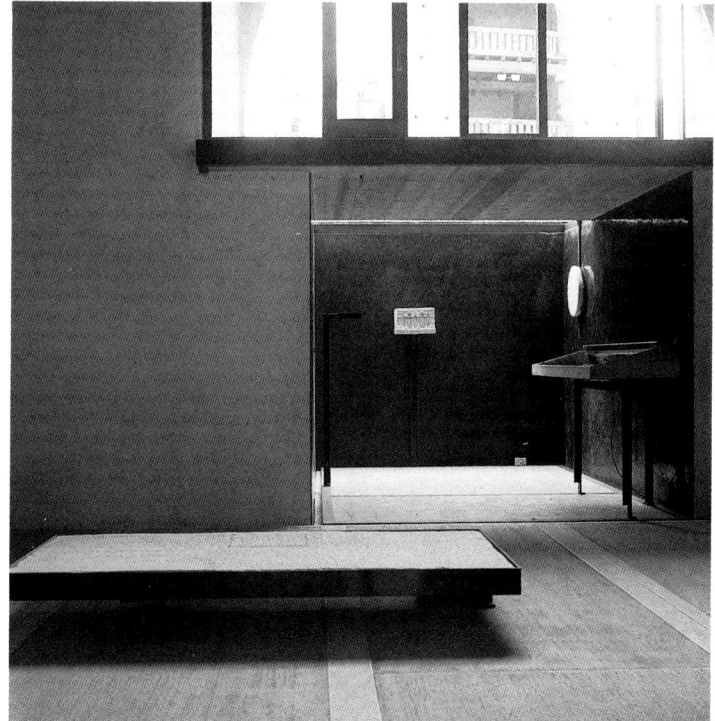

168. Sketch for the interior of the sacellum in the Castelvecchio Museum, Verona. Pencil and crayons on paper

169. The sacellum, interior

169

170

170. Sketches for the sacellum, interior and exterior. Pencil on paper

171. The sacellum, exterior

171

27. Volumes on the Ottolenghi house

172. The volume of the bathroom in the Ottolenghi house, Bardolino (Verona)

173. Studies for the bathroom. Pencil and crayons on tracing paper

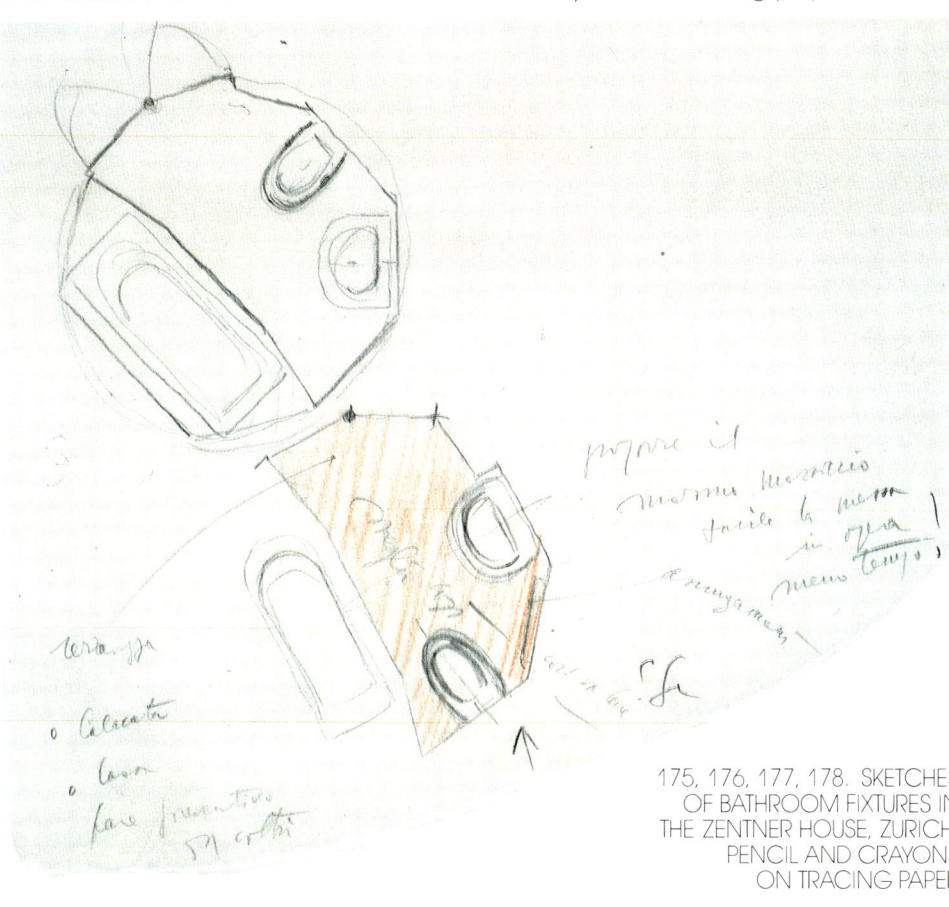

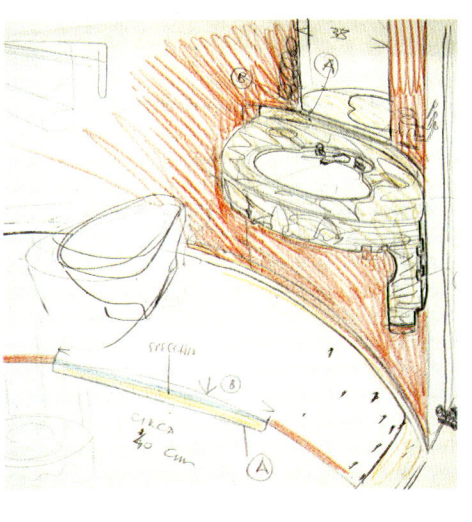

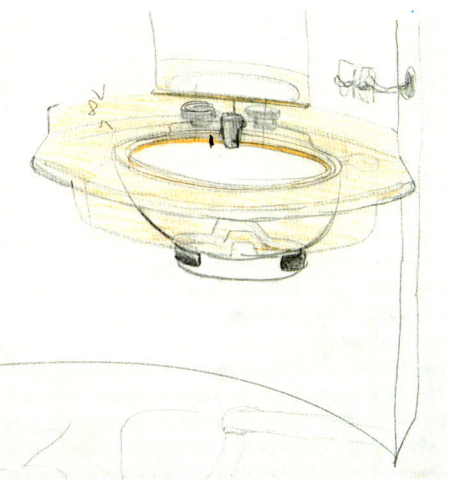

175, 176, 177, 178. SKETCHES OF BATHROOM FIXTURES IN THE ZENTNER HOUSE, ZURICH. PENCIL AND CRAYONS ON TRACING PAPER

174. Study for the bathroom. Pencil and crayons on Bristol board

28. Skylights

179. Skylight on the Canova Casts Gallery, Possagno (Treviso)
180. Play of light in the main hall of the Casts Gallery
181. Interior of the Casts Gallery

182. Study for the skylights on the Venezuelan pavilion in the Biennale gardens, Venice. Pencil on onionskin

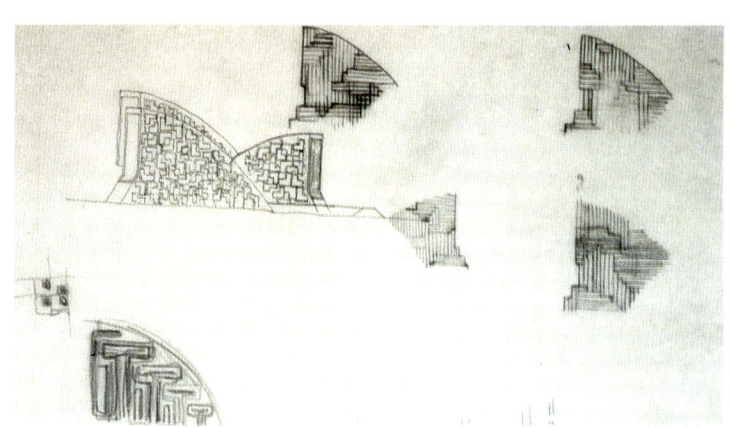

187

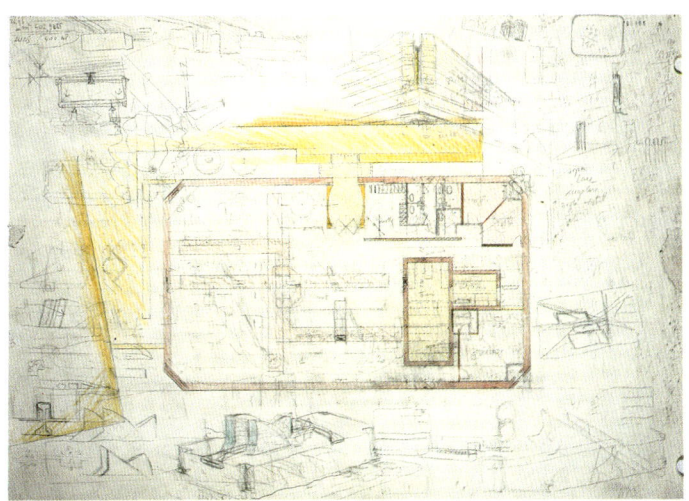

188

183, 184. Sketches of the initial idea for the skylight, project for the branch office of the Banca Antoniana, Monselice (Padua). Pencil and crayons on tracing paper

185. Sketch of the final idea for the skylight. Pencil and crayons on tracing paper

186. Sketches for the revetment of the skylights. Pencil on tracing paper

187. Side elevation, final idea, project for the Banca Antoniana branch office. Pencil and crayons on Bristol board

188. Plan for the same project. Pencil and crayons on Bristol board

189

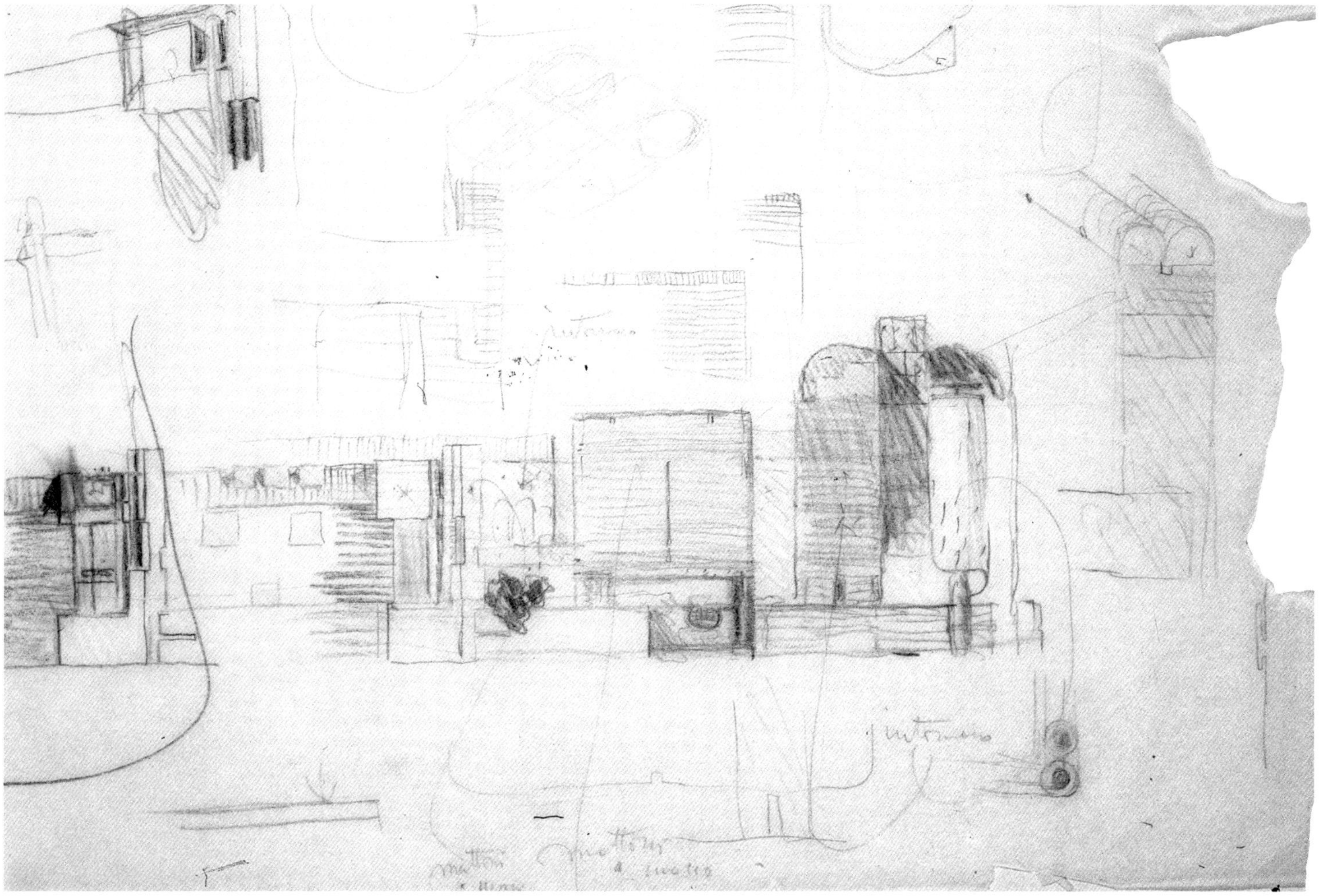

189. Sketch for a front, project for the Bailo Museum in the former convent of S. Catherine, Treviso. Pencil and crayons on tracing paper

190. Transversal section of the extension on the same project. Pencil, crayons and red ball-point pen on Bristol board

190

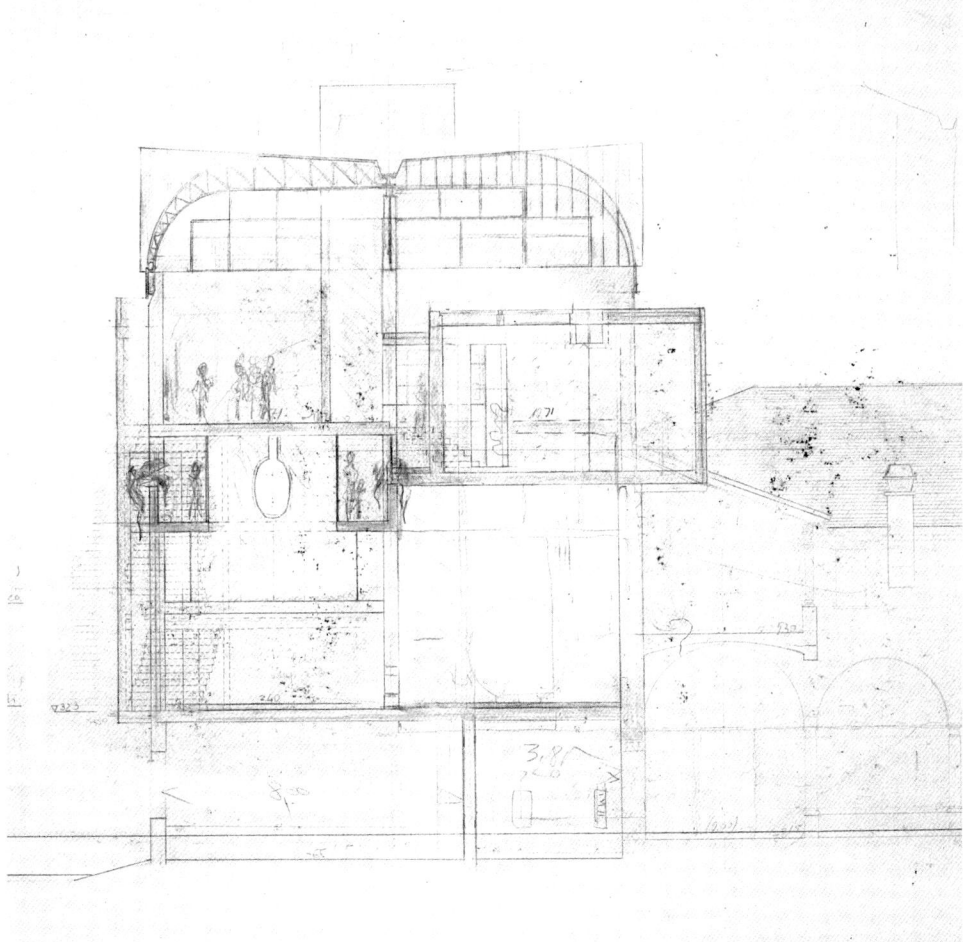

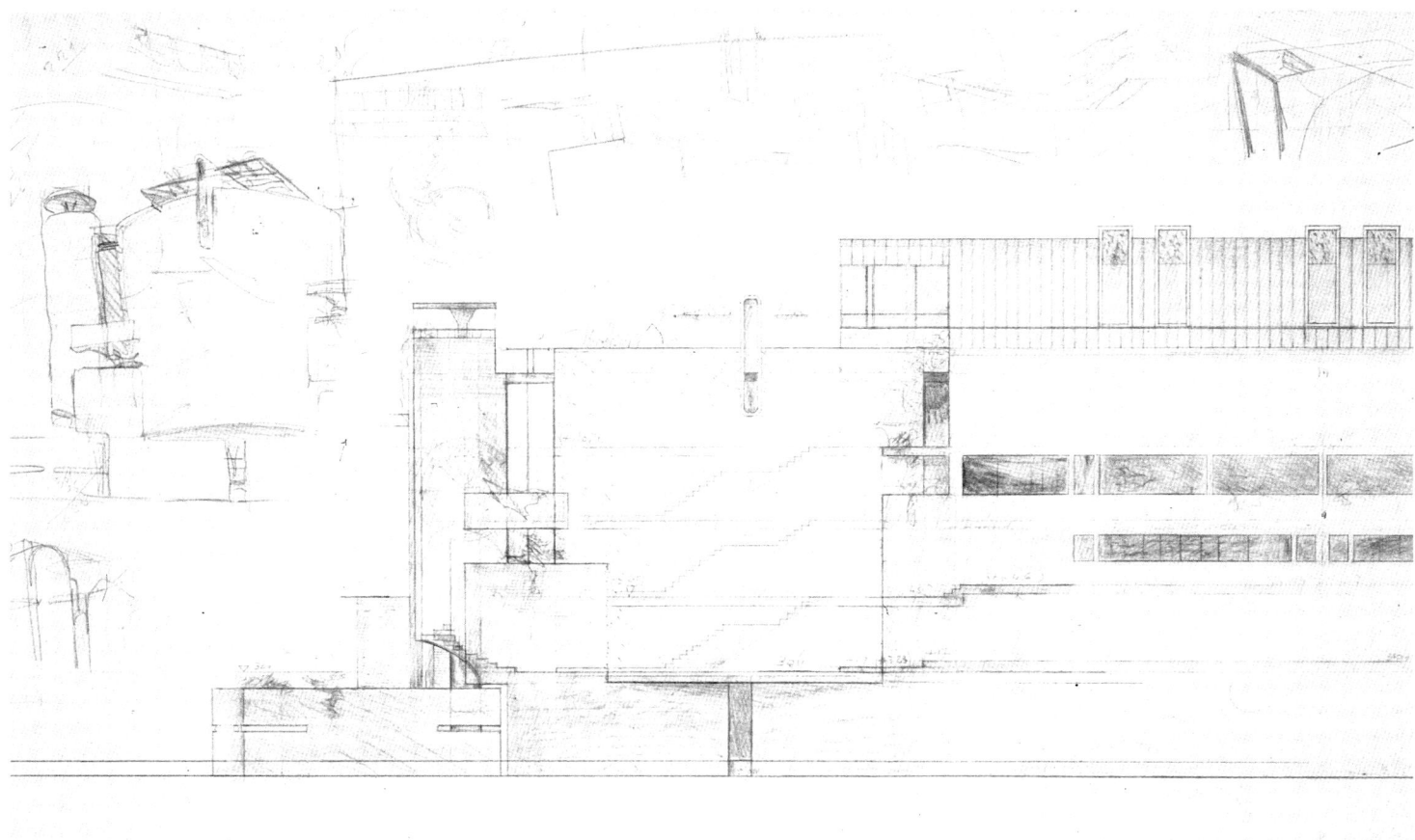

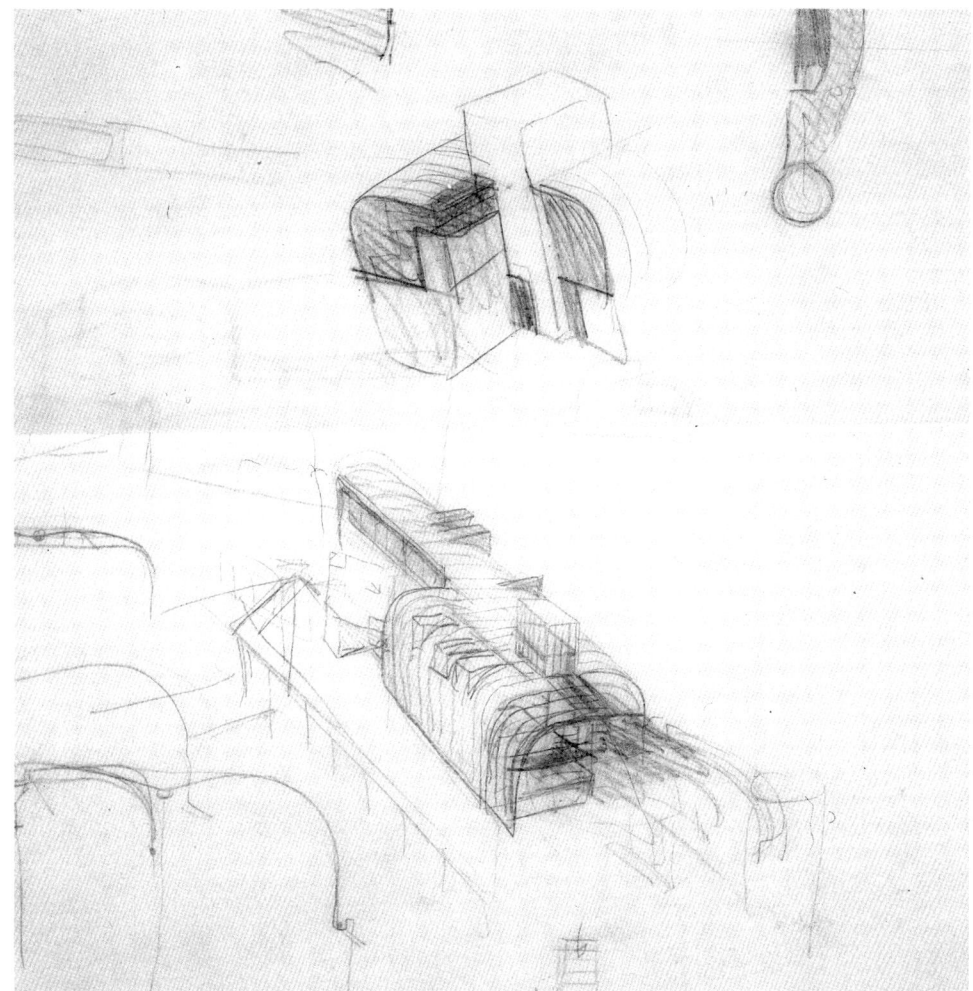

191. Detail of front of the Bailo Museum extension: Pencil, crayons and green ball-point pen on Bristol board

192. Sketches for the roofing, stressing skylights. Pencil on tracing paper

29. Frontage of the condominium at Vicenza

193, 194. Two studies for the window on the condominium at Vicenza. Pencil and crayons on Bristol board

195. Detail of frontage and section. Pencil and crayons on Bristol board

196. Plan. Pencil on Bristol board

197, 198. Two sketches for the façade. Pencil and crayons on tracing paper

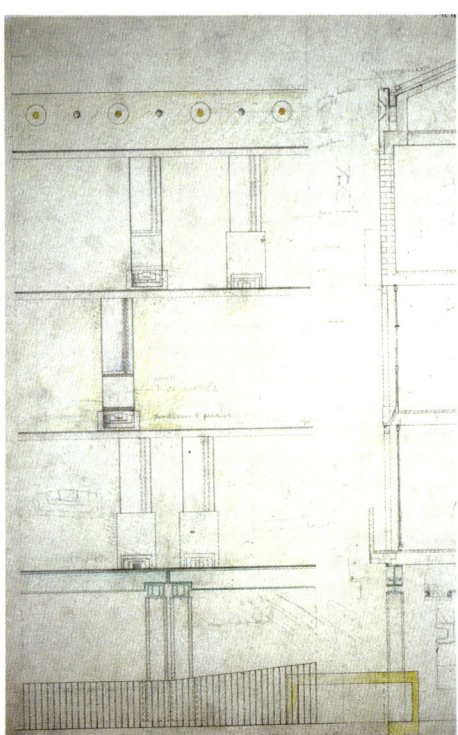

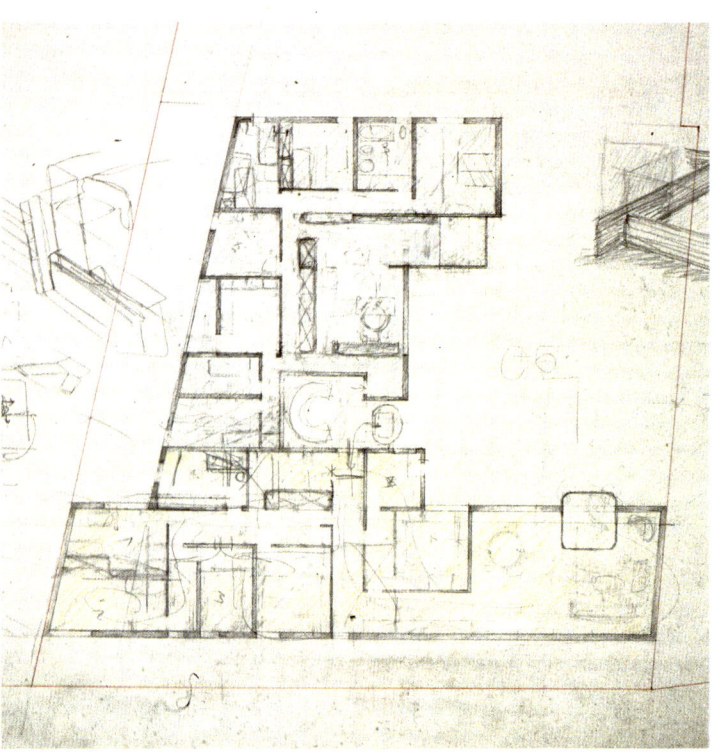

197

198

◁
199. Detail of the condominium at Vicenza

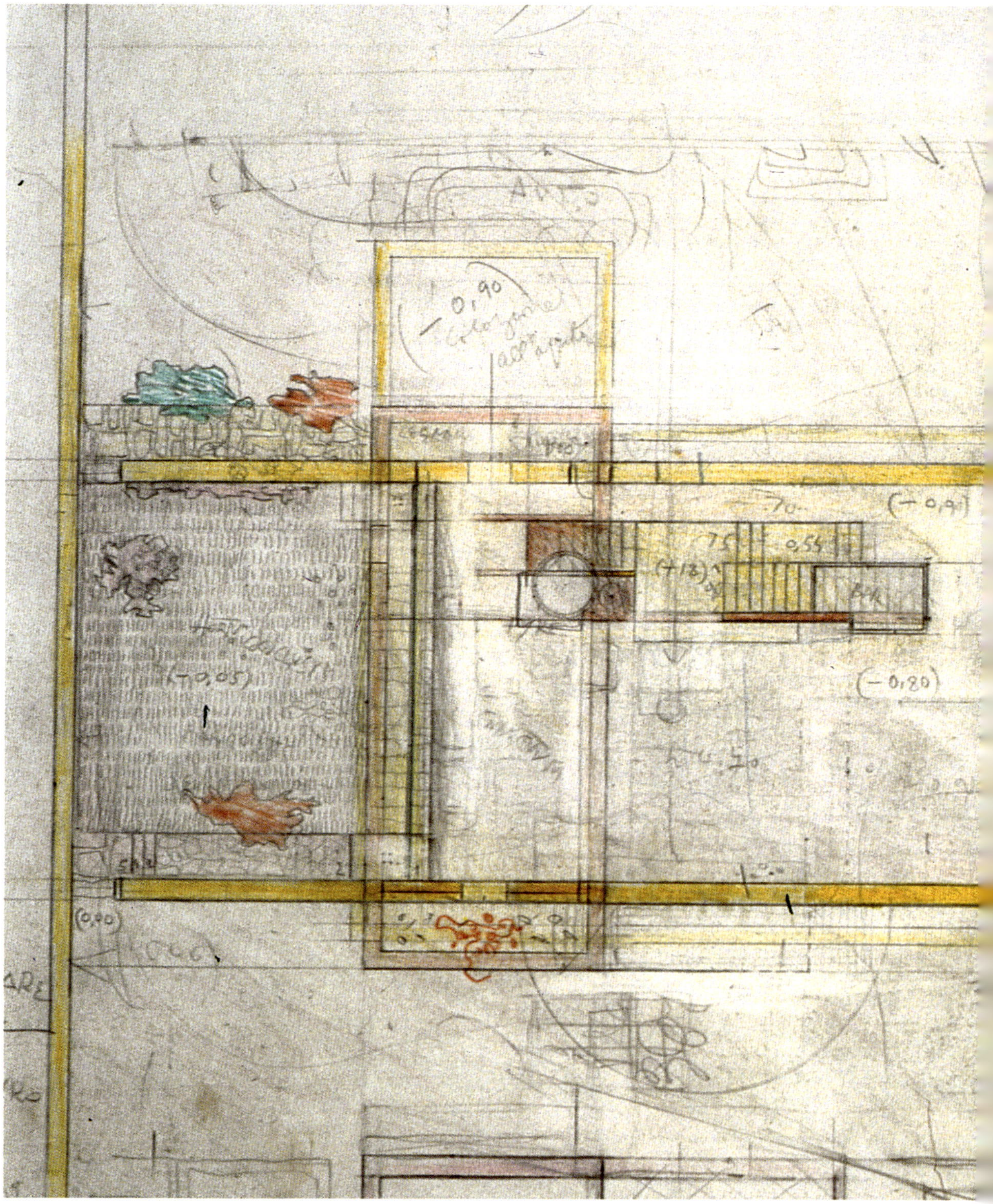

200. GROUND FLOOR PLAN, PROJECT FOR THE CHIESA HOUSE, VICENZA. PENCIL AND CRAYONS ON BRISTOL BOARD

201, 202, 203, 204. SKETCHES FOR THE FAÇADE ON THE SAME PROJECT. PENCIL AND CRAYONS ON TRACING PAPER

201

202

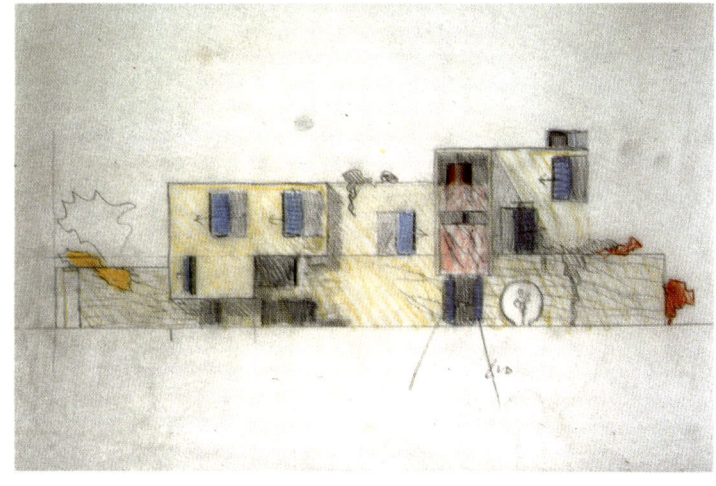

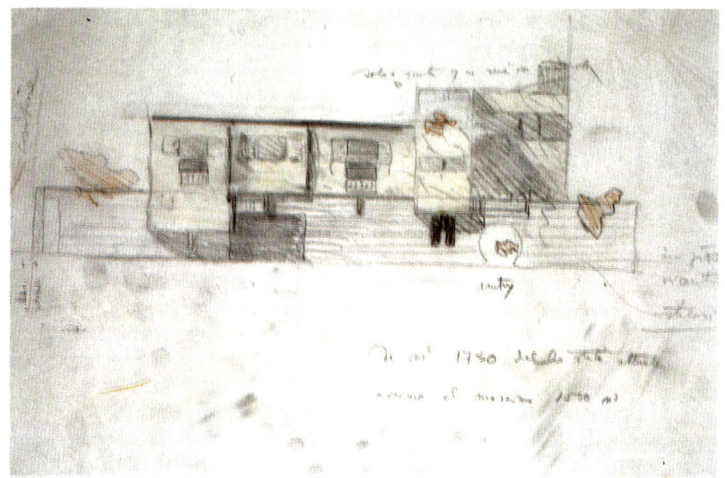

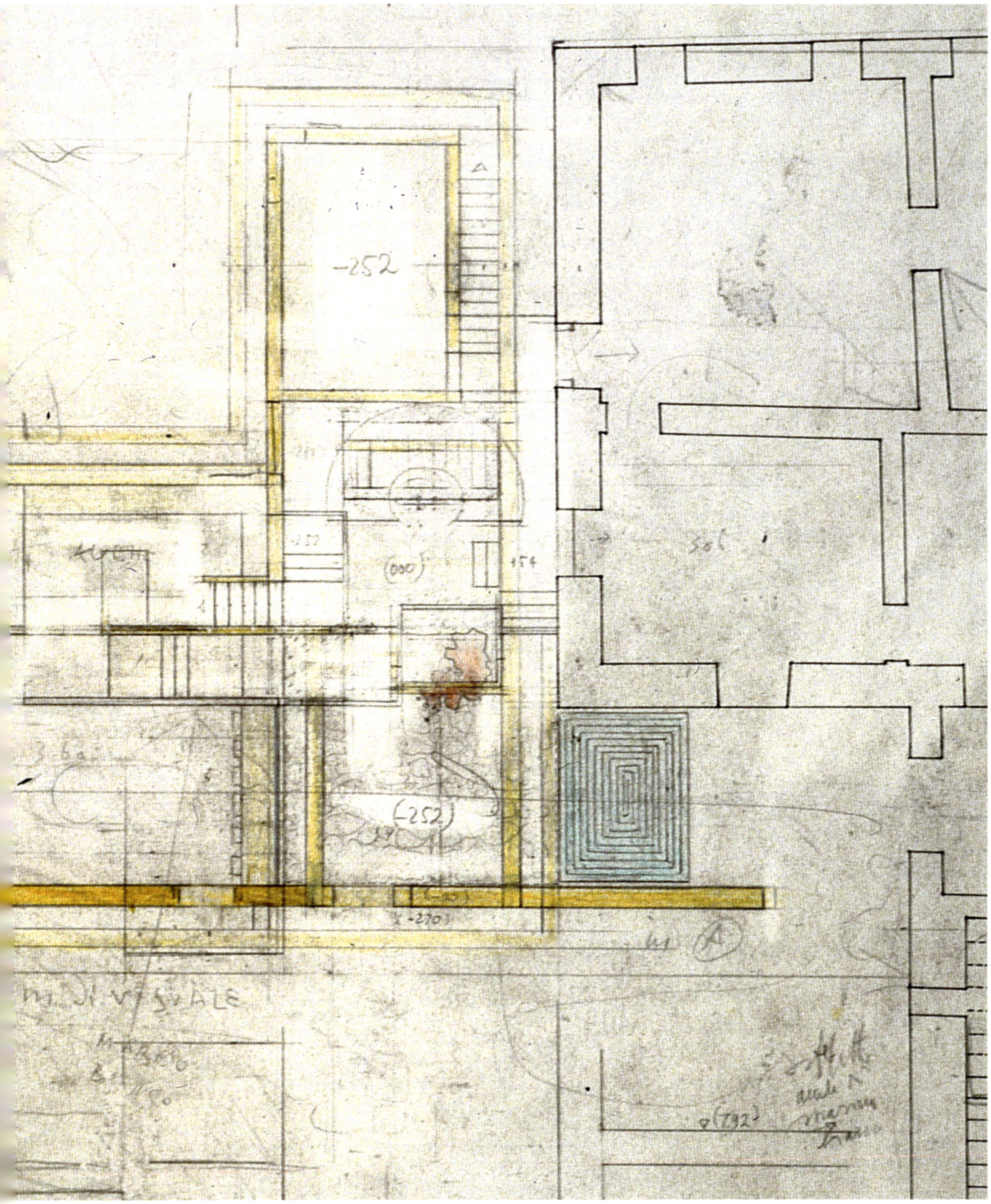

30. Fronts of the Banca Popolare di Verona

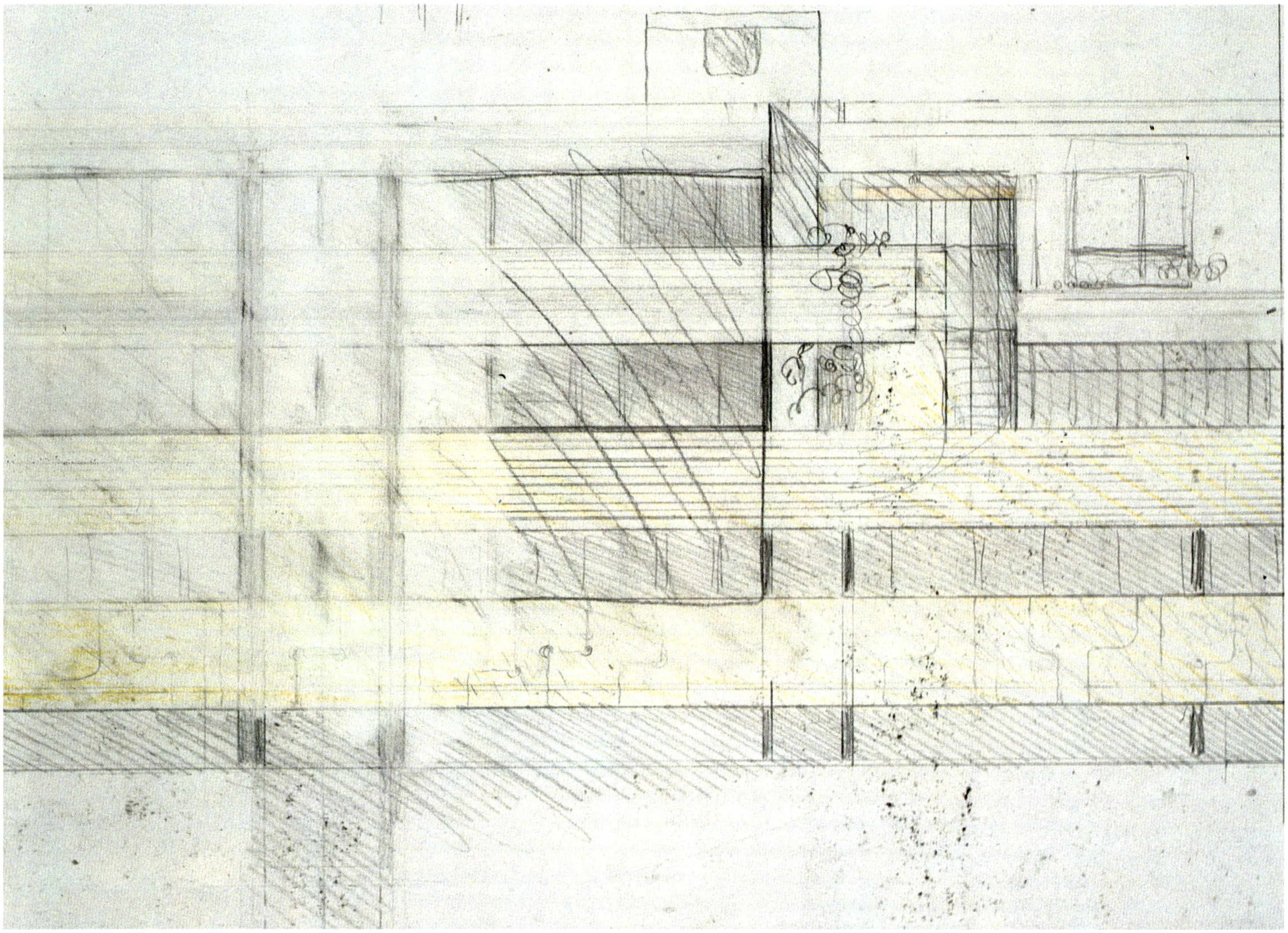

206

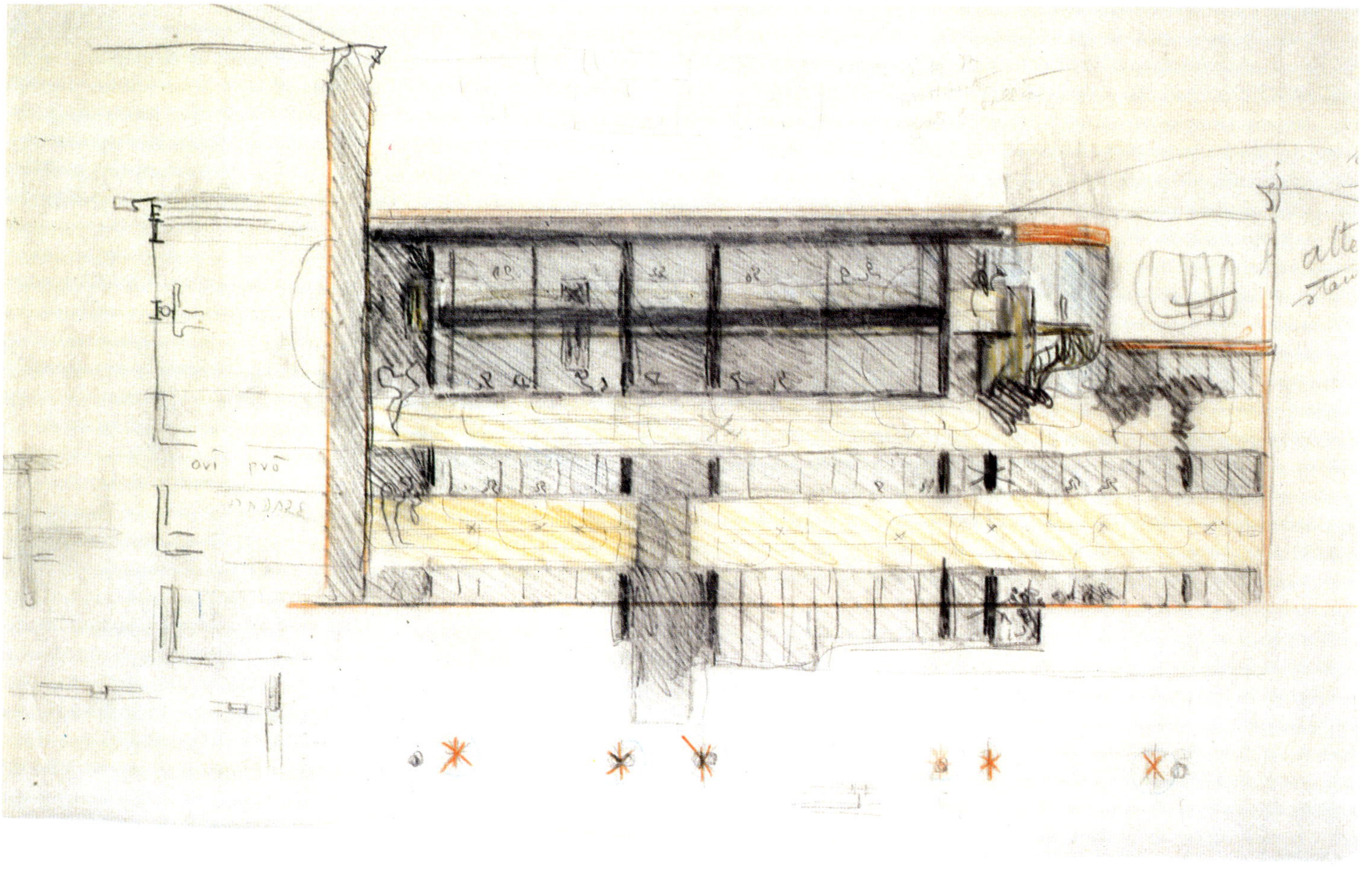

207

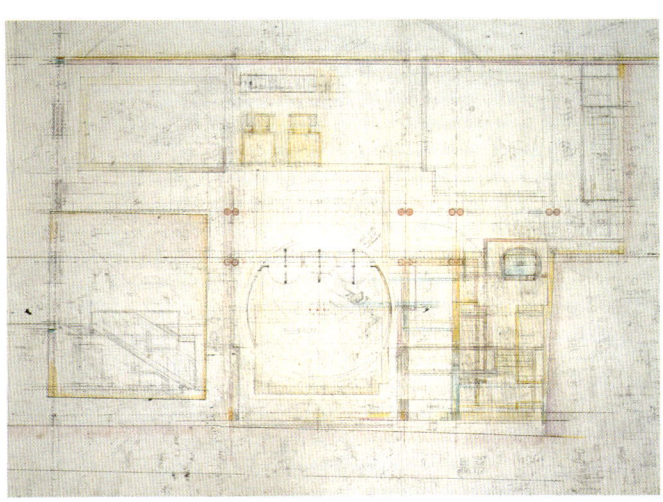

206. Study for the court front, initial idea. Pencil and crayons on Bristol board

207. Study for the court front, initial idea. Pencil and crayons on tracing paper

◁
205. Detail of court front on the Banca Popolare di Verona

208. Studies for the façade. Pencil, crayons with red and green ball-point pen on Bristol board

209. General plan. Pencil, crayons and red ball-point pen on Bristol board

210. Study for the façade, initial idea. Pencil and crayons on tracing paper

211. Detail of the façade with bay windows

▷

212. Sketch for the bay windows on the façade seen from the interior. Pencil and crayons on tracing paper

213. Detail of two windows

MOLDING—PROFILING

Where planes meet or where a plane ends, a simple projection, a fold or a change of material often substitutes for a sharp corner or the cornices on ancient architecture.

Mere millimeters of relief, a thread of shadow or a blurring, a smooth rounding-off, serve to enhance the articulation of a volume or the proportioning of a plane, or to lend definition to an otherwise inconclusive part. These are sought-after vibrations by means of which the light may better animate an object.

The profiling concludes, delineates, links parts and identifies them in the recomposition of planes or spaces that follows the dismemberment that invention entails. A colored fascia, the hard contour of iron, the softer one of wood, even when sanded or singed, are pointers, modern and often accessible expedients that suffice to evoke more sumptuous decors.

31. Round window on the Banca Popolare di Verona
32. The 5.5 x 5.5 motif
33. Cornice on the Banca Popolare di Verona
34. Mosaic
35. Profiling in wood
36. Profiling in iron
INSTANCES EXTRA-DOSSIER

31. Round window on the Banca Popolare di Verona

214

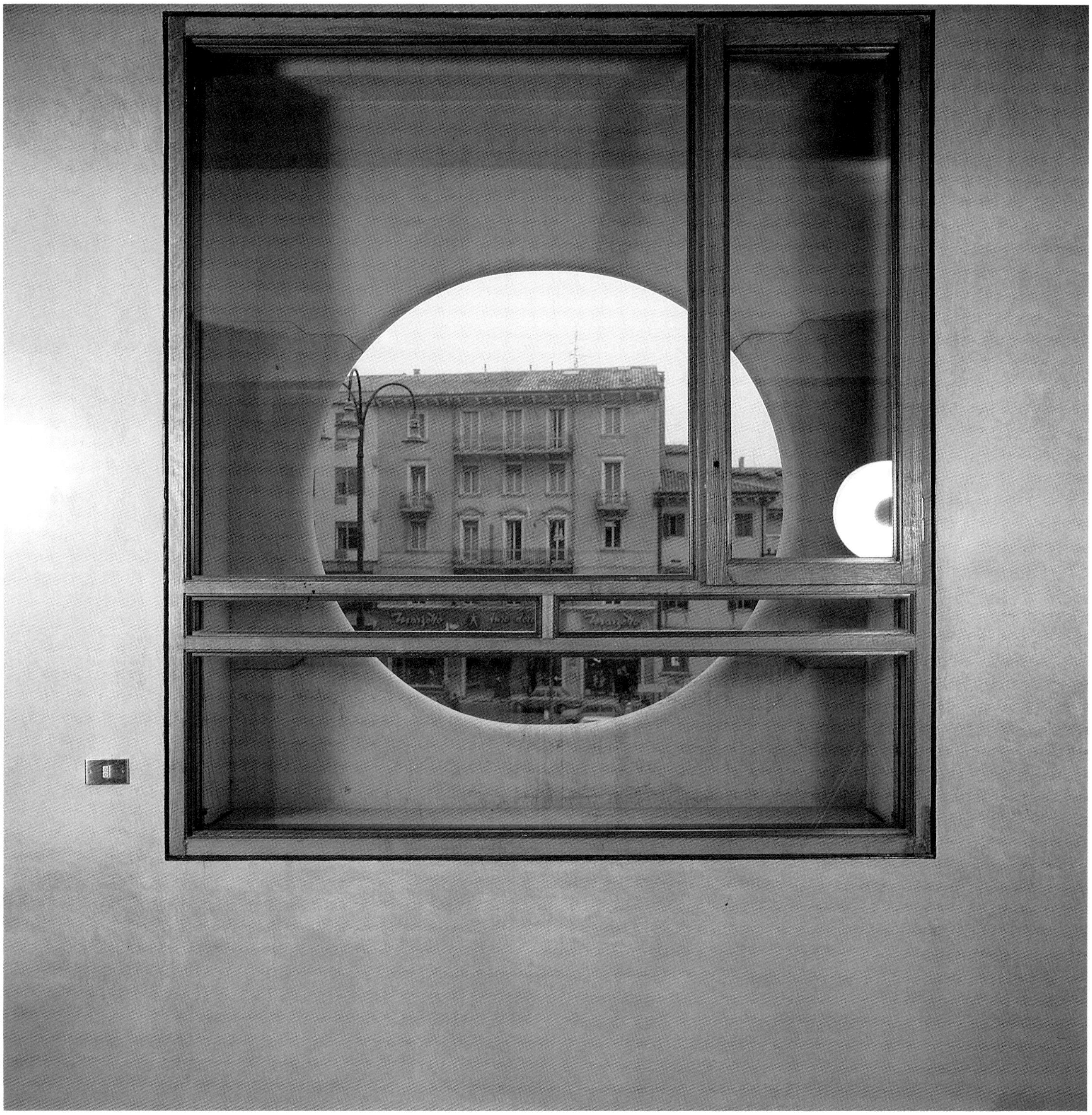

214. Round window on the Banca Popolare di Verona, interior

215. Sketch for the window, interior. Pencil and crayons on paper

215

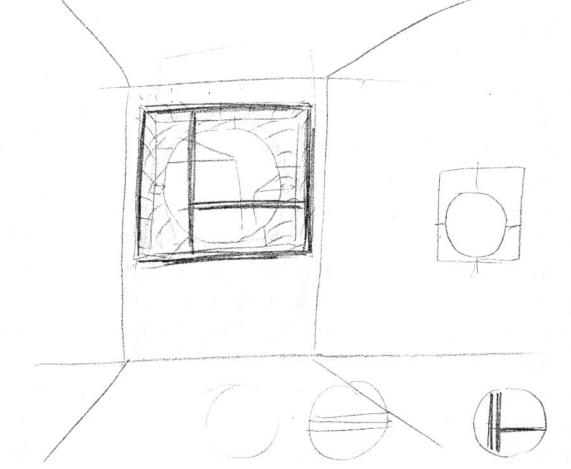

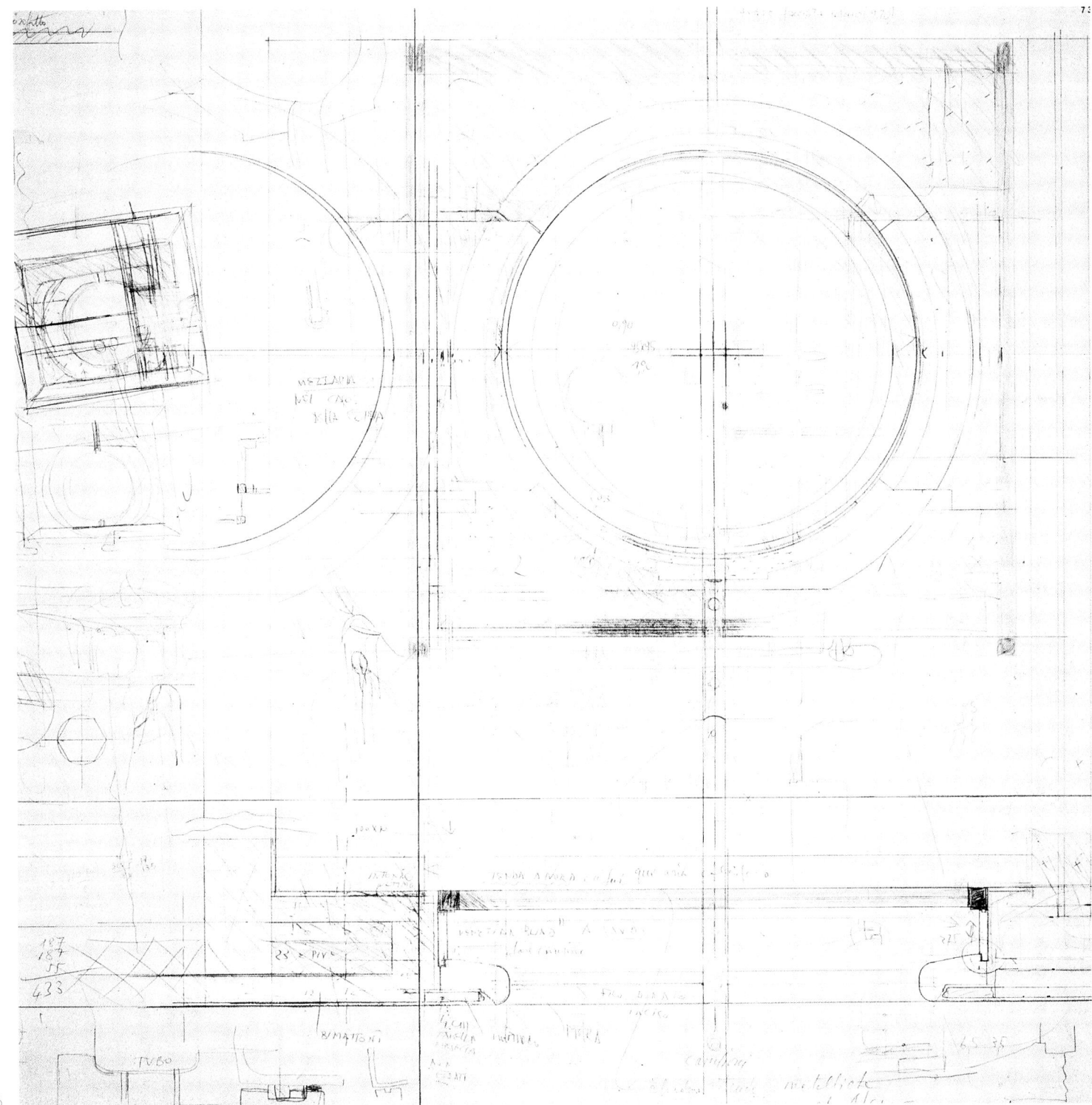

216. Study for the window. Pencil and crayons on Bristol board

217. Detail of the window

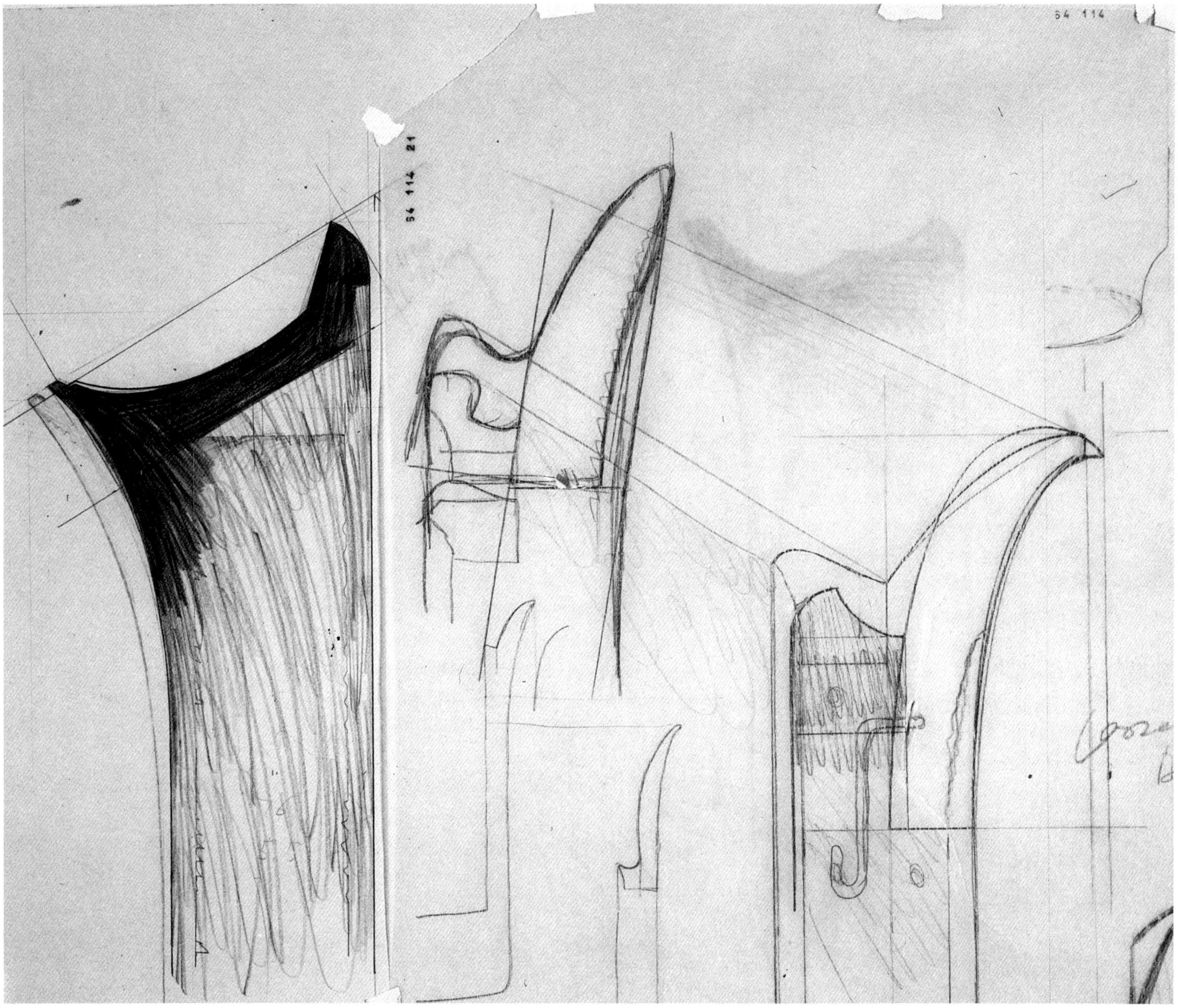

219

219. STUDY FOR THE PARAPET HANDRAIL ON THE BALBONI HOUSE, VENICE. PENCIL AND CRAYONS ON BRISTOL BOARD AND ON TRACING PAPER

220. SKETCH FOR THE GALLERY ON THE BALBONI HOUSE. PENCIL AND CRAYONS ON ONIONSKIN

220

◁
218. DETAIL OF THE HANDRAIL ON THE MAIN STAIRCASE OF THE BANCA POPOLARE DI VERONA

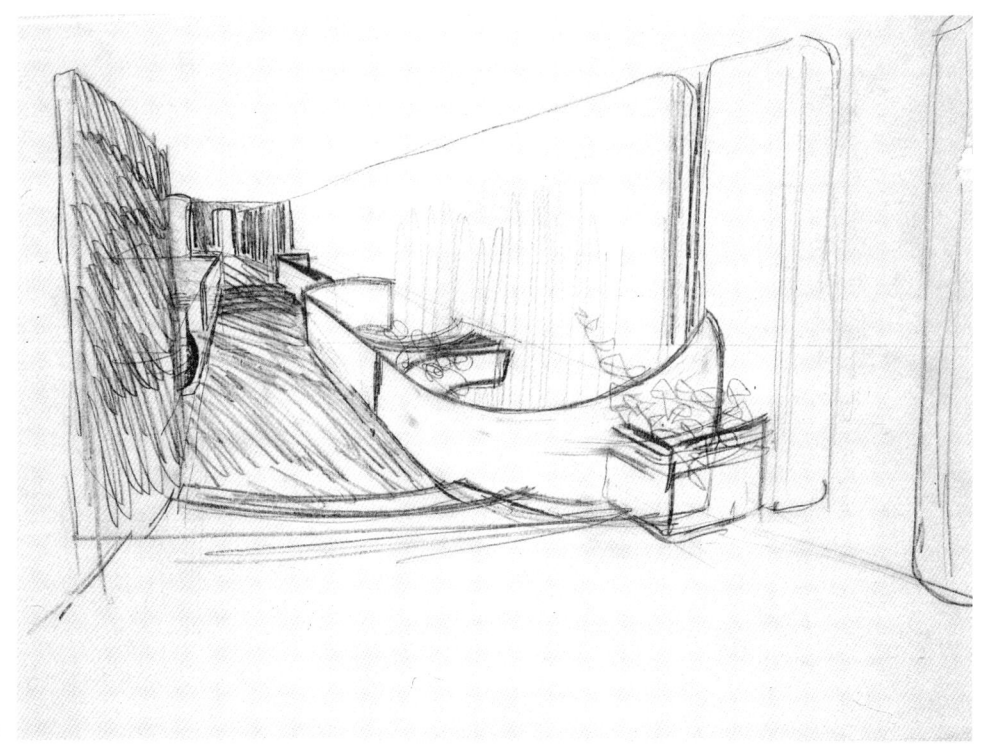

32. The 5.5 x 5.5 motif

221, 222, 223, 224, 225, 226, 227.
Details of molding on the Brion cemetery,
S. Vito di Altivole

228. Detail of sarcophagus in the Brion cemetery

33. Cornice on the Banca Popolare di Verona

229. Detail of the cornice on the Banca Popolare di Verona

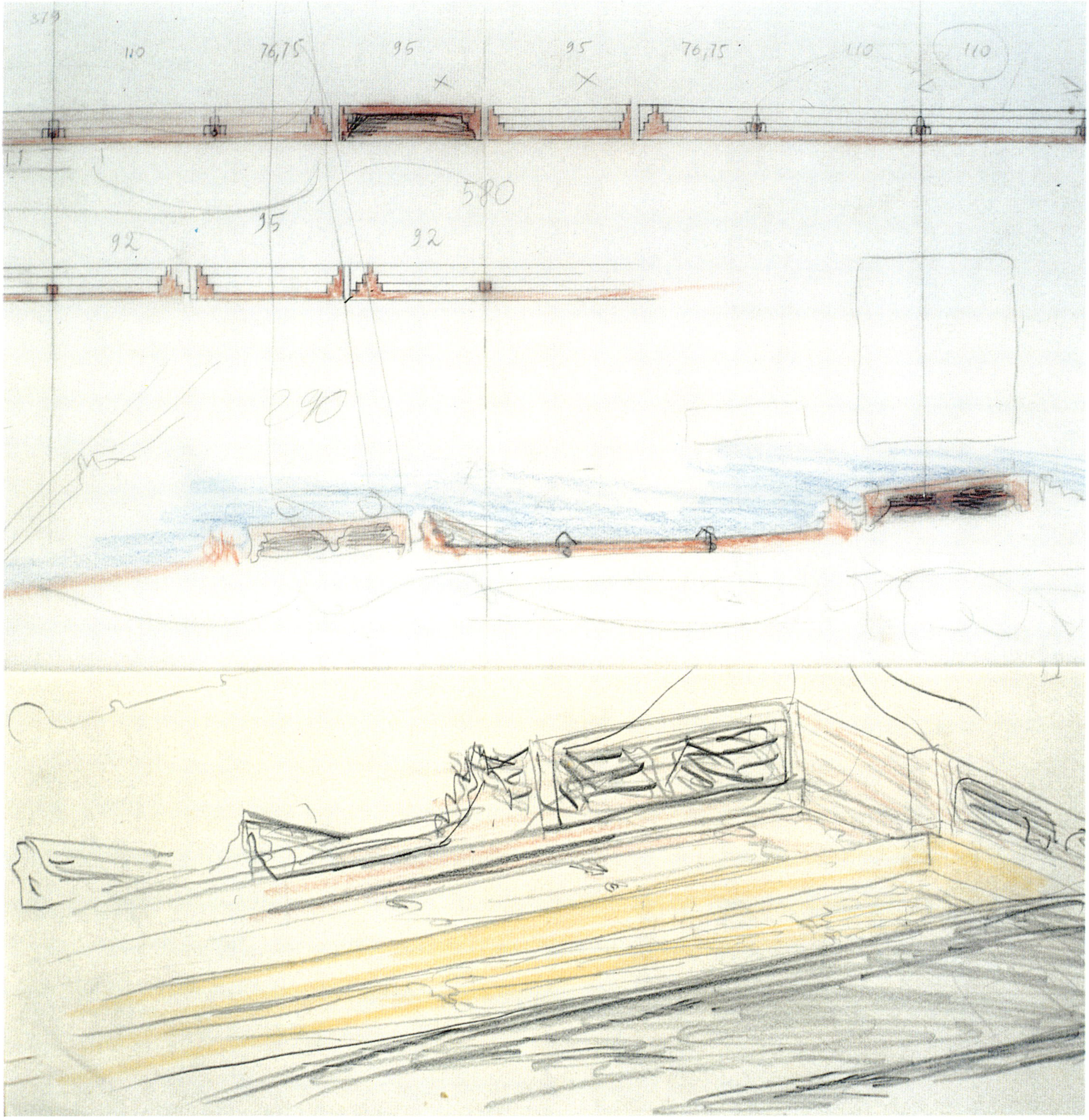
110
76,75
95
95
76,75
110
110
580
92
95
92
290

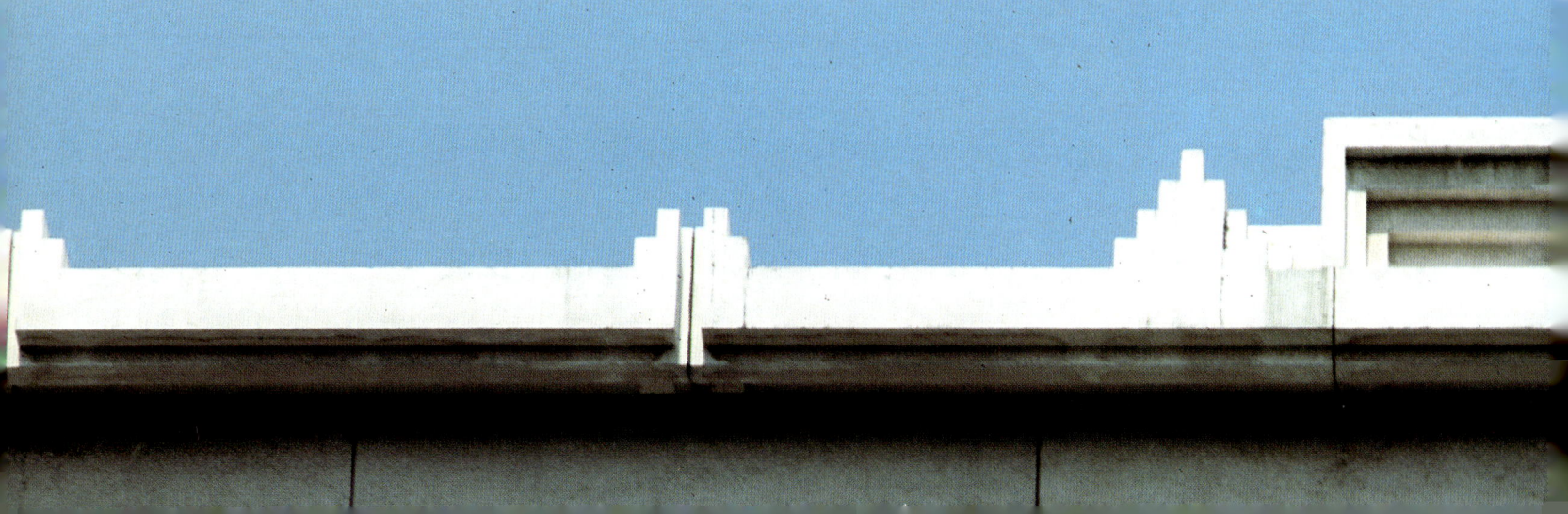

233

234

◁
230. Sketches and study for the cornice.
Pencil and crayons on paper and on tracing paper

231. Study for the cornice, plan and front.
Pencil and crayons on Bristol board

232. Detail of the cornice

235

233. DETAIL OF THE FASCIA OF RED STONE ON THE FAÇADE OF THE BANCA POPOLARE DI VERONA

234. MEZZANINE OF THE MAIN STAIRCASE ON THE BANCA POPOLARE DI VERONA

235. DETAIL OF MOLDING ON THE ENTRANCE TO THE BANCA POPOLARE DI VERONA

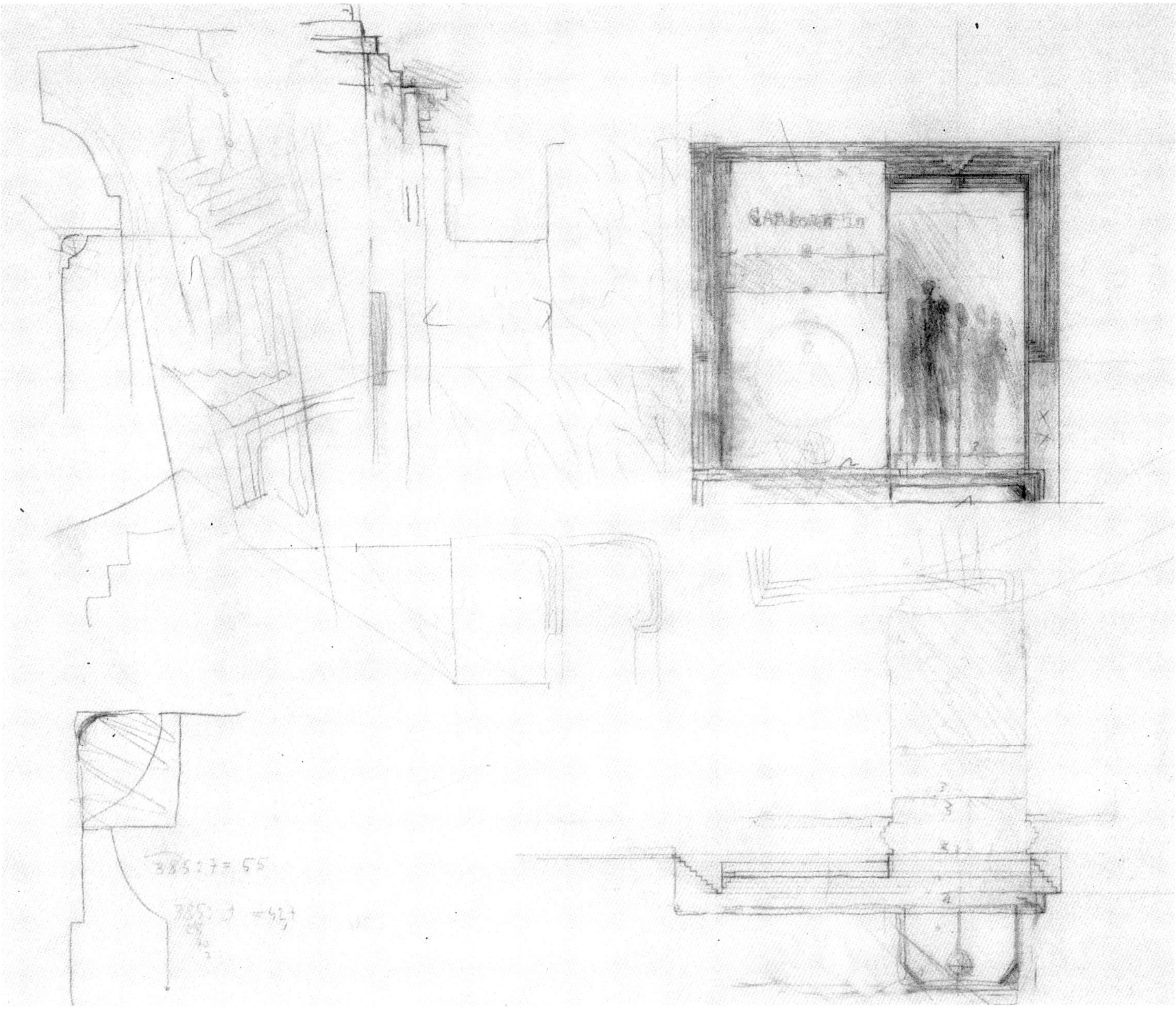

236

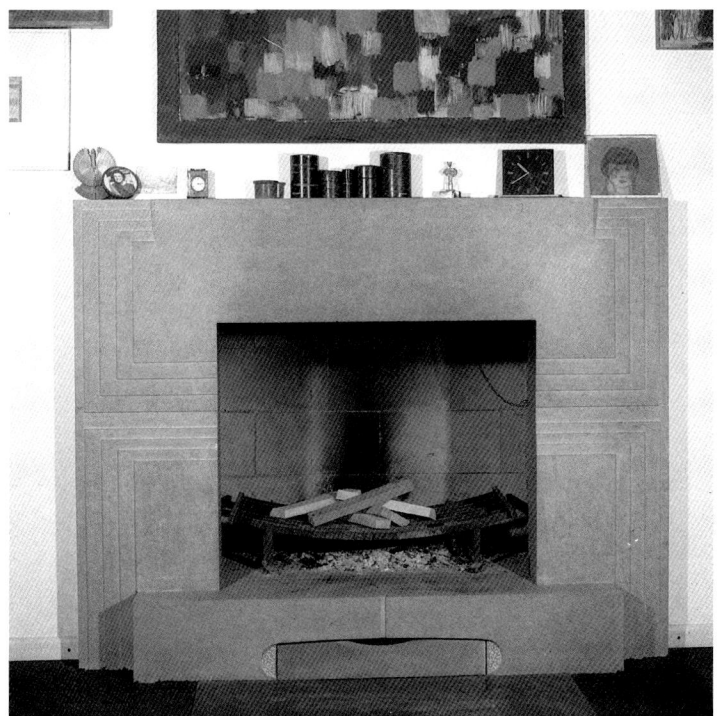

236. STUDY FOR THE MAIN ENTRANCE, PROJECT FOR THE FACULTY OF HUMANITIES AND PHILOSOPHY IN THE FORMER CONVENT OF S. SEBASTIAN, VENICE. PENCIL AND CRAYONS ON HEAVY TRACING PAPER

237. FIREPLACE IN THE SCARPA HOUSE, VENICE

237

34. Mosaic

238, 239. Details of mosaic decorations on the garden wall of the Querini Stampalia Foundation, Venice

35. Profiling in wood

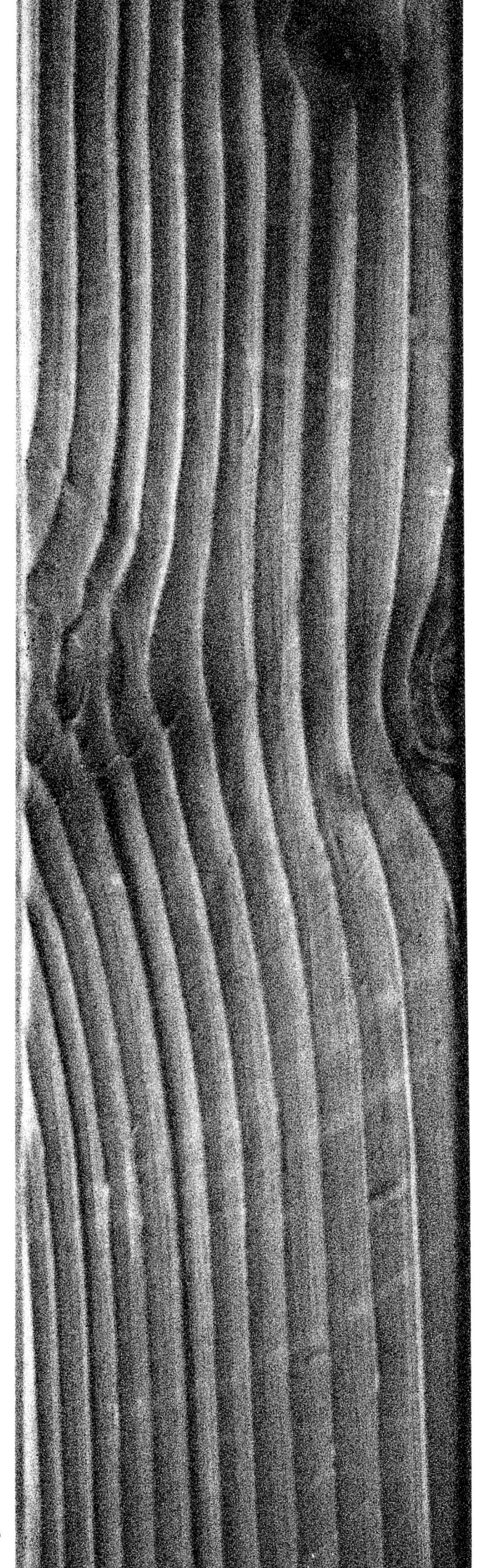

◁
240. Detail of the parapet to the staircase in the Olivetti store, Venice

241. Detail of the same parapet facing the landing

242. Detail of the gallery handrail in the Olivetti store

243. Detail of profiling on a passage between two rooms in Palazzo Abatellis, Palermo

36. Profiling in iron

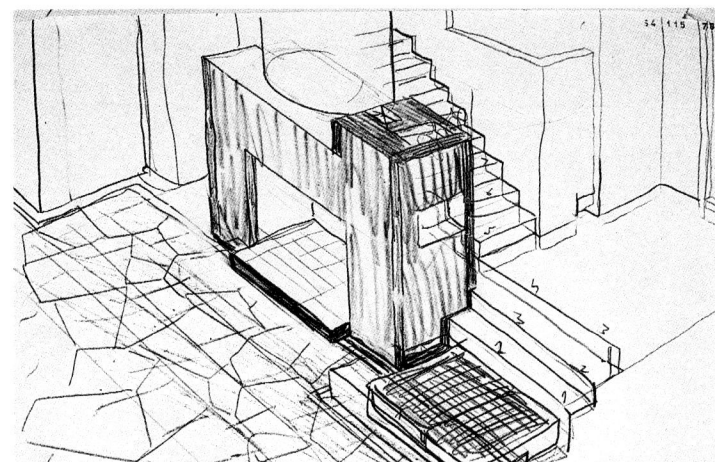

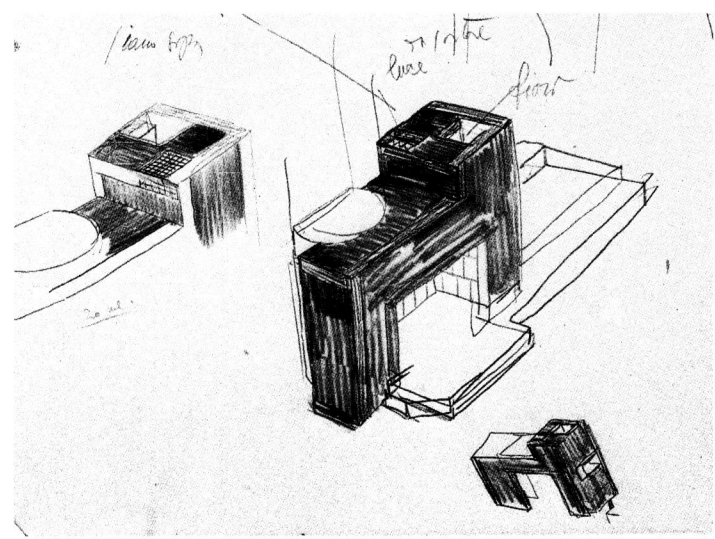

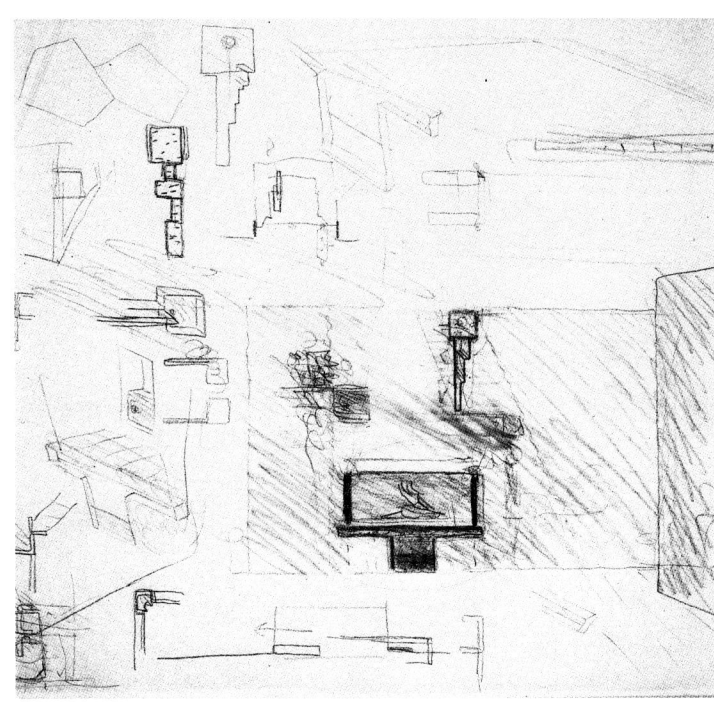

244. Sketch for the fireplace in the Ottolenghi house, Bardolino. Pencil and crayons on tracing paper

245. Two sketches for the fireplace in the Zentner house, Zurich. Pencil and crayons on paper

246. Sketch for a bedroom wall in the Ottolenghi house. Pencil and crayons on tracing paper

▷ 247. Detail of profiling in iron on a passage between two rooms in the Gallery wing of the Castelvecchio Museum, Verona

248. Detail of paving in the first ground floor room in the same museum

249. Iron skirting in a room in the Academy Picture Galleries, Venice

250. Sketch for the profiling on the glazed wall of the Banca Popolare di Verona façade. Pencil and crayons on paper

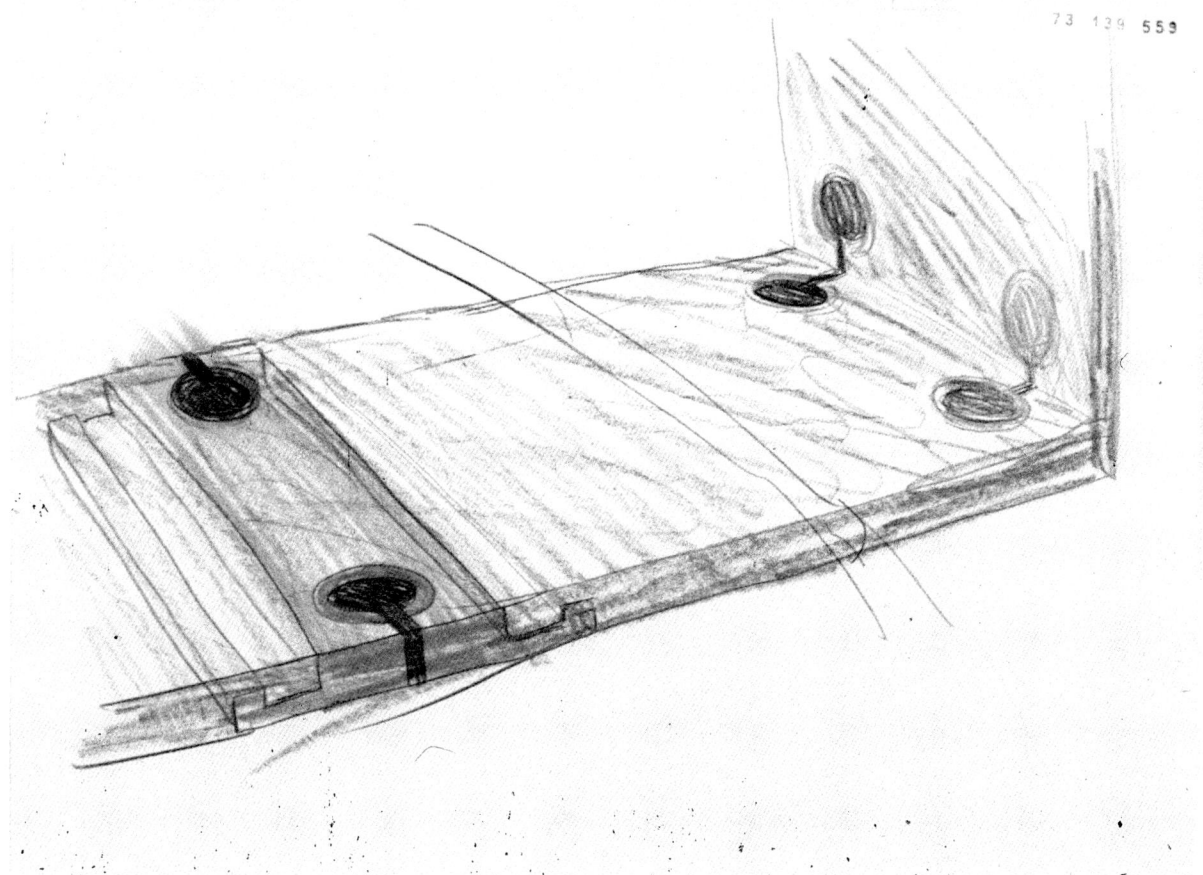

SURFACE

The architectural complement that best lends itself to exploiting light, to enhancing the vital function of color, creating either strong or gentle contrasts. Closer than other spatial components to painting, every style and every epoch has conjured with it. In our case, it inevitably becomes a very versatile means of expression.

The influences of modern pictorial research are evident. But so are the signs of instinctive response to textural values: relationships between the differing granulosities of a rendering, rough offset by smooth, an extraneous material that creeps in to act as a foil, chromatic alternations, nuances or imperceptible variations of tone in a single stone.

Finally, there is stucco, the synthesis of all surfaces by virtue of color, transparency, depth, and the vibrations induced by the compact, elaborate modulations of the trowelling.

37. Stone with stone
38. Stone with other materials
39. Paving of the Olivetti store
40. Paving of the condominium at Vicenza
41. Service staircase in the Banca Popolare di Verona
42. Involucre of the Brion pavilion
INSTANCES EXTRA-DOSSIER

37. Stone with stone

251. Revetment on the entrance to the Banca Popolare di Verona

252. Paving in the entrance hall of the Querini Stampalia Foundation, Venice

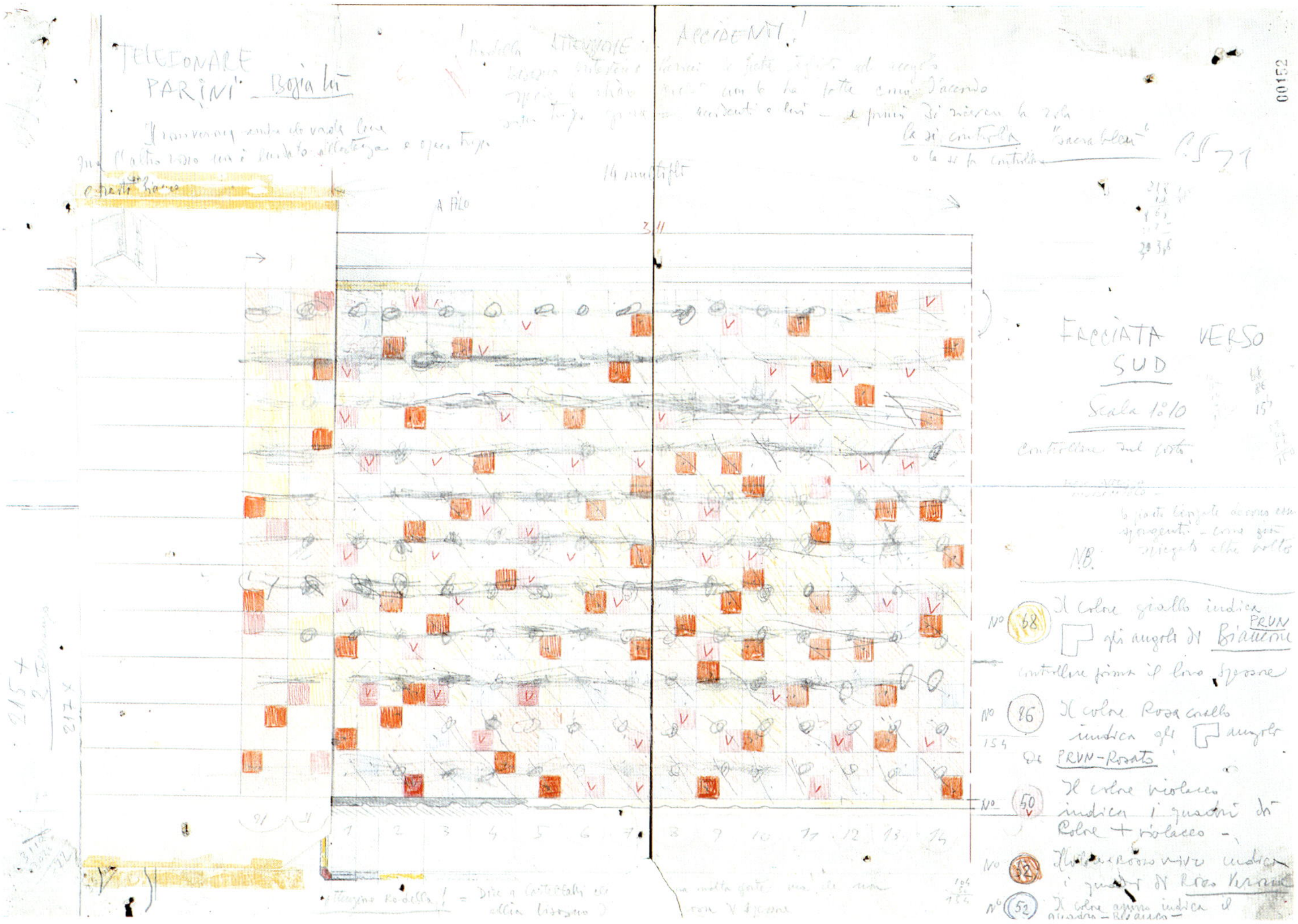

253.

254.

253. Study for the external revetment of the sacellum in the Castelvecchio Museum, Verona. Pencil and crayons on paper

254. Detail of the external revetment of the sacellum. Photo taken immediately after completion in 1965

38. Stone with other materials

255. Revetment of the walls of the ground floor room in the Querini Stampalia Foundation, Venice

256. Paving in the same room

257. Paving of the ground floor rooms in the Castelvecchio Museum, Verona

258. Paving of the Gallery wing in the same museum

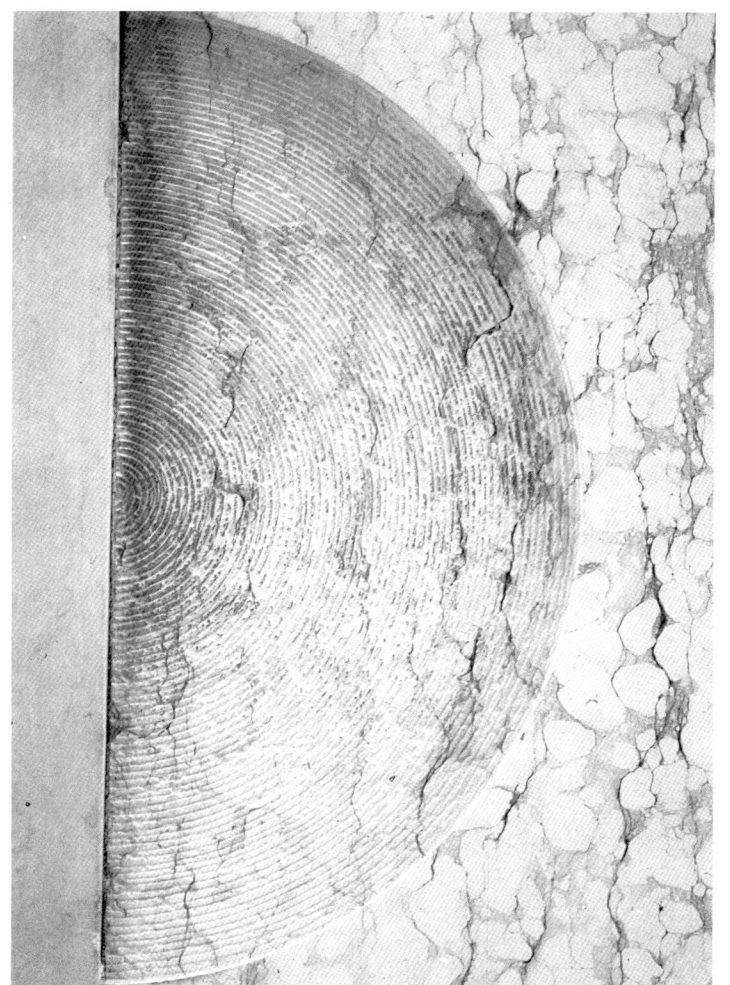

259. Detail of the skirting in the first and second floor rooms of the palace in the Castelvecchio Museum

260. Detail of the jamb on the main entrance to the Banca Popolare di Verona

261. Detail of revetment of a pillar in the Olivetti store, Venice

262. Detail of external revetment of the same store

39. Paving of the Olivetti store

263, 264, 265, 266. Details of paving in the Olivetti store, Venice

41. Service staircase in the Banca Popolare di Verona

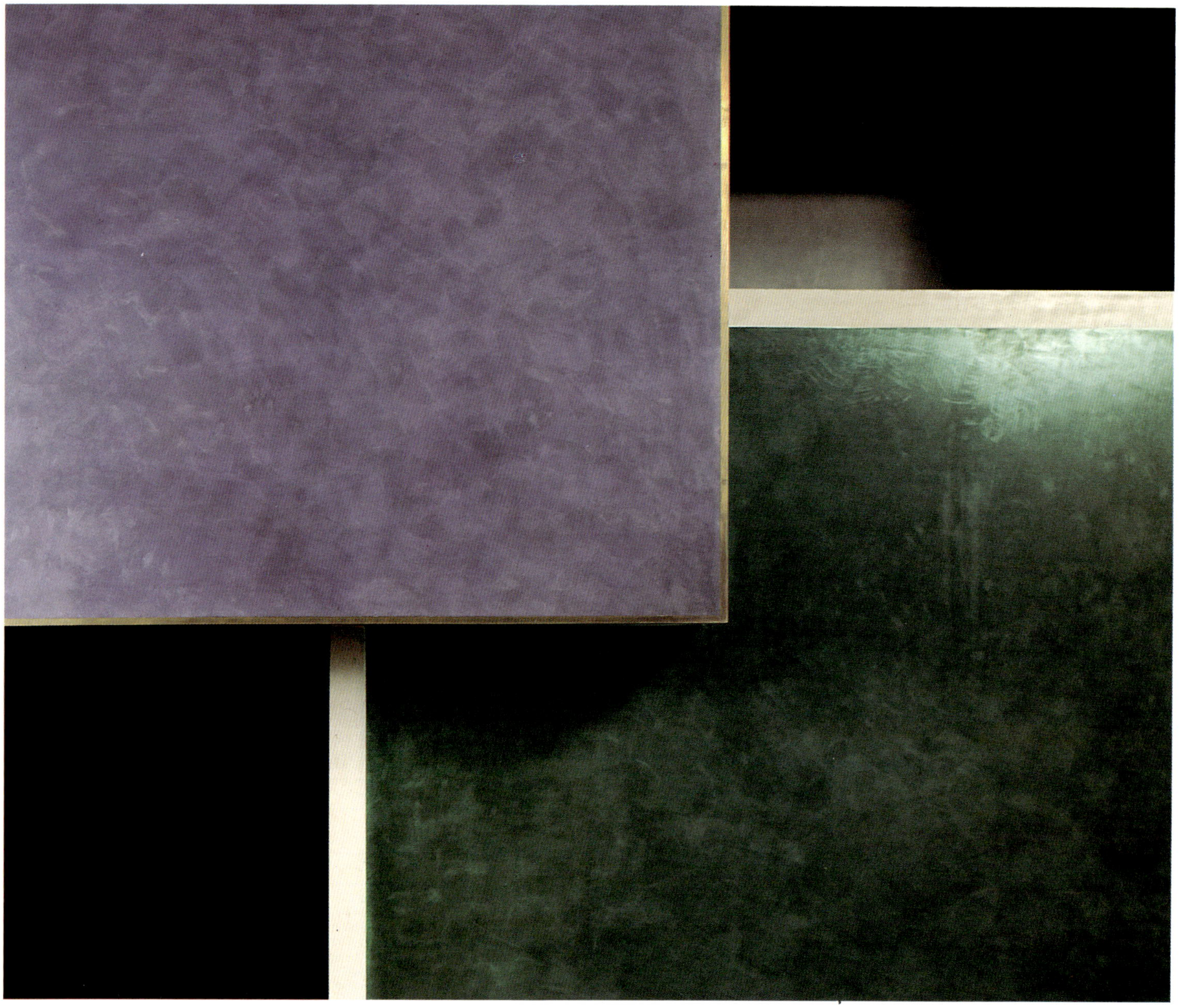

269

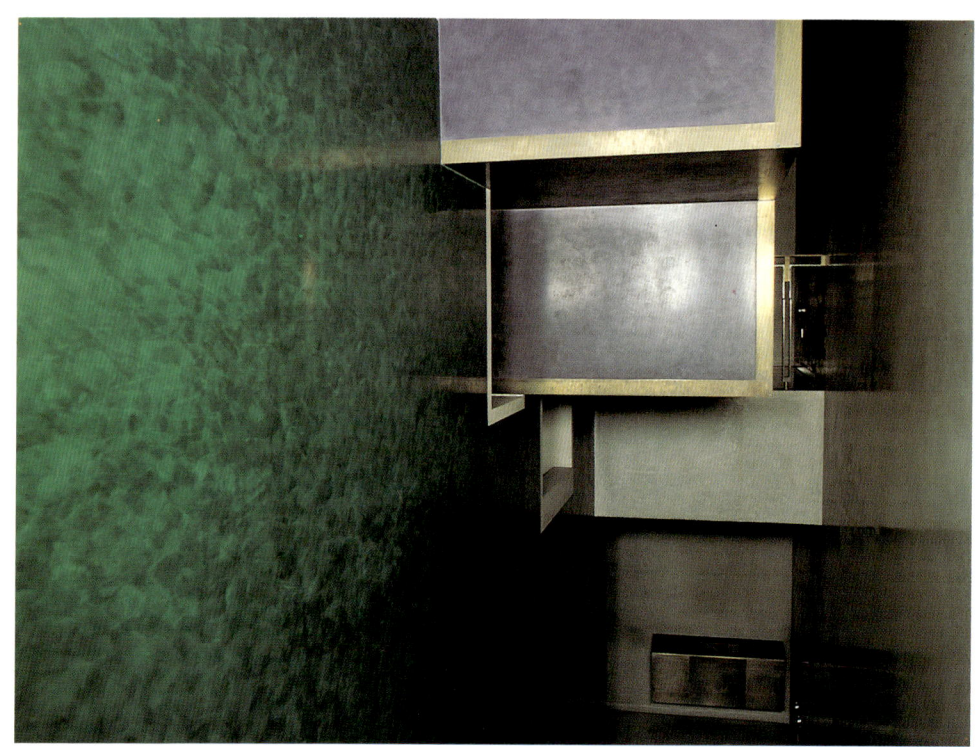

269. Detail of the stucco rendering on the service staircase in the Banca Popolare di Verona

270. The soffit of the staircase

270

◁

40. Paving of the condominium at Vicenza

267, 268. Details of paving in the portico of the condominium at Vicenza

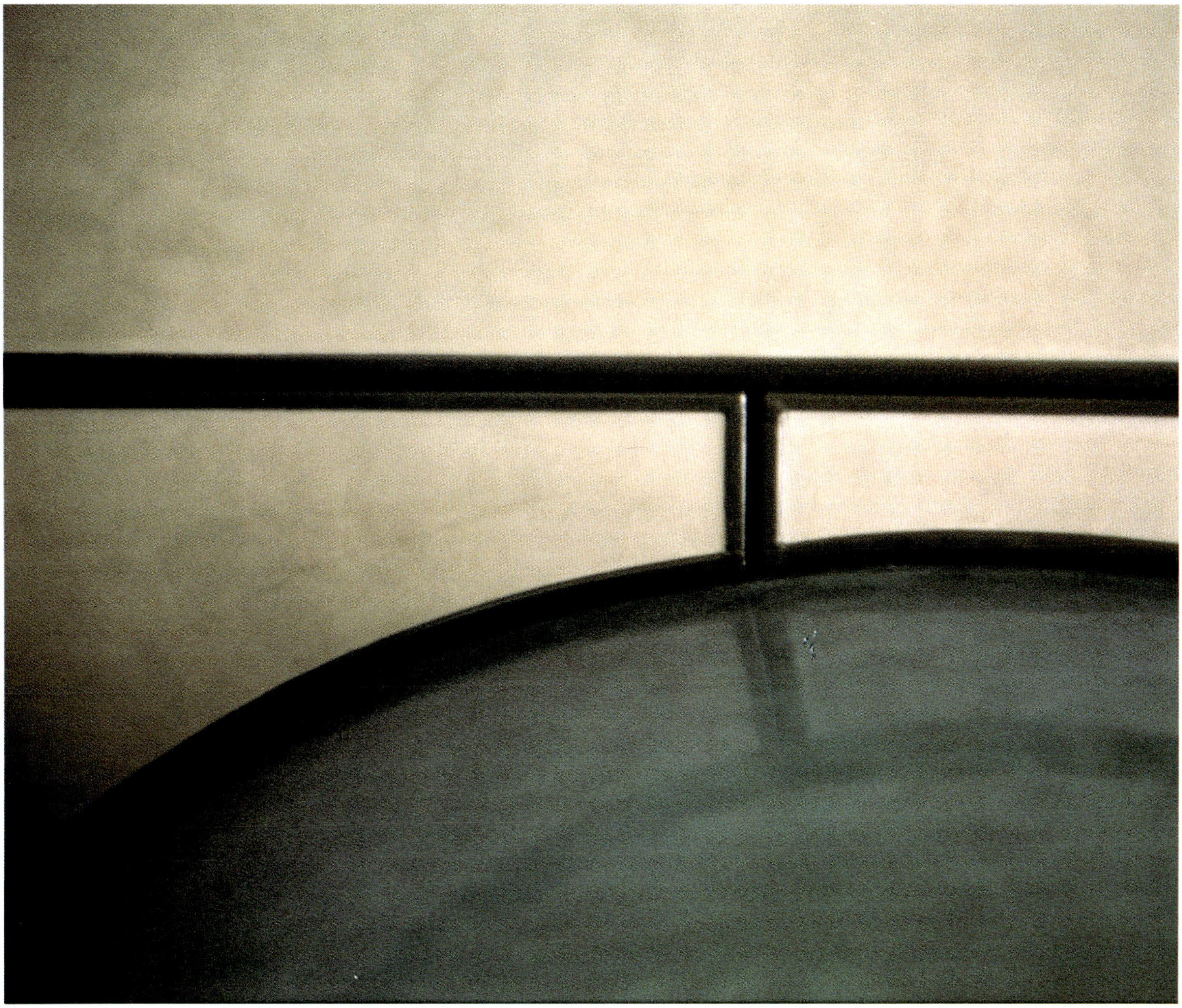
271

272

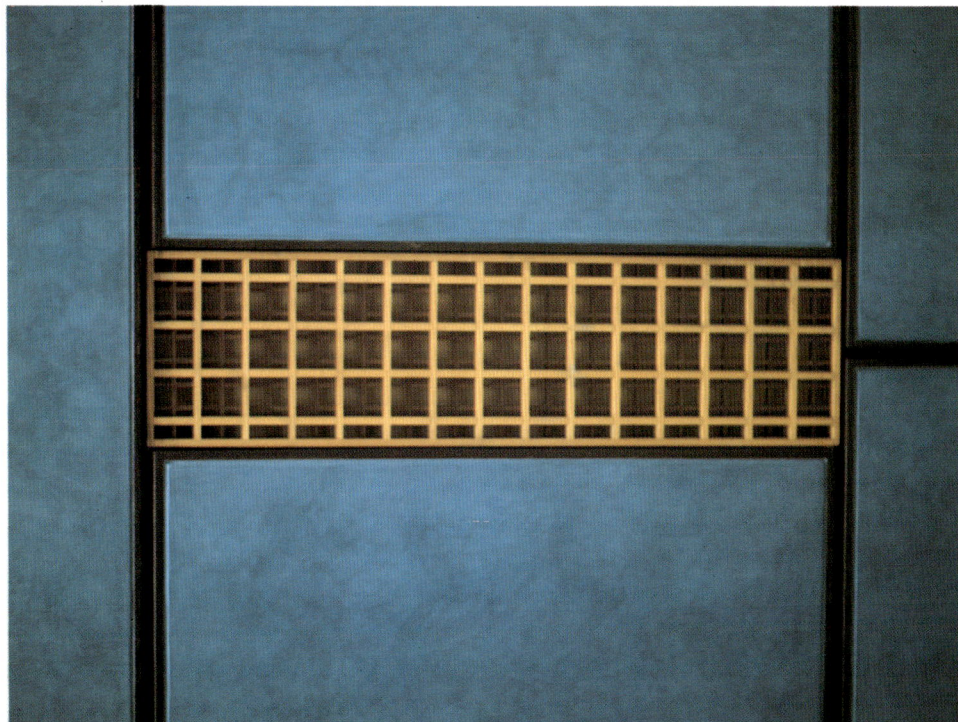

271. FORESHORTENED DETAIL OF THE BLUE ELEVATOR AND FALSE CEILING ON THE BANCA POPOLARE DI VERONA

272. DETAIL OF THE FALSE CEILING AND VENTILATION GRATING IN A ROOM IN THE GALLERY WING OF THE CASTELVECCHIO MUSEUM, VERONA

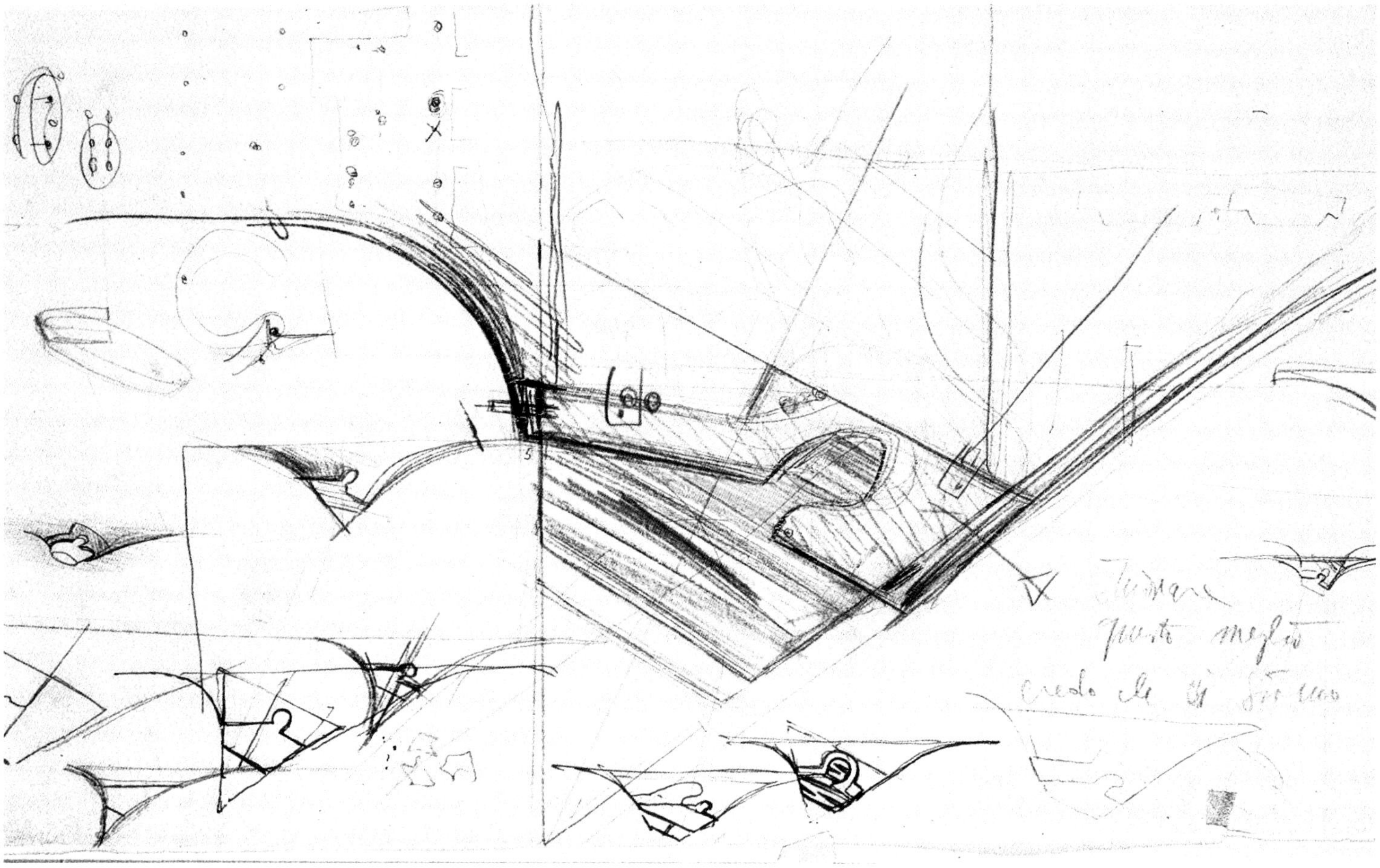

273. STUDY FOR THE CEILING AND LAMP IN THE LIVING ROOM OF THE ZENTNER HOUSE, ZURICH. PENCIL, CRAYONS AND RED BALL-POINT PEN ON ONIONSKIN

274. DETAIL OF THE LAMP IN THE ENTRANCE HALL OF THE BANCA POPOLARE DI VERONA

▷
42. Involucre of the Brion pavilion

275. Detail of the wooden revetment of the Brion pavilion, S. Vito di Altivole

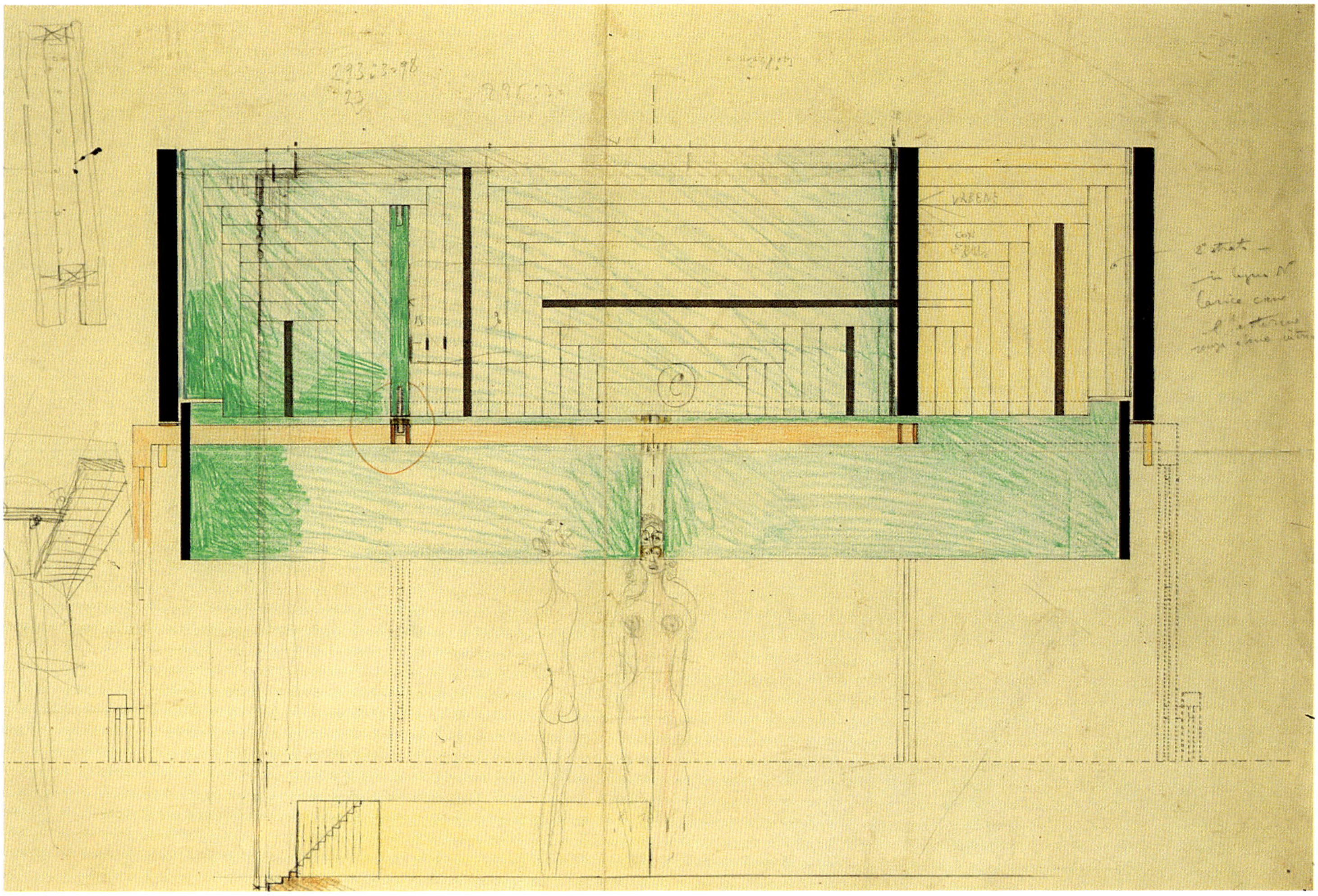

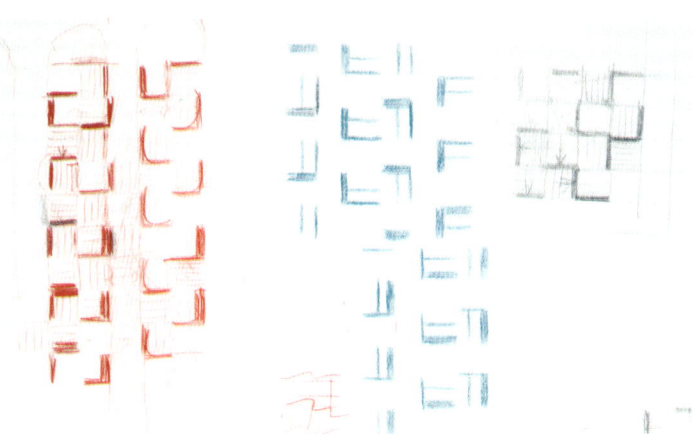

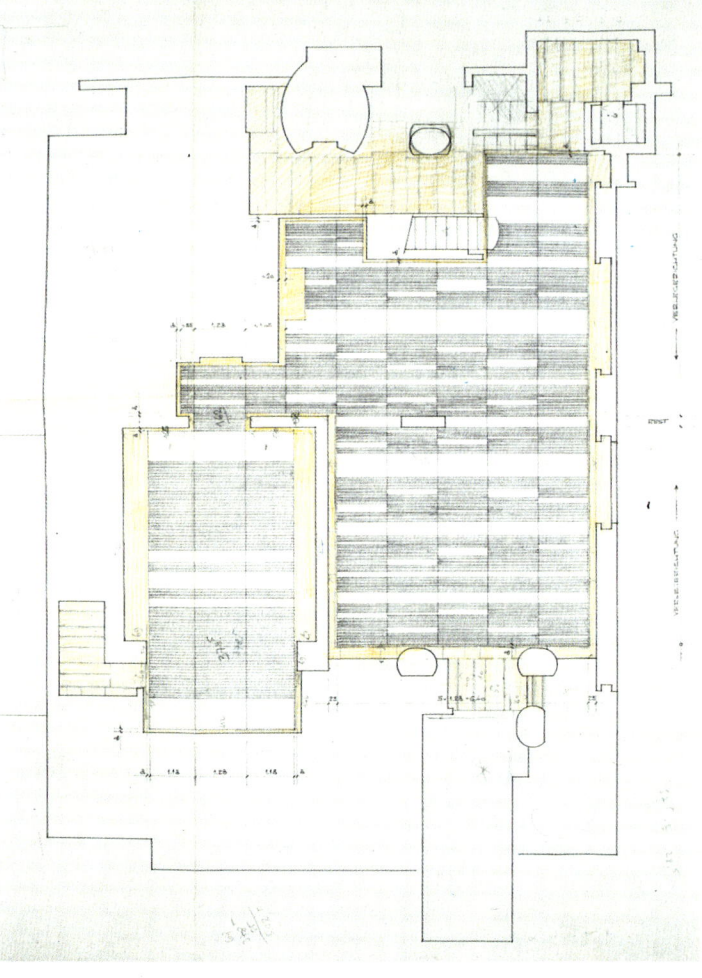

276. Study for the revetment. Pencil and crayons on heliographic print

277. STUDY FOR THE PARQUET FLOORING, PROJECT FOR A PRIVATE HOUSE, MONTECCHIO (VICENZA). PENCIL AND CRAYONS ON TRACING PAPER

278. WORKING DRAWING FOR THE WOODEN FLOORING IN THE ZENTNER HOUSE, ZURICH. CRAYONS ON HELIOGRAPHIC PRINT

279. DETAIL OF A DOOR IN THE CASTELVECCHIO MUSEUM, VERONA

280. WOODEN DISPLAY SCREEN IN THE ANTONELLO ROOM, PALAZZO ABATELLIS, PALERMO

281. WOODEN WALL IN THE OLIVETTI STORE, VENICE

▷

282. INTERIOR REVETMENT OF THE CUPOLA ON THE CHAPEL OF THE BRION CEMETERY, S. VITO DI ALTIVOLE

279

280

281

TRANSPARENCY

The properties of weight and solidity must not read as a barrier.

The underlying thought, elaboration and assembly of each element are directed to dispelling inertness. Space must never be confined.

Transparency in spaces: one glimpses and sees beyond, the air transfigures the light of day and water brings life to that which it flows over. So too it is with glass artifacts: by virtue of color, held in suspended particles or diffused, reflections, irridescent or wavering shadows, flaring, elongated or dilated forms and the essential fragility of the substance.

43. Garden, Querini Stampalia Foundation
44. Glass

43. Garden, Querini Stampalia Foundation

284

285

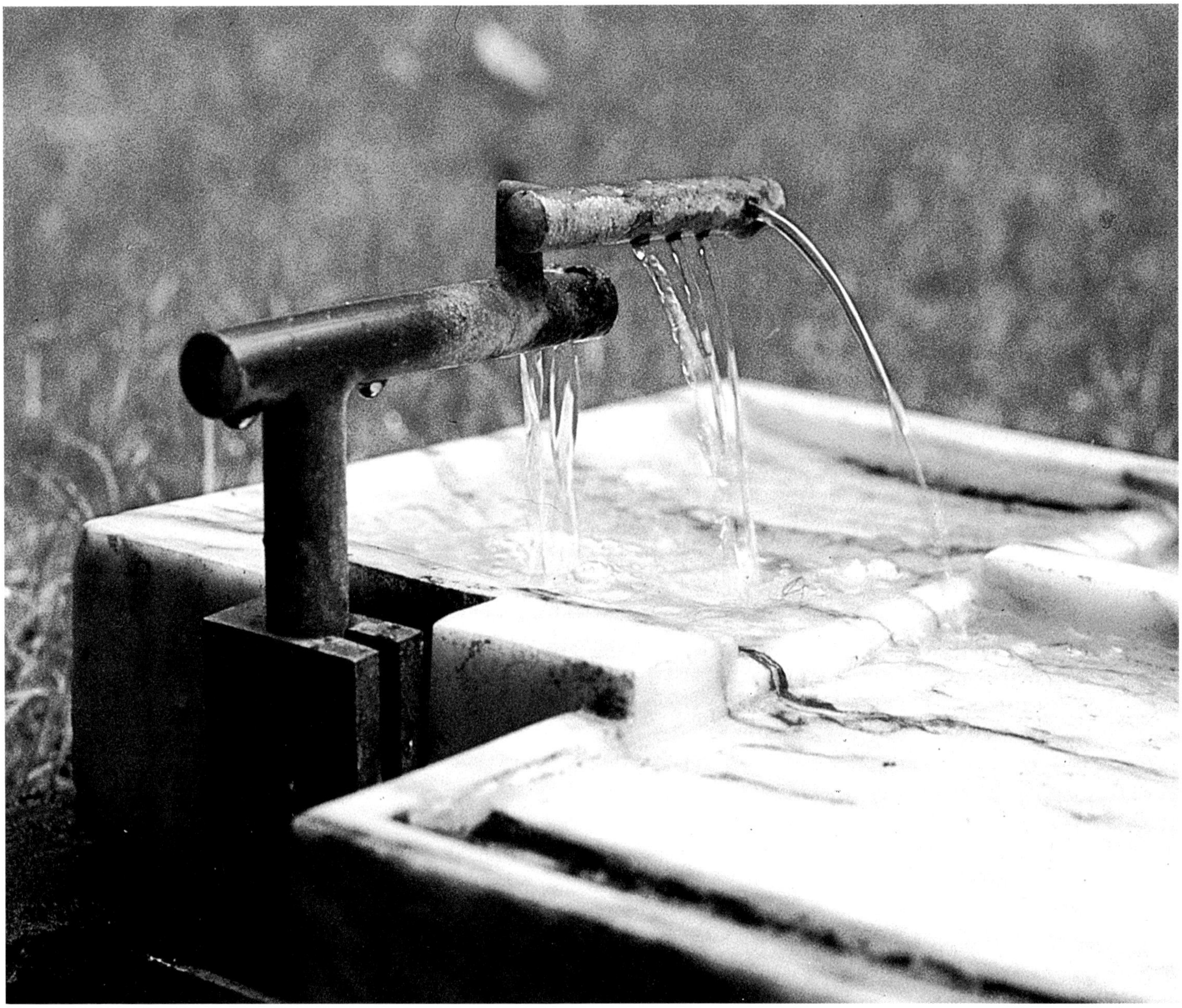

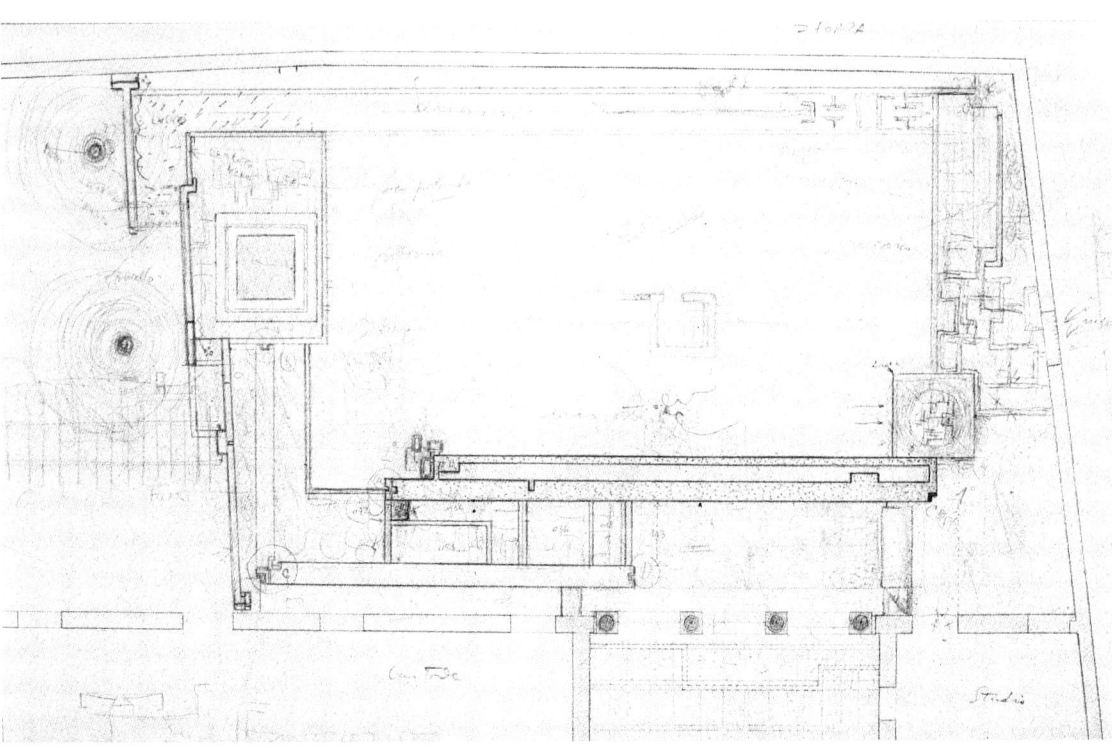

284. Detail of the marble basin

285. Plan of the garden. Pencil and crayons on heliographic print

286. Detail of the garden

◁
283. Detail of the garden to the Querini Stampalia Foundation, Venice

286

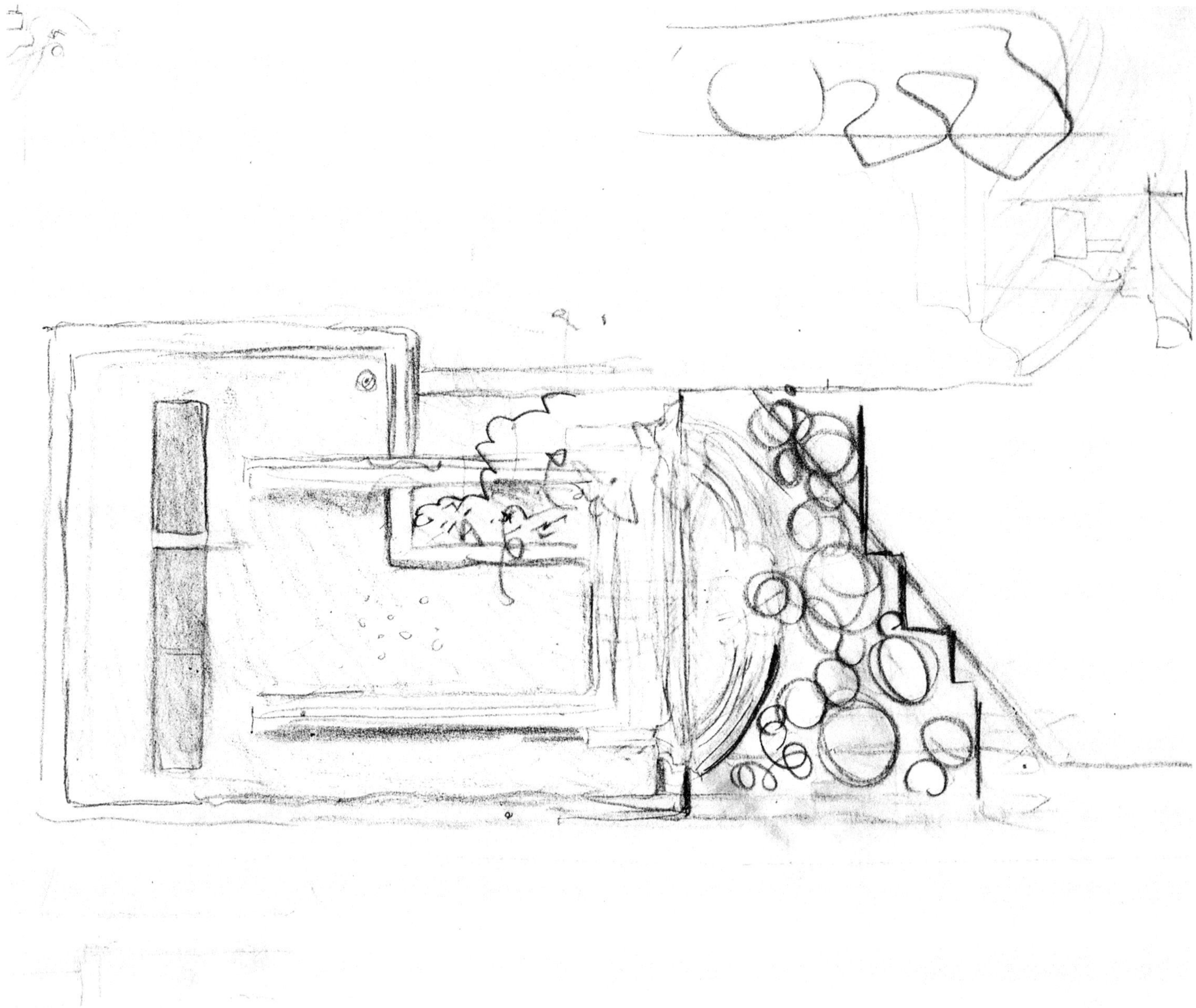

288

288. SKETCH FOR THE BASIN ON THE COURT OF THE ARCHITECTURAL INSTITUTE AT THE UNIVERSITY OF VENICE. PENCIL AND CRAYONS ON TRACING PAPER

289. VIEW OF THE BASIN ON THE COURT OF THE CASTELVECCHIO MUSEUM, VERONA

289

◁
287. Detail of the garden

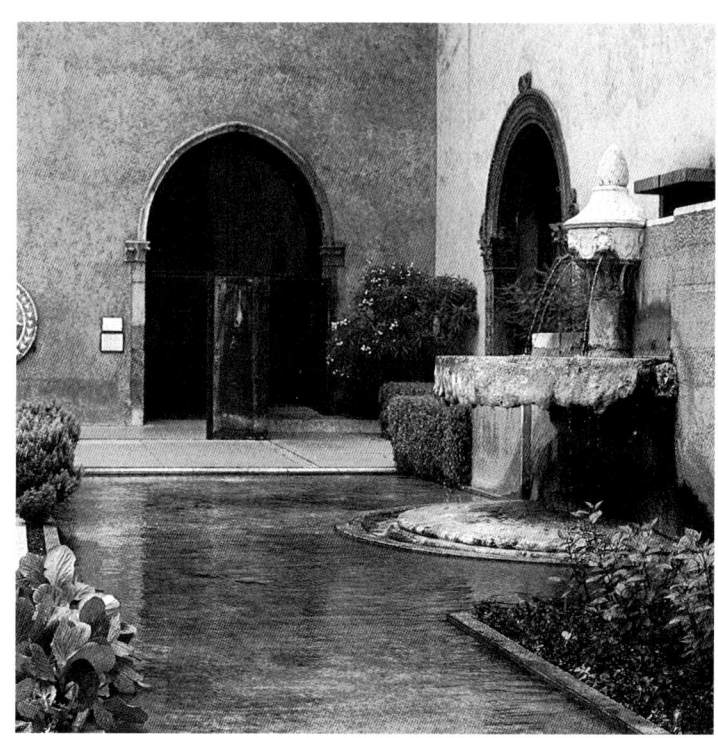

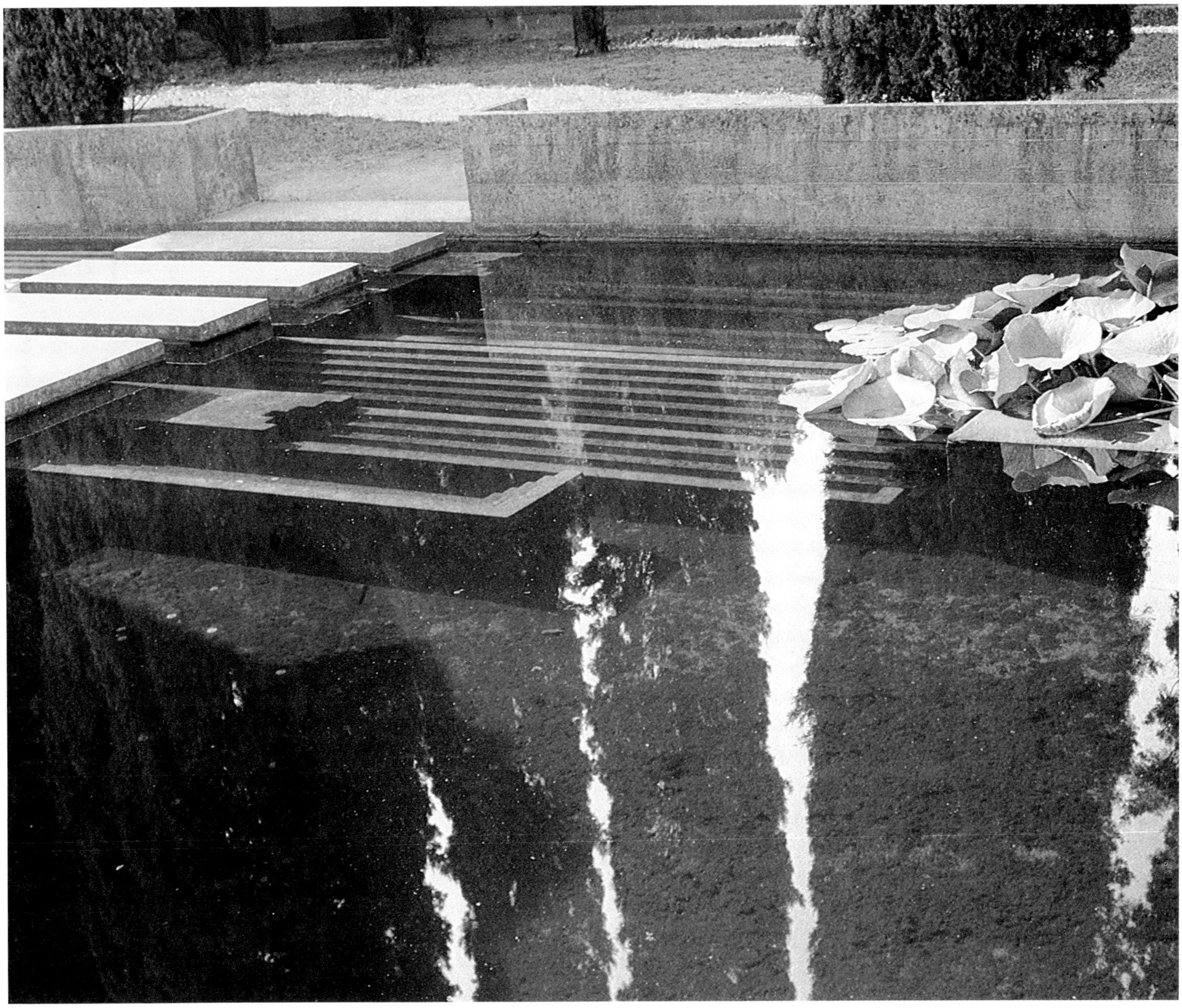
290

291

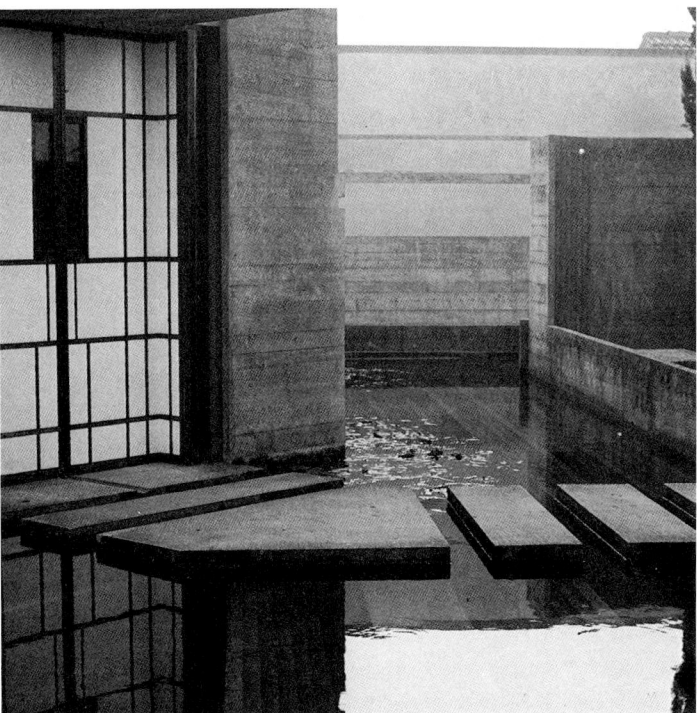

290, 291. DETAIL OF THE POOL AND CHAPEL IN THE BRION CEMETERY, S. VITO DI ALTIVOLE

44. Glass

292. Blue bowl

293. Murrino bowl

294. Vases

Dossiers on the Thematic Elements

SUPPORT

1. PILLAR ON THE OTTOLENGHI HOUSE

The house is a partially sunken construction, screened by the luxuriant vegetation on a hillside sloping down to the shores of Lake Garda, in the zone of Bardolino. It is approached by a flight of steps and a narrow walk that brightens and airs the leeside rooms.

Primary elements in the layout of the project and spatial protagonists of the construction are nine round pillars supporting the roof structures. The soffit was envisaged with a revetment of well buffed black stucco to reflect the green setting and suggest endless continuity of the elements, an allusion to rather than a full classical statement of the trilithic principle.

The pillars (Ø 88-90 cm) are of reinforced concrete, clad with alternating, mixed courses of 11 cm h concrete elements—prefabricated in concrete molds—and 7 cm h stone elements, wasted with a steel point—an operation that proved technically impossible to carry out in situ. Originally exclusive use was made of Prun, a local white stone, but later, in the interests of a subtler chromatic balance, a number of courses of Trani stone were introduced.

Pillars very similar in proportion and constructional technique—though not in the materials used—are to be seen in the Romanesque church of S. Severo at Bardolino itself. Scarpa was not familiar with the interior of this building, however. The source of inspiration of his construction was Frank Lloyd Wright's 1938 project for the Jester house at Palos Verdes, California.

See also dossier 27

SUPPORT

2. SUPPORT ON THE BRION PAVILION

The Brion family tomb stands on a vast, L-shaped plot of land adjoining the cemetery of S. Vito di Altivole, in the province of Treviso.

A covered walkway leads from the country cemetery to what is generally known as the Brion cemetery. This is a public place commemorating Giuseppe Brion, created by his family.

Another entry point beside a cypress grove is reserved for funerals and, like the nearby chapel, may be utilized for all local burials. A covered walkway also leads from the chapel to the proprietors' tombs, spanned by a great arch symbolically uniting them. There is a second chapel in the vicinity, a kind of concrete tent reserved for other Brion family tombs.

A concrete platform in a lily pond at the end opposite the chapel is the only nonpublic place. It is set aside for contemplation—sealed off by a pulley-controlled glass gate. A canopy over this platform creates the small "pavilion." This is an involucre stayed by split-level metal supports, each of which is a composite structure of four solid extruded elements on a square section (side 35 mm, total side per support 9 cm), forming a longer upper segment and a shorter lower one, on two separate axes. The disengaged extremity of each segment is capped with a symbolic motif in cast muntzmetal: a burnished semi-spherical cavity (h 5.5 cm).

Rising directly from the still surface of the pool, the lower segment of each support is underpinned to concrete piles sunk below water level. In relation to the basic rectangle of the "pavilion," the supports are positioned asymmetrically, one to each side, engaging with the unexpressed iron flats that structure the involucre.

See also dossiers 16, 19, 21, 32, 34, 42

SUPPORT

3. TRABEATION ON THE VICENZA CONDOMINIUM

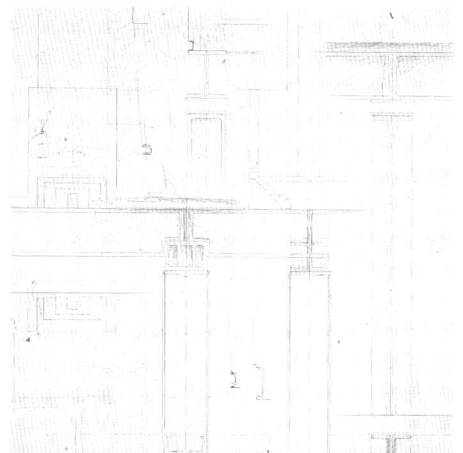

The condominium is situated in Contrà del Quartiere, raised on exposed concrete pillars to allow the park behind it to be seen from the street. Each pillar terminates in a welded aggregate of extruded iron flats, forming a sort of capital.

Iron coupled to concrete in this way is intended to supply the indispensable factor of linkage between the pillars themselves and the horizontal member supporting the three stories of the building. The capitals are grafted onto the welded and riveted iron girder, forming a modern trabeation evocative of the friezes and chiaroscural modulations of tradition.

The loadbearing structure is distributed regularly, but offers a miscellany of formal solutions stemming from the nature of the single supports: reinforced concrete wall on the left, corresponding to the garage entry point, baffle in reinforced concrete with iron capitals facing in from the ground-floor curtain walling, a single pillar flanking the entrance, paired pillars on the porch and corner solution on the far right.

See also dossiers 29, 40

SUPPORT

4. DISPLAY STAND FOR THE BUST OF ELEANOR OF ARAGON

This slender support holds the bust of Eleanor of Aragon, carved by Francesco Laurana (1430—1502), at a convenient height for viewing. It stands in a room in Palazzo Abatellis, where the National Gallery of Sicily is housed.

Contrary to appearance, the display stand, rising perpendicular from the floor, is the fruit of complex formal elaboration, inasmuch as the shaft (129 cm h), consisting of four iron plates (two 70 x 5 mm, two 110 x 5 mm) is assembled and welded butt to side to form the slender box structure (perimeter 115 x 75 mm). It supports an ebony tray (maximum measurements 24.5 x 51 x 5.5 cm), a truncated pyramidal figure, upended and beveled at the perimeter, offering features of both contrast and assonance with the sculpture.

A bronze collar (8 mm deep) is inserted between shaft and tray. Two cylindrical pins hold the bust in place from behind, while, at the front of the tray, a third, rectangular pin, also in bronze, is hollowed out to house a small lead bar at the precise point where purchase for the bust is required.

See also dossiers 5, 11, 35

SUPPORT
5. "SARPI" TABLE

SUPPORT
6. LAMP, QUERINI STAMPALIA FOUNDATION

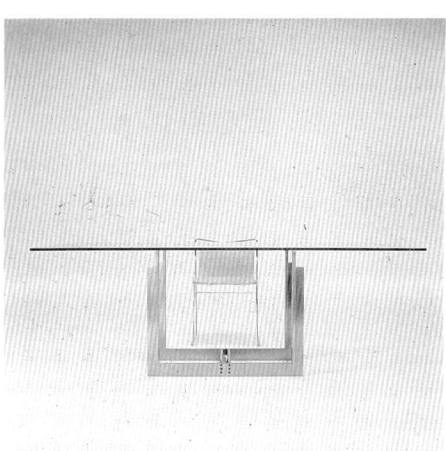

Commissioned by Dino Gavina and named for the Venetian Fra' Paolo Sarpi, the brief specified a support for a table top reinterpreting, on more modest scale, that of the famous "Doge." It also draws on an idea worked out in wood, in 1950, for Ongania, the Venetian antique shop. The "Sarpi" table (72 cm h, rectangular or octagonal top maximum measurements 213 x 133 cm) testifies to successful collaboration between author and client. Whereas the latter contributed by suggesting sparing use of the interlocking structures of extruded steel flats (50 x 15 mm and 40 x 15 mm), the essence of the table, the point where invention really comes into its own, is at the juncture of crystal top and supports. This is resolved by piercing the extremities of the four iron rods to insert small rounded, hollow cylinders of muntzmetal, which, in their turn, house tiny discs of neoprene, a hard, black plastic contrasting sharply with the golden hue of the metal and providing a material better adapted for contact with the crystal top.

It is not by chance that these elements encapsulate the intrinsic idea of the table, in that they are supports obtained from the upper extremities of a structure that is itself seen as a support. The "Sarpi" table is produced by Simon International, Bologna.

An assemblage of iron sections also is frequently used to form display stands for works of art. The support for a wooden crucifix in the main room of the National Gallery of Sicily in Palazzo Abatellis at Palermo is formed of welded and screwed plates rising from a solid lavic stone base.

A landing between two flights of stairs leading up to a first-floor library in the Querini Stampalia Foundation is lit by a lamp of geometrical severity: a simple, oblong stretcher-frame (97.5 x 36 cm) in Brazilian rosewood, its width spanned by a polygonal-section bar (maximum length 126 cm) serving both as horizontal support and securing agent to the facing walls of the landing. Extreme simplicity is pursued here to point up the only indispensable accessory to the object's function: the two plates of opaline glass, engraved with the motif of intersecting rings, screening the lamp.

See also dossiers 9, 25, 34, 37, 38, 43

SUPPORT
7. FRUIT STAND

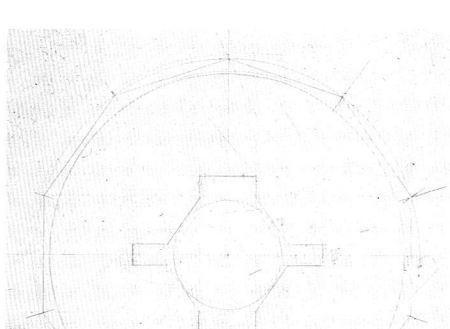

During one of his frequent informal talks on taste Scarpa sketched in the initial idea for this silver fruit stand on the back of a piece of card.

The base (8.2 cm h) is a volume obtained by folding a sheet of silver foil (2 mm thick) to a scheme by means of which two parallelepipeds of differing dimensions interlocking on the orthogonal axes of the edges of a central cube produce a perimeter of sixteen sides alternating two basic widths (2 cm, 4 cm). But this is the simplified version for production in series, inasmuch as, in relation to the prototype, the sketch utilizes different angles in folding the foil. The difference from the original at the executive phase probably derives from the fact that Scarpa had envisaged a base some millimeters shallower and slightly broader. Visually, this effect was obtained by simplifying the scheme, leaving the measurements almost unchanged. Ten facets (each 9.2 cm) define the perimeter of the sheet-silver tray (Ø 29.5 cm) above this base. The slight concavity required of a container is produced by a rise of a few millimeters in two successive stages, forming two concentric circles (Ø 26.4 and 5.5 cm).

A point of mediation between the elegance of Josef Hoffmann and the more austere geometry of Adolf Loos, this "support for fruit" also conveys echoes of architecture and, while responding precisely to what is asked of it, results in a synthesis of complex reflections transcending the object and its use.

The fruit stand was designed for Cleto Munari and is produced by Arcandi e Rossi, silversmiths, of Monticello Conte Otto, Vicenza.

CONNECTOR—LINK
8. FLYOVER ON A SQUARE AT FELTRE

From the first sketch, the girders planned for the cathedral square at Feltre bear a resemblance to bridges or cantilevered structures spanning a divide. They were intended to reinstate a covering for the archeological zone excavated beneath the original paving of the square before the church.

The idea favored was to use iron and concrete joists as a flyover connecting one side of the zone to the other, thereby forming body bolsters for the entire plane of the square: lightweight joists equipped with ties, authoritatively spanning the space like bridgeheads, with a constructional purpose and simplicity of connexion between the single parts far removed from the familiar image of a beam. They are composites of thick steel plates filled with concrete, acquiring both resistance and elegance from the metal ties countering the thrust from below while all but touching the excavated stones.

Regrettably, the project was not implemented because granting adequate headroom for the ancient remains below the flyover meant raising the ground level on each side, albeit by a few dozen centimeters. This would have created a rapid redescent to the frontage—or even into the interior of the church—an operation judged to be overly audacious and innovative with respect to the traditional scheme allowing for a parvise in front of church buildings.

CONNECTOR—LINK

9. BRIDGE, QUERINI STAMPALIA FOUNDATION

The connector between the small square and the Querini Stampalia palace, seat of the homonymous foundation, is a small bridge abutting on the atrium. Entrance via the bridge requires four steps up and five down because the ground level of the building is sunken in relation to that of the facing square. The structure of the bridge consists of a center, describing a tautly curved arch, that springs from the block of Istrian stone and the canal embankment it is secured to.

The center is formed of two semi-arcs, each composed of two large, curved metal plates fitted with square-sectioned, solid iron distancers providing extra bond at the juncture of the semi-arcs. The balustrade, built from welded and screwed iron flats, carries the teak handrail on a support of rods welded to iron tubing. Both the tubing and the handrail terminate in rounded bronze caps.

The balustrade follows a rectilinear trend made up of three distinct segments at slight variance with the arch of the bridge. The steps and the center treads are in solid blocks of larchwood.

See also dossiers 6, 25, 34, 37, 38, 43

CONNECTOR—LINK

10. "TUNNEL" ON THE BANCA POPOLARE DI VERONA

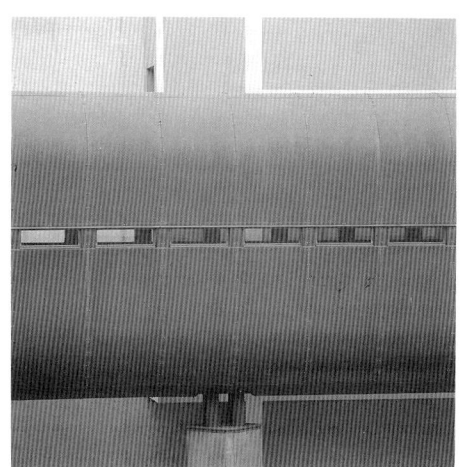

An aerial passage some twenty meters long crosses the court of the Banca Popolare di Verona at the first-floor level. It is a covered walkway with a revetment in sheet copper (2 mm thick) nailed to a curved plywood involucre, secured in turn to a metal frame.

A support in the central section divides the projection into two bays, corresponding to a shift in height between the two blocks of the building it connects. In section a cocoon, the elongated form of the structure, albeit an entirely original concept, recalls either a railway carriage or a plane fuselage.

The first sketches indicate an initial idea for revetment in marine multilayer, later abandoned in favor of copper, for maintenance reasons.

On the death of Scarpa, working drawings were ready, materials had been decided on, and execution was completed faithfully by Arrigo Rudi, the architect who, from the outset, had shared with Scarpa the commission for the entire project of the Banca Popolare di Verona.

See also dossiers 12, 15, 20, 28, 30, 31, 33, 37, 41

CONNECTOR—LINK
11. STAIRCASE IN PALAZZO ABATELLIS

Since the 1954 inauguration of the National Gallery of Sicily at Palermo, the Palladian balance of the small staircase in stone and metal, connecting the ground floor with the mezzanine of the main staircase in Palazzo Abatellis, has attracted comment. In effect, the work is one of the finest exemplars of nonmimetic intervention on ancient buildings: a bold structural insertion of extreme modernity that, by virtue of the dark iron support and the porous surface of the stone, successfully establishes a dialectical rapport with its austere context. On a composite structure of iron flats (60 x 12 mm and 50 x 25 mm), interlocking with strings supplied by two metal beams, the steps are seen as separate entities, their elongated, hexagonal profiles articulating an elegant motif against the wall flanking them, each tread—wasted by a few centimeters—proffering a tray for the visitor's feet.

Blocks of honey-toned Carini limestone (14 cm high, 41.5 cm deep, 120 cm long)—also known as Forest stone—form the steps. As this is a low-rise structure, no need was felt to break the sharply defined silhouette with a balustrade or a handrail.

See also dossiers 4, 5, 35

CONNECTOR—LINK
12. TRABEATION ON THE BANCA POPOLARE DI VERONA

A quite complex architectural system is applied to the top storey of the Banca Popolare di Verona—almost a modern interpretation of an ancient order: supports and architrave in metal, frieze in colored mosaic, and cornice in white Botticino stone. The long ribbon of the architrave, formed of two plate girders of differing dimensions (the larger 600 mm h, the smaller, 180 mm h) joined by riveting plates, is supported at regular intervals by pairs of coupled colonettes in tubular iron (Ø 166 mm), replacing the metal sections of an earlier version.

The colonettes are fitted with muntzmetal collars, acting as linking elements to the architrave above and the base beneath. This is formed of deep flats, cut and milled, riveted to a flat (22 mm deep) laid on the masonry. The tall columns on the court front have a more elaborate muntzmetal link at the base: a motif, frequently used by Scarpa and typical of Indian architecture, by means of which a square plan becomes, by successive divisions, first octagonal, then a sixteen-sided polygonal figure, ending up as a circle. A small block of muntzmetal, recessed to form the symbol of two intersecting rings, gleams against the dark iron above each pair of colonettes. Connectors of the same metal are used at the head and base of the columns to create a single support: these are small elements, distancers, screwed to the tubular shafts, articulating the proportions of the whole.

Inside the building, the faceted, reinforced concrete, round pillars are linked by an analogous element at the top alone, which almost touches the ceiling, and from below, revals two burnished recesses turned in the muntzmetal.

See also dossiers 10, 15, 20, 28, 30, 31, 33, 37, 41

CONNECTOR—LINK

13. STAIRCASE IN THE MURARO HOUSE

This staircase, making use of metal exclusively, connects two floors in a Venetian apartment.

The fifteen steps (maximum measurements of winder 30 x 80 cm, rise 19.5 cm), built with flats (60 x 12 mm) overlaid with colored felt, loop round a thick cylindrical tube forming the newel (Ø 100 mm) and radiate out in the helical trend dictated by the limitations of space.

Support is completed by railing in the structure with smaller tubes (Ø 30 mm), two per step, thereby also ensuring safety of ascent and descent. Simplicity of conception apart, the singularity and interest of this work are derived from the unpretentiously mechanical type of connector used to secure the various parts: the protruding socket head screws and the natural metal surfaces, only lightly coated with transparent anti-oxidizing agent, evoke an image of ease of assemblage, almost of play.

The upper extremity of the newel terminates in two forked ties, formed of flats, inscribing an abstract graphic sign in the aerial space of the involucre.

CONNECTOR—LINK

14. UNPUBLISHED TABLE

The conception of the shaft allowed for alternatives in the choice of materials, which were then tested on the prototype (varying from iron tubing, either exposed or clad in leather, to treated solid wood), but a clear picture of the base emerged at once: a hollow steel cylinder (Ø 160 mm), with faceting deriving from Indian architectural moldings, to which five smaller tubes are joined (Ø 50 mm), radiating on the bisectors of the angles of a pentagon.

It was equally clear from the outset that a linking element would be needed where they joined, but formal definition, as the numerous drawings show, proved difficult until a protective flange, emphasized by blueing, was decided on at the point of insertion of each cylinder.

An expedient worth noting is the frequent use of a length of extruded solid steel cylinder, pierced at the center to lessen weight, as a means of closing iron tubing.

The table top is an ovoid surface on two centers, a composite structure of three superimposed layers of beveled multi-ply, unequal in diameter, either lacquered, left natural or covered with leather, to match the version of the shaft.

The drawings provide clear illustration of the system adopted in joining together the various parts described.

FIXED JOINT—HINGED JOINT

15. METAL STAIRCASE IN THE BANCA POPOLARE DI VERONA

The metal staircase connecting the first and second floors of the Banca Popolare di Verona is situated on the terrace addressing the court. The two rectilinear flights, each composed of nine steps, are housed in an involucre of glass panels that, while suggesting a cylindrical structure, is, in fact, a multi-sided polygonal.

The use of tubular iron to secure the steps was inspired by the extreme simplicity conveyed by an analogous structure on one of the staircases in Pierre Chareau's Maison de Verre in Paris, where inflection of a single tube provides both horizontal and vertical support.

Greater complexity is introduced at Verona by the use of tubing of two sizes (Ø 48 mm, Ø 70 mm), interlocking to form a cage, the steps screwed first to the larger main tube, then to the smaller secondary one.

The steps are latticed plate iron filled in with concrete. The line of the steps determines a bipartite structure in the cage, creating, with a variety of nodes and connector solutions, a rigid mechanistic geometry which challenges the void generated by the cylindrical involucre. The involucre itself recalls Gropius's glass towers at the Cologne Werkbund Exhibition.

With the exception of the muntzmetal for fixed joints, supplying support and interlocking, the entire tubular structure is treated with a special gray-green, metalized calamine solution and a final coat of gloss varnish. Reentrant in respect to the façade partially masking its first-floor terrace location, this transparent volume on the Banca Popolare di Verona is used dynamically as a hinged joint, to express release after a constriction in spatial flow.

See also dossiers 10, 12, 20, 28, 30, 31, 33, 37, 41

FIXED JOINT—HINGED JOINT

16. CANDELABRUM IN THE BRION CHAPEL

The functioning agent of this exquisite object (total h 3 m), is a series of delicate fixed joints. The loadbearing structure, in pear wood, consists of two parts: a single bar (Ø 58 mm), set horizontally into the molding of the chapel ceiling and a vertical assemblage of three smaller bars (Ø 22 mm); elements in cast muntzmetal allow for single-plane rotation—forms totally extraneous both to the symbology of the object and to their specific functions. They consist of a rounded bulb (Ø 66 mm) with a suggestion of a hinge about it, as if to underline the nodal point of release, embellished with copper inserts and a tassel of metal rods (Ø 8 mm, h 170 mm, l max. 110 mm)—a kind of rigid fastener for the parts: abstract elements possibly reminiscent of other objects but also conjuring up new associations and lending extra dimension to their use. The candle holders are in plexiglass, fitted to sections of silver-plated brass rod (Ø 6 mm), with ease of rotation on other elements, in burnished muntzmetal, attached to the bars of wood.

The overall image is one of extreme lightness. Observing the candelabrum as a unit brings to mind some plastic material, crystallized in an equilibrium admitting of a carefully gauged potential oscillation—an instability that would have been counteracted in the original scheme by an iron brace attached to the nearby altar.

See also dossiers 2, 19, 21, 32, 34, 42

FIXED JOINT—HINGED JOINT
17. "TOLEDO" BED

With a name harking back to Spanish traditions in leatherwork, this object is the product of a study for circular-section jointing, a theme already explored at length.

The alternating light and dark toned woods of the frame (Ø 5.5 cm) provide a support for the upholstered panel on which the mattress rests. The original feature is the overhang of the foot of the panel. The headboard may be slanted slightly, which enables the leather padding to adjust to body pressure and to adapt perfectly to the needs of whoever, stretched out or seated, wishes to lean against it.

It was designed as a single bed, but commercial demand has brought out a three-quarter version.

A comment in Scarpa's own hand: "...high production, at high prices, to bring in high returns in royalties—otherwise leave it alone..." is indicative of the spirit in which he approached industrial design—something midway between his habitual, committed research into original forms and a kind or entertaining hand drill expressing amused tolerance toward a presumed futility of the subject. The bed is produced by Simon International, Bologna.

The motif of circular-section wooden jointing, already adopted for a couch project, was returned to, albeit in other guises, for the structure of such pieces as the "Scuderia" table and cupboard (named after the extension to the Villa Valmarana ai Nani in Vicenza, where ultimately his studio was installed), and the "Kentucky" chair, so-called because the inspiration came from a publication dealing with the furnishings of Quaker communities in North America. These latter pieces are produced by Bernini, Carate Brianza, Milan.

FIXED JOINT—HINGED JOINT
18. PROTECTIVE BARRIER AT BRESCIA

Intended to protect a commemorative stone, in Piazza della Loggia, the barrier was designed by Scarpa himself after it became clear that no more elaborate tribute would be made to record the victims of the bomb outrage of 28 May 1974.

The structure picks up a motif, already developed in the past, of a horizontal rail balanced in such a way as to rotate slightly when pushed.

It gains in complexity by the adoption of a system of supports, each composed of two close-set muntzmetal rods (h 110 cm) on hexagonal section (3 cm side), secured to a plate set into the cobbles of the square.

In reality, the horizontal rail itself is an assemblage: a sheaf of three differentiated cylindrical elements in turned teak (Ø 55, 44, 33 mm) fastened together by metal distancers.

In view of the considerable length involved (5.50 m), an attempt was made to preserve perfect horizontality by building the rail in sections, each with a central core of muntzmetal, and joining them with pins. But despite this expedient, there was insufficient time to allow for adequate testing, and it proved impossible to prevent immediate and obvious deformation.

FIXED JOINT—HINGED JOINT
19. DOOR ON THE BRION CHAPEL

From the cypress grove approach to the Brion chapel, the entrance door offers a simple grid pattern delineated by an iron structure with an infill of white concrete. Crossing the threshold, each leaf of the door is seen to be formed of two parts, perpendicular to one another. The door opens on a special muntzmetal hinge external to the leaf.

Where lathe-turned pieces have to withstand a heavy load, muntzmetal is preferred to the usual brass alloy—copper plus zinc 15-18%—which would be too soft. Although it is itself a brass alloy, the higher percentage of zinc in muntzmetal—40%—enhances rigidity, even though it increases fragility.

The hinge is secured to the door by means of an iron element forming a collar to the pivot, which rotates on ball bearings housed beneath the paving. At ground level, round plates of muntzmetal insulate this mechanism.

The brilliant hue of the metal is accentuated by delicate milling to produce a semi-cylindrical section of fluting that stops just short of the slightly rounded upper extremity of the hinge (h 12 cm, Ø 5.2 cm). Each leaf of the door is fitted with a slightly smaller hinge, anchored to the soffit.

See also dossiers 2, 16, 21, 32, 34, 42

CLOSURE—APERTURE
20. GRILLE ON THE BANCA POPOLARE DI VERONA

A monolithic slab of Botticino (14 cm deep), set into the revetment of the façade of the Banca Popolare di Verona in proximity to the main entrance, is pierced by a series of small rectangular openings (16.5 x 5.5 cm), forming a simple lattice pattern, based on a repeated motif. On the frontage, both lath and opening are of the same breadth (5.5 cm), but the lath is chamfered on the interior to let in more light. However, as it is perceived against strong light, from inside the building the design reads as the negative of what appears on the frontage.

The latticework of the grille is built up on the 5.5 cm module and its multiples: each opening is aligned horizontally to others of the same proportions, or abuts on two vertical openings with an intervening lath. The extreme simplicity and severity of the whole, together with the chamfering, owes something to the image of the marble and bronze screen built in 1366 for Orsanmichele in Florence.

The grille is surmounted by two small, elongated rectangular openings (143 x 22 cm) to throw light on the staircase landing. These are mere slits, but, echoing the openings beneath, they point up the factor of aperture without detracting from that of protection and closure required of the grille.

See also dossiers 10, 12, 15, 28, 30, 31, 33, 37, 41

CLOSURE—APERTURE
21. GATE ON THE BRION CEMETERY

This is the element representing closure of the funeral entrance. It is formed of an iron structure with concrete infill and glass inserts. Bronze wheels with concealed ball bearings are fitted to the extremities of a carriage, to slide along rails embedded in the concrete paving.

Only three quarters of the gate slides back, and consequently the large handle formed of solid steel rod (Ø 40 mm) is always visible. As the height (165 cm) is aligned to that of the sloping perimetral walls, the gate forms a constituent part of the barrier when closed. Nevertheless, the barrier is at eye level, and it is possible to see over it, or through it, at a point where a cross motif breaks the upper line, at the center of the gate.

Behind the altar in the nearby chapel, the gates of two low apertures rotate through 90°, skimming the surface of the pool. The gates are formed of an iron loadbearing structure and two marble slabs, black granite on the outside and white Clauzetto stone on the inside, inlaid with Stella serpentine and oriental porphyry to form the familiar motif of two intersecting rings.

See also dossiers 2, 16, 19, 32, 34, 42

CLOSURE—APERTURE
22. WINDOW ON THE OLIVETTI STORE

The Venetian Olivetti store is situated in S. Mark's square, on the Procuratie Vecchie portico. The salient characteristic of the window is that it fits flush with the frontage, without molding, projections, or chiaroscuro: a clearly defined, transparent aperture, held by a solid frame in the curtain wall.

The chamfered glass (14 mm thick) is bordered by muntzmetal sections (35 x 10 mm and 45 x 10 mm) adequately milled to house the chamfer but allowing the pane to advance by a few millimeters in respect to the metal.

The entire unit then is screwed into a frame, laid ready on the masonry support of Istrian stone forming the surround to the window opening, secured to the stone by small bars of muntzmetal and steel pins. Soldered dots are employed to hide the screws used in mounting the unit and in assembling the muntzmetal sections.

The soldered dots introduce a decorative feature, pointing up the necessary presence of screws to provide anchorage. The corners, severed obliquely, lend a refinement to the window pane, later becoming a characteristic feature of other buildings where voids cut boldly into a vast, solid expanse of wall.

See also dossiers 35, 39

CLOSURE—APERTURE
23. GATE ON THE GAVINA STORE

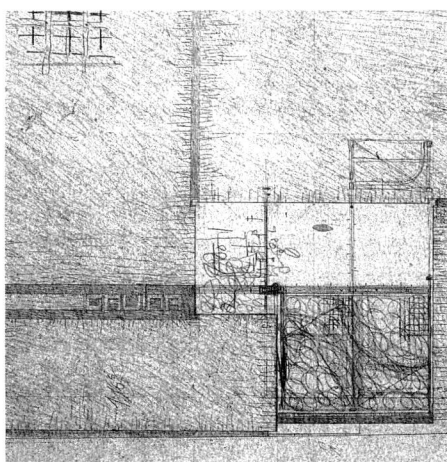

The threshold to the Gavina store, situated in Via Altabella in Bologna, is characterized by a small atrium sealed off by an elegant gate. This is built of extruded iron sections (50 x 10 mm) and, after folding flat on a central hinge, hooks up to a catch on the side wall. With its unassuming dimensions (165 x 134 cm), it is well suited to provide an unusual form of containment for the void in the curtain wall and a polite impediment to entry into the store. But the fundamental complements to the loadbearing structure are the narrowly spaced out vertical elements in walnut (Ø 35 mm), trimmed at the extremities with muntzmetal elements, interlocking with the horizontal iron sections to form a grille that conveys the dual impression of transparency and closure.

The numerous drawings, whether on Bristol board or on paper, and the sketches accompanying the various phases of planning, testify to the commitment urged by its design, inasmuch as the elegantly contrived gate, offering a finely worked and not unaccommodating solution to closure, had been seen to represent the first element encountered on the store frontage.

CLOSURE—APERTURE
24. MAIN ENTRANCE TO PALAZZO STERI

The studies for the solution to be adopted for the main entrance to Palazzo Chiaromonte—dubbed "the Steri palace"—at Palermo, are an elaboration of a favorite motif—the wooden grating—but they introduce basic differences, chiefly due to their juxtaposition with iron. In accordance with a set design, the flats (50 x 10 mm) form a basic web to which a warp and weft of solid wood is applied. While exploiting the voids, the design allows the solids to create a closely woven fabric. Implementation was handled by the architect Roberto Calandra, Scarpa's collaborator on the task of remodeling the palace, and it is to him that we owe the present-day appearance of the sliding gateway to the main entrance and the modulations of the wooden solids to form a more open fabric toward the top.

Calandra was also responsible for carrying out the wooden gratings at the windows; these too were envisaged and partially designed by Scarpa.

It is remarkable how the use of the grating, already frequently employed as framing—though never pursuing quite such complexity—takes on a new meaning at Palermo and lends itself so well to the setting and the Arab-Norman architecture of the Steri.

CLOSURE—APERTURE

25. GATE, QUERINI STAMPALIA FOUNDATION

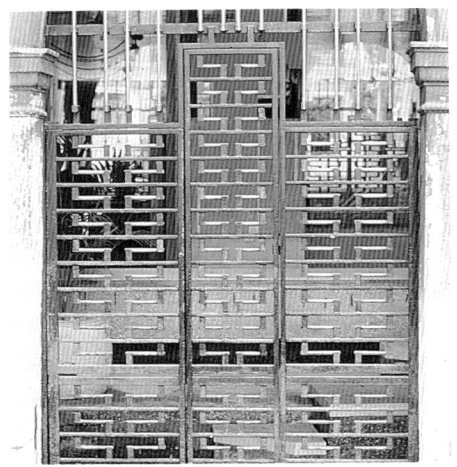

Identical gates close the two archways of the portico giving onto the canal, through which the flood waters generated by high tide flow into the relevant channels.

Each gate is bipartite. On the upper part, vertical rods of solid muntzmetal are housed in iron sockets. On the lower, aggregates of extruded iron elements of varying thickness form three sectors, reminiscent of oriental motifs in the pattern of short cylindrical sections of muntzmetal arranged symmetrically on the horizontal.

By virtue of their transparency the gates further the intent of allowing light, air, and reflections of water to permeate the portico and the garden beyond.

See also dossiers 6, 9, 34, 37, 38, 43

SOLID—VOID

26. SACELLUM IN THE CASTELVECCHIO MUSEUM

A small room in the Castelvecchio Museum at Verona is reserved for the display of objects found in a number of Longobardic tombs. The name it is known by is indicative of the spirit and quality of the intervention. It is a sharply defined form, a simple parallelepiped, projecting from the plane of the façade to make a bold impact on the exterior, but allowing no communication with it, with the exception of the sky, visible in the interior through a transparent light let into the far end of the ceiling. The revetment of the sacellum walls is in Veronese stone, completed on the upper reaches by an iron fascia, masking the skylight and the fixtures providing an outlet for rain water. The volume, condensed by the stone revetment, determines a void on which the spatial flow of the large adjoining room converges. A jewel casket replaces the void, its lining the bottle green rendering of dragged lime. The sheen of the rendering is obtained by repeated and prolonged dragging—no additives or waxes are involved—simply "elbow grease," to use the term of the trusty craftsman responsible, Eugenio De Luigi.

See also dossiers 36, 37, 38, 41, 42

SOLID—VOID

27. VOLUMES ON THE OTTOLENGHI HOUSE

The dilated, almost cylindrical form, with its glossy white walls, in reality is obtained in plan by a geometrical construction, two circles with close-set centers, typical of Scarpian poetics. The volume is an evident spatial protagonist, separating the master bedroom from the rest of the house. It is also one of the clearest demonstrations of his way of using the spaces themselves as separators, contrasts between forms, solids set against, or within, voids. It is a fairly established stylistic feature, and we see it variously applied whenever he feels compelled to circumscribe a particular short-term function or isolate a portion of an organism to point up its role, or subject it to a more systematic order: it is, perhaps, a means of heightening the expressive potential of a space, and at the same time rationalizing and articulating it. The study of the insertion of identifying accessories in these container spaces is of great interest. In this instance, the book illustrates the sketches for the bathroom wash basin and supporting surfaces, identical to those at Bardolino but planned much earlier, for the Zentner house at Zurich.

In this same Ottolenghi house, we also find the use of volumes in the negative: two conical surfaces cut into the narrow walled approach to relieve spatial congestion at that point contribute a sense of airiness, as if the wall had been gently modulated by some vortex in the atmosphere.

See also dossier 1

SOLID—VOID

28. SKYLIGHTS

Two recurrent trends can be identified in planning skylights: the type of pure glass volume with little or no supporting frame, first introduced in the cubiform skylights on the exterior of the Canova Casts Gallery at Possagno and the reentrant parallelepiped variety adopted for the hall. This trend is later reproposed in the bay windows on the façade of the Banca Popolare di Verona. The sketches always emphasized projection of the glazed volumes on the exterior.

The second trend is that of a free, original volume that gradually evolves from its initial use for the skylights on the Venezuelan pavilion at the Venice Biennale, still restricted to only two perpendicular planes. In the project for the Bailo Museum in the convent of S. Catherine at Treviso, the jut of the skylights states an irregular rhythm, sharply expressed against the keeled roof of the building. In the later project for the branch office of the Banca Antoniana at Monselice, the skylights become a commanding feature characterizing the small building. Admiration for many works by Alvar Aalto is not irrelevant here, but there is also no difficulty in acknowledging the originality of the form and the inspiration for the revetments in various graphic motifs by Paul Klee.

SOLID—VOID
29. FRONTAGE OF THE CONDOMINIUM AT VICENZA

The organization of the frontage on the condominium at Vicenza responds on the one hand to the need to establish a gestaltic balance between the solid of the curtain wall and the voids of the windows, and, on the other, to the particular attention called for in view of its location in the historical center of Andrea Palladio's town.

The first idea had been to place a perfect Miesian volume on the site, but for volumetric reasons, and to conform to the height of adjacent housing on the street frontage, depth for the block became an additional necessity. Nonetheless, it reads as a pure geometric volume from the street, where, as the parallelepiped it forms is set on a colonnade, there is a view of the parkland behind. Le Corbusier's solution for the Maison du Brésil at the Cité Universitaire in Paris came to mind here.

An avant-corps in exposed concrete maintains alignment with the adjacent buildings, thereby creating a reentrant base to the façade.

The design of the window, dressed in Vicentine stone, runs the full height of the recess, excluding only a low stringcourse in concrete, finished with an iron U-section introducing a slight factor of chiaroscuro in the pale rendering of the façade. All these elements are reminiscent and modern reinterpretations of many architectural features in the historical center of Vicenza.

See also dossiers 3, 40

SOLID—VOID
30. FRONTS OF THE BANCA POPOLARE DI VERONA

The main office of the Banca Popolare di Verona is situated in the historical center of the town. It offers only two fronts, one addressing the square, the other the internal court.

The early sketches show all the elements appearing on the building itself; elements that gradually took shape in the course of long study and graphic elaboration, by means of which an extraordinary balance between two opposing tendencies is created. Of these, one is classical and static, established by the several vertical axes of symmetry, each of which is an autonomous entity, and the horizontal alignments between the various parts. Its antagonist is dynamic, deriving from the apparent instability of the round windows, the broad zigzagging trend of the loggia and the stone fascia, to which may be added the general asymmetric effect suggested by the entire façade.

From the stone revetment at the base, there is a progressive shedding of weight on the façade, starting with the curtain wall, which is pierced with rectangular windows, a number of them projecting (13 cm), the round windows higher up, and culminating in the second-story loggia.

The front on the court subsequently assimilated a number of motifs from the main façade, such as the two types of fenestration and the stone fascia, here on a rectilinear trend, retaining, however, the void in proximity to the spatial release of the staircase on the terrace.

See also dossiers 10, 12, 15, 20, 28, 31, 33, 37, 41

MOLDING—PROFILING

31. ROUND WINDOW ON THE BANCA POPOLARE DI VERONA

The round window is sharply defined against the *cocciopesto* wall. The effect originally aimed at was that of a neatly perforated membrane. In reality, the wall is all of 50 cm deep and houses casings and plumbing units. The window is formed of five close-set blocks of Botticino stone, of which only a rounded lip (14 cm) is stated on the front to underline unity of plane between opening and rendering. Play of light on the lip points up the form. Below, a strip of red Veronese marble (11 cm) contains the down pipe of the rain water gully.

Inside the building a square-frame window casing is set flush in the wall, opposite the round aperture on the exterior. The windows are of two sizes, the larger (r 90 cm, h 180 cm, l 191 cm) and the smaller (r 77 cm, h 154 cm, l 165 cm) both drawn on two centers at 11 cm distance.

Profiling in white Clauzetto stone, smooth and rounded, is used at many other points inside the building: for the handrail, the steps (tread 27.5 cm, rise 16.5 cm), and the socle (h 11 cm). There are striking and not too distant echoes of the ancient stones on the bridge of Tiberius at Rimini in the trend of the handrail, its section and the corner solution.

Profiling in stone also can be seen on the Balboni house in Venice, where white Lasa on an asymmetrical section forms the rounded coping to a curved parapet.

See also dossiers 10, 12, 15, 20, 28, 30, 33, 37, 41

MOLDING—PROFILING

32. THE 5.5 x 5.5 MOTIF

The entire Brion cemetery is conceived, scaled, and built on the simple module of 5.5 x 5.5 cm and its multiples and submultiples. Such is its bearing on relating scale and proportion of the parts and in determining the form of the single elements, that it has become the salient characteristic of the place. It adapts to an almost endless series of compositions and variations, but at the same time it is also a constraining factor.

It is a geometrical yardstick, a self-imposed discipline that Scarpa rationally applies to the whole: an abstract matrix yielding an expressive order for the city of the dead, which in terms of plastic form enhances the metaphysical sense.

The same type of molding, but in the proportion of 3.5 x 3.5 cm, is adopted for the parts in marble.

See also dossiers 2, 16, 19, 21, 34, 42

MOLDING—PROFILING

33. CORNICE ON THE BANCA POPOLARE DI VERONA

A module of 5.5 x 3.5 cm, its proportions directly descended from the Brion cemetery, is applied here to the cornice forming two superimposed series of close-set blocks of Botticino stone. Correspondence at the junctures of the blocks is avoided to preserve the separate identities of the two series and to prevent water from infiltrating the full depth of the stone. It was possible to reduce one of the measurements, making the heavy blocks easier to mount, because the stone yielded to deeper cutting.

The upper series has carving at the top, with the exception of one upended block mounted over the interaxes of the loggia. Carved in high relief, the cornice, despite its innovatory content and originality, continues the Venetian tradition of crowning ancient palaces: in particular, the projecting surfaces suggestive of a trapezium, trapping the strong light, are inspired by the crowning of the Fondaco dei Turchi in Venice.

Stonework to which the 5.5 x 3.5 cm module also has been applied can be seen in the fascias on the fronts, corresponding to the bay windows, where red Veronese marble has been employed, and inside the building, on the well of the main staircase, in the elements in Clauzetto stone. As a "signature," the motif also is applied in the study for the main entrance to the Faculty of Humanities and Philosophy in the former convent of S. Sebastian in Venice.

See also dossiers 10, 12, 15, 20, 28, 30, 31, 37, 41

MOLDING—PROFILING

34. MOSAIC

The glass tesserae on the Brion cemetery form the revetment of the intrados of the arch spanning the two sarcophagi: the elaborate concrete molding forming the arch is offset by a colored plane surface using tesserae in tones of blue, green, and yellow that were made to order at Murano, in homage to the vault in the Martini chapel in the church of S. Job, the only Della Robbia work in Venice.

A colored mosaic fascia is introduced in wall surfaces on several works, both as profiling to edges and as a single continuous fascia, as in the garden to the Querini Stampalia Foundation, on the garden frontage of the Zentner house at Zurich, and in the cemetery itself, in the area where the wall is high and runs perpendicular to the ground.

The function of the mosaic fascia is to define the wall itself, establish its height and proportion, and, in the case of the cemetery, to continue the horizon line, coincident with average eyelevel, the height of the inclined perimeter wall (h 165 cm), on a higher surface.

MOLDING—PROFILING
35. PROFILING IN WOOD

Wood, too, is occasionally used to delineate a surface and protect the revetment.

The mezzanine parapet in the Olivetti store in Venice is a metal structure faced on both sides with plywood panel, veneered in teak on the landing and rendered with soft-sheen Venetian stucco to face the store below. The resultant depth is capped by the handrail, also in teak.

In the National Gallery of Sicily, in Palazzo Abatellis in Palermo, a corridor between two rooms has a protective frame of singed oak.

MOLDING—PROFILING
36. PROFILING IN IRON

An iron section set flush to the plaster to delineate a plane surface, by an effect of outline augments the volumes. Such an outline, in the presence of the soft-sheen of tinted stuccoes, by contrast, points up the refinement of the material.

Elsewhere it has been used to balance the composition of a plane surface or to edge walls abutting on passages, reinforcing the corners and protecting the plaster, or else to build a door frame, thereby avoiding the unwelcome presence of cover fillets.

In certain exhibition rooms in the Academy Picture Galleries in Venice, the Uffizi in Florence, and the Canova Casts Gallery at Possagno, the skirting is formed of an iron flat, raised from the paving and isolated from the walls by distancers housing the screws.

The paving of the sacellum in the Castelvecchio Museum at Verona, in levigated Florentine earthenware tiles, is bordered by an angle iron framing the small surface, setting it off like a carpet and sharply distinguishing it from the walls and the paving of the adjacent room.

SURFACES
37. STONE WITH STONE

SURFACES
38. STONE WITH OTHER MATERIALS

Stones of different provenance have often been used in revetments, exploiting the chromatic values of their varying hues to point up certain important parts of a building.

The revetment of the entrance to the Banca Popolare di Verona is in two colors, large white surfaces in Clauzetto alternating with fascias of Alpine green. The proportion changes on the sloping surfaces beneath the staircase, where there is a predominance of green.

A mosaic of Veronese stone is used for the external revetment of the sacellum of the Castelvecchio Museum, incorporating small blocks of stone of varying hue, ranging from white to red, inspired by modern art motifs. The smallest block, an 11 cm square, is combined with a surface equivalent to three such squares, thereby forming a square twice its length, variously repeated and rotated. The diversity of the stones in the revetment is further accentuated by alternating rough and smooth surfaces.

An analogous design with squares (side 7 cm) is utilized for the paving in the entrance of the Querini Stampalia Foundation in Venice, where the motif gains in complexity by the use of four colors, representing stone from Lasa (white), Verona (coral pink), the Alps (green), and Cattaro (somber red).

The decision to employ stone with other materials has been taken on many occasions: stone and concrete produce floors resistant to use, easily kept in trim and appropriate to the chosen setting. The stone, laid out as a grid, enhances the surface, not only lending it luminosity, but also bolstering the concrete against the formation of fissures at inopportune points. In the ground-floor rooms of the Castelvecchio Museum, a levigated concrete floor is subdivided by fascias and curbed in Prun stone, forming a dropped level in proximity to the wall, to articulate the corner.

In the great hall of the portico on the Querini Stampalia Foundation, fascias of Repen subdivide the paving of concrete and gravel aggregate, a subdivision reproduced on the walls to form a tall dado of the same materials: this paving is a modern interpretation of the stone and pebble work to be seen in the courts and porticos of palaces both in Venice itself and in Venetia.

The revetment of the walls above the dado is formed of two superimposed fascias of Rapolano travertine with an intervening brass section. They also house the neon tube lighting, screened by opaline glass, set flush with the stone surface.

SURFACES
39. PAVING OF THE OLIVETTI STORE

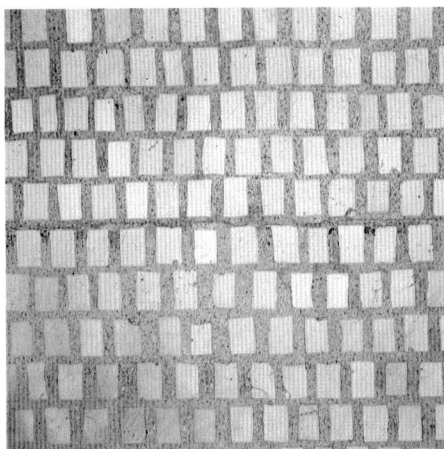

Constantly imitated, this stands as an exemplary intervention in perfect accord with its setting. The glass tesserae from Murano, arranged in four different colors, each distinguishing a separate zone in the store, are sunk into a light ground to create precise but deliberately irregular alignments, drawing on the pictorial schemes of Paul Klee: mobility of image results, evoking the effect of flood waters playing over the surfaces. These are distinguished not only by color, but also by size: whites 3 x 4.5/5 cm; reds 2/2.5 x 3 cm; blues and yellows 2.5 x 3.5 cm.

The entire paving is delimited by fascias and bordered in Roman stone.

See also dossiers 22, 35

SURFACES
40. PAVING OF THE CONDOMINIUM AT VICENZA

The paving of the portico on the Vicenza condominium exploits the chromatic effects resulting from setting brick against stone. A combination already tested elsewhere, but the innovation here lies in utilizing perforated bricks, with an infill of white concrete in the four holes.

This is a simple, low-cost solution, requiring no special precautions to carry out.

It was a deliberate choice for a condominium, as a demonstration that fine finish may be obtained without recourse to costly or even particularly elaborate methods and materials.

This same solution also was envisaged for the walls of a building at Scarperia nel Mugello, Florence, a scheme carried forward to a fairly advanced stage of elaboration, and also planned to incorporate a dark concrete fascia on the exterior revetment.

See also dossiers 3, 29

SURFACES
41. SERVICE STAIRCASE IN THE BANCA POPOLARE DI VERONA

Access to the employees' locker and service rooms is down two parallel flights of steps, from the mezzanine to the basement. The upper flight, isolated to express a communicating space, rests on the side wall of the lower flight. This superimposition of their respective walls is pointed up by the strongly contrasting tones of intense green and violet tinting the plaster.

The steps and the skirting are in white Clauzetto stone, to accentuate the brightly colored sheen of the plaster in the original Venetian stucco.

These and other surfaces rendered in stucco on the Banca Popolare di Verona were carried out after Scarpa's death, faithfully respecting his choices of color tonalities—inspired by the works of one of his favorite painters, Mark Rothko.

The double ceilings in the Gallery wing of the Castelvecchio Museum are gray and light blue panels with a high sheen, offset by profiling in wood; in the Zentner house at Zurich, the chimneypiece is dark red, the light beige ceilings, gloss-finish reflecting surfaces are modelled at strategic points to incorporate special lamps focused on the walls to illuminate the proprietors' collection of modern art.

See also dossiers 10, 12, 15, 20, 28, 30, 31, 33, 37

SURFACES
42. INVOLUCRE OF THE BRION PAVILION

The involucre of the "pavilion" in the Brion cemetery is reveted in larch wood, inlaid with ebony. The short, unplaned planks are nailed to a continuous surface beneath, juxtaposed, after prolonged study for each of the four sides, in such a way as to recall the familiar graphic motifs of Paul Klee. The gray tonality of the wood after years of weathering was foreseen; indeed, it was a determining factor.

Green-lacquered drop panels, reentrant relative to the revetment, screen vision down to the eye level of whoever lingers in contemplation on the platform.

For numerous wooden floors, definitive choice favored light offset by dark woods, planks of differing lengths in random juxtaposition, as in the living room of the Zentner house at Zurich, or laid to form a panel motif, repeated and rotated, as was studied for a private house at Montecchio (Vicenza). In the Castelvecchio Museum, a flooring of large planks of Mansonia was installed in the rooms on the first and second floors of the palace; in every case, the use of wood is accompanied by stone skirting.

Larch or oak, a frequent choice for doors and windows, is treated by singeing or sanding, to enhance the grain of the wood.

See also dossiers 2, 16, 19, 21, 32, 34

TRANSPARENCY
43. GARDEN, QUERINI STAMPALIA FOUNDATION

Light permeates the interior of the Querini Stampalia Foundation from the garden behind it, visible as much from the flanking canal as from the facing square. The presence of light is most noticeable in the ground-floor portico, where it floods in from two sources to mingle with the reverberations from the canal and the garden pools.

The garden forms a rectangle roughly corresponding to two squares, each 12 m per side, cut by a concrete dividing wall. It is largely laid out with lawn and shrubs. A square copper container for papyrus plants is inset in a larger pond reveted with mosaic tesserae; here water collects before rechanneling. Isolated from this, a small basin (75 x 33.5 x 4.5-6 cm), formed of Apuan marble of a purplish hue, collects the water dripping into it from a small pipe and channels it into a miniature maze, where it fills a series of shallow concavities before flowing into a long, deep water course in which water lilies flourish. At the end opposite the small basin, serving as a bird bath for the winged inhabitants of the garden, a low cascade lends impetus to the flow of water, carrying it into proximity with an ancient and now dry wellhead. A short path with a number of steps completes the garden layout, branching off from the glazed wall of the portico to lead the visitor either toward the papyrus pool or in the direction of the wellhead.

See also dossiers 6, 9, 25, 34, 37, 38

TRANSPARENCY
44. GLASS

From the thirties onward Scarpa worked for two Murano firms, initially for Cappellin and Co. and subsequently for Paolo Venini, for whom he created the two objects illustrated here, selected for their contrasting qualities, but both representative of his expressive and formal research. The blue vase (Ø 16 cm, h 9 cm) allies purity of form with unusual effects of color, enhanced by diversity of surface finish, lustrous on the inside, more opaque outside.

The exemplar of *murrino* ware (Ø 16 cm, h 6 cm), on the contrary, exploits transparency and the response of its variegated colors to the light. It may be remarked that the objects in glass, the majority of which have been collected together by his wife, Nini Scarpa, are emblematic of Scarpa's methodology and of the repertory of forms recognized today as typically his.

Index of Illustrations

1950-59	REPLANNING OF THE ACADEMY PICTURE GALLERIES, VENICE	Skirting	249
1953-54	REPLANNING OF PALAZZO ABATELLIS, SEAT OF THE NATIONAL GALLERY OF SICILY, PALERMO	Display stand for the bust of Eleanor of Aragon	19
		Base for a crucifix	22, 23, 24
		Staircase in stone and metal	56, 57, 58, 59
		Door and hinge	118, 119, 120
		Profiling on a passage between two rooms	243
		Wooden display screen	280
1954-56	VENEZUELAN PAVILION IN THE BIENNALE GARDENS, VENICE	Skylights	182
1955-57	ANNEX, CANOVA CASTS GALLERY, POSSAGNO (TREVISO)	Skylights	179, 180, 181
1956-64	RESTORATION AND INSTALLATIONS OF CASTELVECCHIO MUSEUM, VERONA	Beam	18
		Small bridge over the ditch	47, 48
		Footbridge near the Cangrande	49
		Barrier	114
		Grating	166, 167
		Sacellum	168, 169, 170, 171, 253, 254
		Profiling on a passage between two rooms	247
		Paving	248, 257, 258
		Skirting	259
		Double ceiling	272
		Door	279
		Basin	289

1957-58	OLIVETTI STORE, VENICE	Store window	136
		Shutter	158
		Radiator screen	159
		Parapet handrail	240, 241, 242
		Pillar revetment	261
		External revetment	262
		Paving	263, 264, 265, 266
		Wooden wall	281
1961-63	REPLANNING OF THE QUERINI STAMPALIA FOUNDATION, VENICE	Lamp	25, 28
		Entrance bridge	38, 39, 40, 41, 42, 43, 44, 45, 46
		Staircase window and hinge	121, 122
		Gate	161, 162, 163, 164, 165
		Mosaics on garden wall	238, 239
		Paving	252, 256
		Revetment of walls	255
		Garden	283, 284, 285, 286, 287
1961-63	GAVINA STORE, BOLOGNA	Pillars	9
		Gate	140, 141, 142, 143, 144, 145, 146, 147, 148, 149
1964	REPLANNING OF THE BALBONI HOUSE, VENICE	Window	139
		Parapet handrail	219, 220
1964-68	REPLANNING AND PARTIAL RESTRUCTURING OF THE ZENTNER HOUSE, ZURICH	Window	137
		Elevation	138
		Canopy	160
		Bathroom fixtures	175, 176, 177, 178
		Fireplace	245
		Ceiling with lamp	273
		Flooring	278
1966-67	PROJECT FOR THE ENTRANCE TO THE ARCHITECTURAL INSTITUTE OF THE UNIVERSITY OF VENICE, VENICE	Basin	288
1969-78	BRION CEMETERY, S. VITO DI ALTIVOLE (TREVISO)	Pavilion support	10, 11, 12, 13, 14, 15
		Candelabrum in chapel	94, 95, 96, 97, 98, 99, 100, 101
		Door on the chapel and hinge	115, 116, 117
		Grille, perimetral wall	127, 128
		Sliding gate	129, 130, 131, 132
		Low gated apertures	133, 134, 135
		5.5 x 5.5 motif	221, 222, 223, 224, 225, 226, 227, 228
		Involucre of the "pavilion"	275, 276
		Cupola on the chapel	282
		Pool	290, 291

1973-78	CENTRAL OFFICE BUILDING OF THE BANCA POPOLARE DI VERONA, VERONA	Tunnel	50, 51, 52, 53, 54, 55
		Trabeation	60, 61, 62, 65, 66, 67
		Internal pillars	63, 64
		Metal staircase	77, 78, 79, 80, 81, 82, 83, 84, 85, 86, 87, 88, 89, 90, 91, 92, 93
		Grille and small windows	123, 124, 125, 126
		Fronts	205, 206, 207, 208, 210, 213
		Plan	209
		Bay windows	211, 212
		Round window	214, 215, 216, 217
		Handrail	218
		Cornice	229, 230, 231, 232
		Stone fascia	233
		Molding on main staircase	234, 235
		Profiling, glazed wall	250
		Revetment, entrance	251
		Jamb, main entrance	260
		Service staircase	269, 270
		Elevator wall	271
		Lamp	274
1974-75	PROJECT FOR RESTORATION AND ANNEX ON THE FORMER CONVENT OF S. CATHERINE FOR THE BAILO MUSEUM, TREVISO	Skylights	189, 190, 191, 192
1974-76	MONUMENT IN PIAZZA DELLA LOGGIA, BRESCIA	Protective barrier	109, 110, 111, 112, 113
1974-77	CONDOMINIUM, VICENZA	Trabeation	16, 17
		Window	193, 194
		Façade	195, 197, 198, 199
		Plan	196
		Paving on porch	267, 268
1974-78	PROJECT FOR RESTORATION AND ANNEX ON THE FORMER CONVENT OF S. SEBASTIAN FOR THE FACULTY OF HUMANITIES AND PHILOSOPHY OF THE UNIVERSITY OF VENICE, VENICE	Pillar	7
		Main entrance	236
1974-75	PROJECT FOR THE CHIESA HOUSE, VICENZA	Plan	200
		Façade	201, 202, 203, 204
1974-78	OTTOLENGHI HOUSE, BARDOLINO SUL GARDA (VERONA)	Plan	1
		Pillar	2, 3, 4, 5, 6
		Volumes and container spaces	172, 173, 174
		Fireplace	244
		Bedroom wall	246
1975	STAIRCASE IN THE MURARO HOUSE, VENICE	Staircase	69, 70, 71, 72, 73, 74

1975-77	PROJECT FOR THE FLYOVER ON THE CATHEDRAL SQUARE, FELTRE (BELLUNO)	Girders	30, 31, 32, 33, 34, 35, 36, 37
1976-77	PROJECT FOR THE BRANCH OFFICE OF THE BANCA ANTONIANA DI PADOVA, MONSELICE (PADUA)	Pillar Skylights Plan	8 183, 184, 185, 186, 187 188
1977	STUDY FOR THE REPLANNING OF PALAZZO STERI, PALERMO	Mullioned window Main entrance Windows	68 150, 151, 152, 153, 157 154, 155, 156
1977	PROJECT FOR A PRIVATE HOUSE, MONTECCHIO (VICENZA)	Flooring	277
1930-78	OBJECTS		
		1930-47 Glass	292, 293, 294
		1974-75 "Toledo" bed	102, 103, 104, 105
		1975 "Sarpi" table	20, 21
		1976 Unpublished project for a table	75, 76
		1977 "Scuderia" table and cupboard	106, 107
		1977 "Kentucky" chair	108
		1977 Stone fireplace	237
		1978 Fruit stand	26, 27, 29

Acknowledgments

The authors wish to thank:

Signora Nini Scarpa, whose hospitality, aid, and goodwill made this book possible,

Afra and Tobia Scarpa, for placing the Carlo Scarpa Archives at our disposal and for consenting to photography,

the architect Stefan Buzas, for his encouragement and permission to use a number of photographs from his files,

the Directorates of the National Gallery of Sicily in Palazzo Abatellis at Palermo, the Castelvecchio Museum at Verona, the Academy Picture Galleries, and the Querini Stampalia Foundation in Venice, for permission to photograph the interiors of their respective seats,

Dr. Tarcisio Marchesini of the Directorate of the Banca Popolare di Verona, who gave, and renewed, permission to photograph the interior of the central bank,

the Venetian craftsmen Saverio Anfodillo, Eugenio De Luigi, Paolo Zanon, Luciano Zennaro, for the invaluable information offered and their kind collaboration,

Prof. Alberto Ottolenghi, who agreed to publicity about his house at Bardolino,

the architect Arrigo Rudi, Giancarlo Bernini, Cleto Munari, and all those who furnished information of various kinds and contributed to the production of this book, and

Dino Gavina, who gave his enthusiastic support to the initiative that led to this publication.

Authorship of Texts:

Bianca Albertini: Scarpa at work
Trimming and tallying—axes, alignments and Gestalt
Cross references within the canon
Memory and invention II
5.5 x 5.5 as a signature
Building traditions
A single form and its potential

Sandro Bagnoli: Premise
A profile
On predilections
The models and the module
From tracing paper to Bristol board
Genesis of the working drawing
Memory and invention I
Large scale, small scale
Neither craftwork nor design
Thematic elements

Compilation of Dossiers:

Bianca Albertini: 2, 9, 10, 18, 20, 25, 26, 28, 30, 33, 34, 35, 36, 37, 38, 40, 41, 42, 43, 44

Sandro Bagnoli: 4, 5, 6, 7, 8, 11, 12, 13, 14, 15, 16, 17, 19, 22, 23, 24, 27, 31, 39

Giuseppe Tommasi: 1

Maristella Tonin: 3, 29

Fabrizio Zuliani: 21, 32

Photo Credits

Bianca Albertini, Siena: 13, 16, 38, 43, 48, 55, 83, 109, 113, 125, 126, 132, 166, 171, 199, 205, 211, 217, 233, 235, 238, 248, 257, 258, 260, 267, 268, 272, 274, 275, 283, 287, 289.

Sandro Bagnoli, Siena: 19, 22, 23, 24, 39, 41, 42, 56, 57, 58, 59, 67, 77, 79, 80, 81, 82, 84, 93, 99, 100, 101, 115, 117, 118, 119, 120, 127, 128, 135, 140, 141, 142, 143, 144, 156, 157, 161, 162, 163, 164, 218, 234, 240, 241, 243, 249, 261, 262, 271, 280, 281, 282, 284, 286, 291, 294.

Maurizio Brenzoni, Verona: 18, 51, 64, 65, 114, 167, 213, 214, 247, 259, 269, 270.

Stefan Buzas, London: 10, 14, 26, 49, 60, 131, 169, 179, 180, 181, 221, 222, 223, 224, 225, 226, 227, 228, 229, 232, 239, 254, 279, 290.

Eliofoto, Venice: 25, 69, 70, 72, 73, 122, 136, 158, 159, 175, 176, 177, 178, 237, 242, 255, 256, 263, 264, 265, 266, 285, 292, 293.

Foto Giuseppe Fini, Treviso: 1, 2, 5, 6, 7, 8, 9, 11, 12, 15, 17, 28, 29, 30, 31, 32, 33, 34, 35, 36, 37, 44, 45, 46, 47, 50, 52, 53, 54, 61, 62, 63, 66, 68, 71, 74, 78, 85, 86, 87, 88, 89, 90, 91, 92, 94, 95, 96, 97, 98, 110, 111, 112, 116, 121, 123, 124, 129, 130, 133, 134, 137, 138, 139, 145, 146, 147, 148, 149, 150, 151, 152, 153, 154, 155, 160, 173, 174, 182, 183, 184, 185, 186, 187, 188, 189, 190, 191, 192, 193, 194, 195, 196, 197, 198, 200, 201, 202, 203, 204, 206, 207, 208, 209, 210, 212, 215, 216, 219, 220, 230, 231, 236, 244, 245, 246, 250, 251, 252, 273, 276, 277, 278, 288.

Decio Grassi, Busto Arsizio: 106, 107, 108.

Giorgio Pellati, Bardolino: 3, 4, 172.

Franco Pizzocchero, Milan: 20, 21, 75, 76, 102, 103, 104, 105.

Senno and Sutto, Venice: 40, 165.

Umberto Tomba, Verona: 168, 170, 253.

Mario Toselli, Manerba del Garda: photo on page X.

Photosetting by
ELLEDUE
Milano

Color separation by
GRAPHICOLOR
Milano

Printed by
LEVA SPA ARTI GRAFICHE
Sesto S. Giovanni (MI)

Bound by
LEM
Opera (MI)